# Playing for A Hoagie and A Beer

## Life on the Outer Fringes of Football with the Semipro Central Pennsylvania Whitetail Bucks

## Mark Speck

**St. Johann Press**
Haworth, New Jersey

ST. JOHANN PRESS

Published in the United States of America
by St. Johann Press
P.O. Box 241
Haworth, NJ 07641
www.stjohannpress.com

Copyright © 2016 Mark Speck

The paper used in this publication meets the minimum requirements of the American
National Standard for Information Sciences—Permanence of Paper for Printed Library
Materials, ANSI/NISO Z39/48-1992

Composition by Susan Ramundo (susan@srdesktopservices.com)
Cover design by G&H Soho Inc., Elmwood Park, NJ
Cover photo: Courtesy of the Collection of Tom Miller

ISBN 978-1-937943-36-3

Manufactured in the United States of America

# CONTENTS

# FOREWORD

As the years have fallen away, the memories still remain vivid among the players, coaches and in the minds of the fans who loved and cheered for the Central Pennsylvania Whitetail Bucks.

Written in the heat of late summer evenings, and in the cool, brilliantly colored autumn days, the Bucks forged a legacy for four years, and we made our case as some of the best in semipro football for that era in America.

In the mid-seventies, Penn State football wasn't the only game in town, because in 1975 the Whitetail Bucks would take our rightful place in Central Pennsylvania sports history.

Mark Speck tells our story through the eyes of the players themselves. He chronicles the embryonic years of Buck football and relates many stories of the men who devoted so much love for the game and their teammates.

The Bucks were a colorful group with varied personalities and backgrounds. The team was composed of some of the area's most outstanding and well-known players who had carved out record-setting performances during their playing days. One has been enshrined in the Semipro Football Hall of Fame, one played briefly in the NFL, many others had NFL tryouts, and one played in the Orange Bowl with Penn State after returning from a tour of duty in Vietnam. Several others also returned to the playing field after served their country in Vietnam.

Some of these men were All-State selections and Big 33 players, while several had big time college experience at Division One schools. Most however, were players from small area colleges, as well as local high school grads who labored in the steel mills of Johnstown, the railroad shops of Altoona and the coal mines in Philipsburg and who still believed they were born to play football.

This book honors our legacy as Whitetail Bucks, and gives the reader a look into the world of semipro football and the athletes themselves.

—Darrel Rutter
Central Pennsylvania Whitetail Bucks, 1975–78

# ACKNOWLEDGMENTS

Researching the Central Pennsylvania Whitetail Bucks turned out to be somewhat of a daunting task. Typing the words "Central Pennsylvania Whitetail Bucks" in the Google search engine will get you a lot of information and images . . . about deer and deer harvests in the Keystone State. Not so much, however, on a semipro football team from the 1970s. But once I got a little creative, I was able to find quite a bit of facts and data online concerning the football team.

The former Bucks were very cooperative when it came to interviews. However, since quite a few years—40 to be exact—had passed, some of them had difficulty remembering specific information, and understandably so. This was especially true with players who had suffered concussions and related to me their difficulty in remembering things.

Then there was the player I tried to contact—who shall remain nameless—who responded to my inquiry: "I did play for the team for their first two years, but I'm afraid I won't be much help. It was the 70s and I was high and/or drunk most of the time, so I don't remember much. I wish you the best with your book."

It was indeed the '70s.

I do have to acknowledge the fact that I had quite a bit of help on this project, and many people deserve a "thank you."

First off, a big thank you to Dave Biesel of St. Johann Press, for having the faith to believe in yet another quirky idea/project of mine.

Another thank you to my wife, Elise, for her continued support and patience as I regaled her on stories about the Bucks and sat hunched over the computer for hours typing, writing and researching.

Next, a shout out to some of the people involved with the team who generously gave of their time, such as Jay Siegel, Al Siegel's son who was one of the team managers; Mike Leone, who served as team manager in 1975; Harry Breon, Centre County historian and author; Julian Ziff, son of team investor Herman Ziff; Ron Bracken, who served as a sportswriter for the *Centre Daily Times*; and Tom Schott, former Sports Editor for the *DuBois Courier-Express* and now a member of the DuBois Historical Society.

The biggest thank you of all, however, goes to the former Bucks themselves, a fine group of men who were gracious and generous with their time and eagerly shared their experiences and recollections of what was a very valued time in their lives with someone who was at first a complete stranger. Thank you, Ken Rutter, Darrel Rutter, Ron Roefaro, Tom Miller, Tom Marlett, Joe Wales, Bill Luther, Pat Little, Hugh Gibbons, George Walker, Wayne Rockmore, Paul Kanagy, Mike McNeish, Rod Ullein, Carl Brown, and Ron "Bull" Rehmeyer.

# INTRODUCTION

Clearfield. DuBois. Curwensville. Bald Eagle. Coalport. Bellefonte. Philipsburg. Port Matilda. Madera.

These are some of the small towns and quaint communities that are sprinkled around the landscape of an area known as Central Pennsylvania, a region known for its gently rolling hills, beautiful, pristine forests and rich farmland.

Like many other areas of the country, it's also known for its love of football. Friday nights (and Saturday afternoons if your stadium had no lights) was high school football. Rooting and cheering for the young men playing for the local schools, such as Chestnut Ridge, Glendale, Bald Eagle Area, Northern Bedford or Moshannon (known in the area as Mo) Valley.

Saturday was the day for the college boys, rooting for Penn State, Pitt, or any of the small colleges around the area.

Then Sunday of course, was set aside for the pros, the NFL, rooting for the Pittsburgh Steelers, the Philadelphia Eagles, or whatever team you had aligned yourself with.

Somewhere between high school, college and the pros, there was another level of football that existed, a level that tried to survive on the outer fringes of the game. This level was the minor leagues, the semipros, the players and teams that tried to make a go of it on the coal-littered, rock-strewn fields of the region. They were quaint little operations, kind of like Mom-and-Pop stores, who used things like raffles, bake sales and fund-raisers to try and compete against the formidable chain store that was the NFL. It's been said that professional athletes are paid to perform under conditions of adversity. It could be said, therefore, that the semipros face the same adversity; they just don't get paid for it.

The semipros, you could say, are players who play and toil and sweat and hurt not for fame, not for glory, but for simply the love of a game they had not yet gotten out of their systems, some of them even after fighting in a far-off war.

In the fall of 1975, while I was in high school, I discovered one such semipro football team, and lo and behold, it was practically in my own back yard: the Central Pennsylvania Whitetail Bucks.

1

The Summer and Fall of 1975 was the Bucks' inaugural season, and I was fascinated by the fact that our area had its own professional football team. It didn't matter that they were labeled "semipros." This was our own team, a team made up of local players from local schools. Players from Altoona, Philipsburg, Clearfield, State College and Tyrone. I read about their exploits in the local newspapers, intrigued by the team. Although the years passed, and the Bucks faded away into the mists of history, the memory of the team remained with me. I often wondered about the team, what had happened to them, and where they had gone.

This is their story.

Minor league football has been played all across the country, in big cities and small towns alike, from Rumford, Maine to Huntington Beach, California.

These teams have plugged away in conglomerates such as the Dixie League, the Cook County League, the Northwest Alliance, and the Mason-Dixon League. While these all too often loosely structured associations featured teams named after NFL squads like the Steelers, Bears, Cowboys and Jets, they also included teams with interesting monikers like the McKensie's Raiders of Costa Mesa, California, the Walker County Comrades of Jasper, Alabama, the NW Fighting Turkeys of Chicago, the Kentucky Trackers of Louisville, and the Eastside Express of Cincinnati.

Minor league football has always seemed to have a culture all its own. Its history is filled with colorful, offbeat and interesting stories.

In November of 1937, an independent team from McKeesport, Pennsylvania played the prison team from Rockview. According to an article in the November 2nd edition of the *Reading Eagle*, officials were puzzled when the McKeesport team came onto the field dressed in uniforms of various colors. The prison team easily defeated the strangely attired visitors, 24-0. After the game, a Corporal Raymond of the state motor police contacted Deputy Warren Rhoads at the penitentiary and told him to "hold that team." Raymond wasn't sending Rhoads an idea for a new cheer, but was conveying an order from Police Chief John J. Whalen of McKeesport to detain the semipro outfit. Unfortunately, the order came too late and the team had already departed. Whalen sent the order because he wanted to investigate the odd selection of uniforms the team was wearing. Seems the gymnasium of St. Peter's Catholic Church had 11 uniforms stolen. This after gymnasium officials had denied a request by the McKeesport team to borrow the uniforms. Two members of the McKeesport squad later met voluntarily with Chief Whalen and denied any knowledge of the missing uniforms.

In 1952 all 37 members of the Stonewall A.C. team from Washington, D.C. spent the night in jail for stealing liquor from a Hagerstown, Maryland store. The players purchased several items but had also walked off with 14 fifths of liquor, a couple cases of beer and several cartons of cigarettes. Police stopped the bus about six miles outside of town and found the missing items. A hurried call was made to team headquarters and club officials arrived at the jail with over $600 in cash stuffed in paper bags to pay the fines.

In 1980, Rich Fehling played linebacker for the Chambersburg Cardinals while working on a master's degree in business administration at Shippensburg State and clerking for a Federal Judge in Harrisburg. Fehling hadn't played competitive football since 1973 while at Yale.

In 1988, the Harrisburg Patriots were looking forward to opening their season with a new $1.38 million field and scoreboard. Only one thing was missing—the stands. Seems a company from Texas had shipped the sections of bleachers to another city.

The schedules prepared by semipro teams have often been fluid affairs, with game times and locations changing at the last minute. Teams have frequently moved or folded up their tents in mid-season. Games are often played on rock-strewn lots, sometimes with no amenities such as showers available.

The players have always been an odd mix of guys who run the gamut from kids who looked like they just graduated high school to men who look like they received their AARP card in the mail earlier that day.

These players will often play both offense and defense in an effort to save money and secure jobs. Others will serve as player/coaches or even do double duty as a general manager or part owner.

Despite the conditions and frequently low pay, some men have played the minor league and semipro game for many years, with some careers lasting decades.

Bob Blechen played the last game of his 41-year career in 1997 with the Los Angeles Mustangs. Paul Scopetski hung up his cleats in 2008 at the age of 61 after playing for 39 years. He appeared in a minor league-record 360 games.

Dick Barnes played from 1955 to 1989, finally retiring at age 68. Steve Moser, who played against the Bucks in 1975 (with Beaver County) and 1976 (with Sharon), bounced around the minors from 1971 to 1998, finally calling it a career at age 65.

Due to the uncertainty of teams and leagues, and in most cases just being too stubborn to quit, some players have toiled for an incredible number of teams over their careers. Rick Buffington and Skyler Sandoval, for example, both played for 14 teams during their time in the minors. Buffington managed to play for three teams in 1964 alone, but the record for most teams played for in a season is five, held by Tony Daliesso, who in 1958 played five games, one with each team, in one week!

Men play the game so long that there have been six incidents where a father and son were on the same team together. Wayne Marviglio played for the 2012 Glens Falls Greenjackets with his sons Ryan and Casey. Paul Scopetski hung around long enough that he and son Scott were both on the roster of the 1998 Leominster Lions.

Some of these men toiled for years on the hardscrabble fields of the minor leagues holding out hope that a scout might happen to see them and sign them up for the big-time. They were inspired by the stories of players such as Johnny Unitas, John Henry Johnson, Gino Cappelletti, Bob Tucker, Vince Papale, Lou Piccone, Jeff Van Note and Joe Klecko, who managed to turn the limited exposure in the minors into a career in the NFL, some of which led to Canton and the Hall of Fame.

Many of the others just played for the sheer love of the game, working in the factory or mill or office during the day and then practicing at night and playing on the weekends. Playing for the sheer joy of playing, still trying to get the game, which had drawn them in as a child, out of their blood.

They hung on by their fingernails; much like the teams they played for, they went from game-to-game surviving just to get back on that field, to play in one more game, to score one more touchdown, to sip one more taste of glory.

The Central Pennsylvania Whitetail Bucks were no exception. Like so many other men playing semipro football, they were, in the words of Leslie Kruk in Penn State's *Daily Collegian*, "a group of non-paid athletes doing what they love best—playing football."

# THE CAST OF CHARACTERS AND OTHER INTERESTED PARTIES

**Ken Andrews**
1976
Altoona
Johnstown High School

**Alex Anto**
1976–77
Guard/Linebacker
DuBois
Slippery Rock State College, 1973
Second team All-Southern Division
    selection at linebacker, 1977

**John Appleton**
1978
Player/Coach
Offensive/Defensive Tackle
Curwensville

**Ed Ardary**
1977
Defensive end
Lumber City

**Tom Arnelle**
1975
Defensive End/Tackle
State College
State College High School, 1971

**Randy Arthur**
1978
Offensive Guard/Linebacker
Altoona

**Jim Averill**
1978
Assistant Coach
DuBois

**Carl Baer**
1976
Ramey
Moshannon Valley High School,
    1975

**Tom Baer**
1975
Irvona

**Bill Bailey**
1977
Linebacker
Hyde
University of Pittsburgh
First team All-Southern
    Division selection at
    linebacker, 1977

**Lee Baughman**
1975
Defensive Lineman/Linebacker
Penn State

**Gary Baumgardner**
Head Coach, 1975
Assistant Coach, 1976

**Dave Belfield**
1976
Running Back
Altoona
Altoona Area High School, 1975

**Jeff Best**
1975–76
Linebacker
Irvona
Glendale High School

**Jeff Blowers**
1977
Defensive Tackle
Clearfield High School, 1972

**Scott Bowes**
1975
Guard
Clearfield
Indiana University of Pennsylvania

**Glen Brandimarte**
1976
Defensive back
Altoona
Altoona High School
Princeton

**Carl Brown**
1977
Tight end
Clearfield High School
Millersville State College
All-Southern Division first team
    selection at tight end, 1977

**Allan Butler**
1977
Defensive Back
Clearfield

**Mike Camuso**
1975
Running back/Linebacker
DuBois
Brockway High School, 1971

**Ted Castle**
1977
Wide Receiver
Bellwood

**John Challingsworth**
1978
Defensive back
St. Mary's

**Bill "Clicker" Clark**
1977–78
Running Back
DuBois High School

**Alan Claycomb**
1975
Running Back
Altoona

**Joe Crestani**
1977–78
Tight End/Offensive Tackle
Milesburg
Bald Eagle Area High School, 1967
Two tours of Vietnam with
    U.S. Navy
Brother of Len Crestani

**Len Crestani**
1977–78
Defensive Back
Brother of Joe Crestani
Julian, Pa.
Bald Eagle Area High School

**Bob Crook**
1977
Juniata College, 1975

**Phil Crotzer**
1978
Wide Receiver
Clearfield

**Mel Curtis**
1975
Philipsburg-Osceola High School,
    1970

**Ron Davison**
1978
Linebacker
Cresson

**Fred DeHaas**
1978
Linebacker
Bellefonte High School, 1972

**Arthur Delp**
1975
DuBois

**Don DeSantis**
1976
Assistant Coach

**Kevin Detwiler**
1977–78
Quarterback/Wide receiver/
    Defensive back
Tyrone High School, 1972

**George Dick**
1976
Linebacker
Irvona
Glendale High School

**John Dobo**
1975
Defensive Back
West Branch High School

**Mike Dobo**
1975
Linebacker
West Branch High School

**Steve Dobo**
1975

**Phil Flipse**
1975–76
End
Boalsburg
State College High School

**Al Folmar**
1975
Center
State College High School

**John Frantz**
1977
Defensive Tackle
DuBois

**Elton Futrell**
1976
Wide receiver
Altoona
Indiana University of
    Pennsylvania, 1973

**Dave Garito**
1975–76
Clearfield
Clearfield High School

**Hugh Gibbons**
1975–76–77–78
Wide Receiver
State College
State College High School
Penn State

**Joe Good**
1976–77
Running Back
Philipsburg
Philipsburg High School
All-Southern Division second
    team selection, 1977

**Bill Gordon**
1975–76
Halfback/Defensive Back
Curwensville
Served in United States Army

**Kevin Graham**
1978

**Terry Graham**
1975–78
Defensive tackle
Lockport (New York) High School

**Dave Gregg**
1976–77–78
Linebacker
Burnside, Pa.
Purchase Line High School, 1971

**Gary Griffith**
1975–76
Defensive Back
Hollidaysburg
Bloomsburg High School

**Dirk Grissinger**
1975–76–77
Defensive Tackle/Linebacker
Pine Grove Mills
State College High School, 1973
Slippery Rock State

**Ken Grove**
1975
Offensive Guard/Linebacker
State College High School, 1971
Thaddeus Stevens Tech

**Tom Hipp**
1975
Running back
Bishop Guilfoyle High School,
  1968
Memphis State

**John Hirt**
1975
Running Back
Bellwood-Antis High School

**Fred Hollin**
1976
Hollidaysburg
Hollidaysburg High School

**Guy Houghtaling**
1976
Fullback/Linebacker
Hollidaysburg
Altoona Area High School, 1972
Westminster College

**Doug Hrenko**
1975
Center/Guard
Philipsburg
Philipsburg-Osceola High School,
  1970
Thaddeus Stevens Tech

**Tim Irvin**
1975
Defensive Line/Linebacker
State College
State College High School

**Jeff Irvine**
1975
Irvona
Glendale High School

**Hyland Jeffries**
1976–77
Guard
Altoona

**Alge Jones**
1975–76–77
End
Philipsburg
Philipsburg-Osceola High School,
  1969

**Paul "Buck," "Bam-Bam"**
  **Kanagy**
1975
Linebacker
State College High School,
  1974

**Dale Keith**
1975–76
Center
Houtzdale
Glendale High School

**Kurt Kessler**
1976
Linebacker
Altoona
Bishop Guilfoyle High School,
  1975
Potomac State College

**Ron Kimberly**
1975
Defensive Back
Flinton
Glendale High School

**Gary Kizina**
1975–76
Wide Receiver
Coalport
Glendale High School

**Dan Kline**
1976
Defensive End
Hastings
Bishop Carroll High School

**Doug Kritzer**
1975–76, 78
Running Back
Clearfield
Clearfield High School

**Denny Kurtz**
1976–77–78
Defensive back
Clearfield
Served in United States Army

**Craig Kyler**
1975
Running Back
Philipsburg
Lenoir-Rhyne College,
    1969–72

**Larry Lane**
1978
Linebacker
State College

**Jeff Leone**
1975
Hastings

**Mike Leone**
1975
Team Manager

**Brian Lightner**
1978
Quarterback
Coalport
Glendale High School
Lock Haven State College

**Pat Little**
1975–76
Wide Receiver
State College
State College High School, 1971

**Bill Luther**
1975
Lineman/Kicker
Bellefonte
Penn State

**Mitch Mancuso**
1975–76
Defensive End
DuBois

**Tom Marlett**
1976–77
Linebacker
Altoona
Altoona Area High School, 1972
Shippensburg State College

**Harry Martz**
1976
Brockway
Brockway High School

**Jeff McCartney**
1975–76
Defensive Tackle
Altoona
Big 33 Selection

**Kevin McClincy**
1977–78
Guard/Offensive Tackle
Clearfield High School, 1972

**Les McCoy**
1975–76–77–78
Defensive End/Offensive Tackle
Clearfield
Clearfield High School

**Mike McNeish**
1975–76
Founded and organized team, 1975
Guard/Co-General Manager/
    General Manager/Assistant Coach
Philipsburg
Philipsburg-Osceola High School,
    1967
Columbia University

**Kevin Mickey**
1978
Running Back
Altoona

**Rob Miles**
1975
Running Back/Wide Receiver
Coalport
Glendale High School

**Tom Miller**
1975–76–77
Quarterback/Player Coach/
    Offensive Coordinator/
    Head Coach
Head Coach 1976
Tyrone High School, 1961
Colorado State

**Roy Mock III**
1975
Altoona

**Tom Monahan**
1978
Linebacker

**Mike Morgan**
1977–78
Wide receiver
Clearfield
Clearfield High School, 1975

**Terry Morgan**
1977
Tailback/Defensive Back
Curwensville High School, 1968

**Jon Morrison**
1976
Guard/Linebacker
Irvona
Glendale High School

**Bill Mumma**
1977
Linebacker
DuBois Area High School, 1976

**Jim Naddeo**
Team Owner
Clearfield Attorney

**Rick Nagel**
1977
Defensive back
Hastings
Glendale High School

**Viv Natoriani**
1975
Field Manager

**David Noel**
1976
Linebacker
Coalport
Glendale High School

**Rusty Noel**
1978
Defensive back
Altoona

**Joe Paddock**
1977
Defensive End

**Dave Paganetti**
Assistant Coach, 1975–76

**Gary Passarelli**
Assistant Coach, 1977
Head Coach, 1977 (replaced
   Don Turley)
Curwensville High School,
   1970

**Ken Pearson**
1977
Kicker
Tyrone

**Ed Peters**
1975
Defensive lineman
Philipsburg

**Gary Pheasant**
1976–77
End/Linebacker
Altoona High School, 1972
Purdue University

**Allen Pletcher**
1976
Offensive Tackle/Defensive
   Tackle
Bellefonte
Bellefonte High School

**Jeff Poorman**
1977
Defensive End
State College

**Allen Potter**
1975–76
Defensive back/Punter
State College
State College High School, 1972

**Tom Primerano**
1978
Running Back
Johnsonburg

**Ron Rehmeyer**
1978
Fullback
Boalsburg
University of Miami

**Steve Robinson**
1975
Running back
Tyrone

**Wayne Rockmore**
1975–76–77–78
Running Back
Assistant Coach, 1978
Head Coach 1978 (Replacing
    Al Siegel)
Clearfield
Clearfield High School, 1971
Rushed for 1,000 yards in 1976
All-Southern Division first team
    selection, 1976–77

**John Roefaro**
Ball boy in 1977
Son of Ron Roefaro

**Ron Roefaro**
1975–76–77
Offensive Tackle
Altoona
Bishop Guilfoyle, 1965
Mansfield State College, 1970

**Greg "Bear" Rowles**
1977
Center/Guard
Wrestled and played football at
    Clearfield High School
Served with the United States
    Army during the Vietnam
    Era

**Mark Rusnak**
1978
Center
Madera
Moshannon Valley High School,
    1978

**Darrel Rutter**
1975–76–77–78
Defensive End
Brother of Ken and John Rutter
Claysburg
Altoona High School
Penn State University

**John Rutter**
1977
Defensive end
Altoona
Brother of Darrel and Ken Rutter

**Ken Rutter**
1975–76–77–78
Wide receiver
Brother of Darrel and
    John Rutter
Altoona

**Larry Rydbom**
1975–76
Quarterback
Brother of Terry Rydbom
Irvona
Glendale High School, 1970

**Terry Rydbom**
1975
End
Brother of Larry Rydbom

**Larry Shank**
1976
Trainer

**Denny Shaw**
1978
Linebacker
Warriors Mark

**Jerry Shivery**
1977–78
Running Back
Bellefonte High School, 1968

**Ritchie Shoop**
1975–76–77–78
Running back/Kicker/Punter
Hollidaysburg High School

**Al Siegel**
1975–76–77–78
Center/Offensive Tackle/Tight
    End/Defensive End/Guard/
    Co-General Manager/General
    Manager/Assistant Coach/
    Head Coach
Brooklyn, New York
All-Southern Division first team
    selection at guard, 1977
Head Coach, 1978

**Jay Siegel**
Team Manager/Assistant Trainer
Son of Al Siegel

**Charvi Skillings**
1975–76–77
Running back/Kicker/Defensive
    Back
Brother of Rich Skillings
Tyrone
Tyrone High School, 1972

**Rich Skillings**
1976
End/Kicker
Brother of Charvi Skillings
Tyrone
Tyrone High School

**Jim Slabon**
1975–76–77–78
Quarterback/Defensive Back
Osceola Mills
Philipsburg-Osceola High School,
    1971

Shippensburg State
All-Southern Division selection at
 defensive back, 1976–77
Assistant Coach, 1978

**Kerry Snow**
1978
Quarterback/Kick returner/
 Wide receiver
Bucknell University

**John Socoski**
1977
Guard
Brother of Nick Socoski
Philipsburg-Osceola, 1976

**Nick Socoski**
1977
Guard
Brother of John Socoski
Philipsburg-Osceola, 1976

**John Sommer**
1975
Linebacker
Defensive Captain
Bishop Guilfoyle High School, 1968
Clarion State College

**Gary Spizzirri**
1976
Defensive End
Brookville
Redbank High School, 1972

**Jim Steinbugl**
1975

Defensive End
Bishop Guilfoyle High School,
 1973
Wesley Junior College

**Mark Stewart**
1977
Linebacker
Osceola Mills

**Jim Stoneberg**
1977–78
Quarterback
Cambria Heights

**John Stoneberg**
1977–78
Defensive Tackle/End
Ashville
All-League, 1977

**Jim Stricek**
1976
Assistant Trainer

**Don Turley**
Head Coach, 1977

**Rod Ullein**
1976
Defensive End/Tight End
Altoona
Altoona Area High School
U.S. Naval Academy

**Jack Volpe**
1978
Defensive back

**Tom Walburn**
1977
Defensive Back
DuBois

**Albe Wales**
1975–76–77
Guard/Linebacker
Brother of Joe Wales
Altoona
Taft College, California

**Joe Wales**
1976–77–78
Guard/Defensive End
Brother of Albe Wales
Altoona
Altoona High School, 1969
Served in Marine Corps, Okinawa,
    Vietnam 1970 to 1973

**Dan Walker**
1976
Defensive End
State College High School,
    1975

**George Walker**
1976–77–78
Offensive/Defensive Tackle
Pine Grove Mills

**Greg Walker**
1976, 78
Defensive Lineman
Bellefonte

**Dave Wayland**
1977
Defensive End
Clearfield
Clearfield High School

**Jerry White**
1975
Running back
Brother of John White
West Branch High School

**John White**
1975
Defensive lineman
Brother of Jerry White
West Branch High School

**Howard Wilcox**
1978
Defensive back
State College

**George "Peachy" Williams**
1978
Linebacker
Clearfield High School

**Joe Williams**
1977–78
Linebacker
Mingoeville

**John Withers**
1975
Quarterback/Linebacker
Altoona High School, 1970
West Virginia University, 1973

**George Wisor**
1977
Defensive back
Clearfield

**Scott Yocum**
1976
State College, Pa.
Penn State

**Stanley Paul "Stash" Yastro**
1975
Defensive Lineman
Osceola Mills
Philipsburg-Osceola High School,
    1967
Lycoming College, 1971

**Herman "Hymie" Ziff**
Team Owner
General Manager, 1977
Part-owner, Ziff clothing stores

# CHAPTER

# 1

"Sometimes it seemed like we were playing for a hoagie and a beer."
—RON ROEFARO, BUCKS OFFENSIVE TACKLE

The Whitetail Bucks were certainly not the area's first experience with minor league or semipro football.

Central Pennsylvania's history regarding semipro football stretches all the way back to the late 19th century. In fact, professional football developed in the 1890s in Pennsylvania, as local athletic clubs first engaged in competitive football games. Soon, teams representing Altoona, Johnstown, Huntingdon, and Punxsutawney were playing in various leagues throughout the last decade of the century.

Semipro outfits such as the Johnstown Capital Club and the Punxsutawney State Police continued to represent towns and cities of the region into the 1900s. In the 1920s and '30s, Portage alone had three semipro teams—the Quakers, the Light Olympics and the Bulldogs. The most successful of these teams were the Bulldogs, who played from the time they organized shortly after World War I until 1956. The team was much like the Whitetail Bucks, made up of miners and steel workers and other laborers whose work schedules made it necessary for the team to play on Sundays. Like the Bucks, they played a rough-and-tumble game where pay was doled out sporadically, if at all. The Bulldogs did not lose a game during their first eight years, and even played a home contest against the NFL's Pittsburgh Steelers (then known as the Pirates) in September of 1935. The game, a 46-0 win by the Pirates, drew 3,000 fans to Moose Field, the Bulldogs' home field located behind the Conemaugh Health Center on Route 53.

According to local historian Harry Breon, the Osceola Indies played semipro ball during the 1930s. "The Osceola team had a cheer called 'Eat 'em up Osceola,'" says Breon.

Breon also recalls another local team from the '30s called the Bellefonte Governors, so named because Bellefonte has been home to five of Pennsylvania's governors as well as two other governors.

Breon says the Governors played from 1930 to 1934, and were fairly successful on the field. In 1930 the team had a record of 7-1, losing only to the Lock Haven Centrals by a score of 12-0. Breon remembers that a year later the Governors got some revenge by edging Lock Haven 7-0. They also nipped a team from South Williamsport, 7-6 and managed to tie Portage 6-6 before several thousand fans, a gate that guaranteed each Governor $119, a princely sum in those days. In 1932, Breon recalls that the Governors struggled a bit, losing twice to Lock Haven, once on the road on Thanksgiving Day, and dropping a 47-0 decision to the Williamsport Amateurs before 800 fans. The Governors also lost star player Carl Moerschbacher in that game, as the big tackle tore ligaments in his arm and finished the season with his arm in a sling.

Another highlight for the team was a 7-6 win over arch-rival Lock Haven in 1934. Breon says that although Lock Haven's Fritz Lucas returned an interception 70 yards for a touchdown, the Governors managed to pull the game out on a 7-yard touchdown run by Max Kelly. "Some of the other players over the years," Breon says, "included Cam Heverly, Paul Crust, Norbert Derstine, Press Garbick, Jim Carpeneto, Lank Wasson, Dutch Waite, and Dick Ulrich."

Following World War II, the Altoona Mountaineers began play in the Pennsylvania Pro League. The Mountaineers played for two years, 1946 and '47, finishing with a record of 6-7 in their first year and 8-5-1 in their second. The team, coached by former Altoona High star Maurice "Babe" Patt, regularly drew crowds of up to 5,000 people to Cricket Field, which sat at the intersection of Chestnut Avenue and Seventh Street.

One of their opponents were the Johnstown Clippers, who played one year, 1947, in Point Stadium, fashioning a 4-3-2 record.

In the late 1950s and early 1960s, the Clearfield Hornets played in a semipro league called the Pennsylvania-Maryland League. Besides the Hornets, this loop included other Pennsylvania teams such as the Lebanon Valley Golden Gophers, the Lower Paxton Rangers, the Verona Rams, and the Pittsburgh South Side Merchants. The Hornets, like the Bucks, were made up of local talent, with players from Clearfield, Cooper Township, Philipsburg, Curwensville, and

Morris Township. These men had experience of varying degrees at either the high school or collegiate level.

Just like the Bucks and other semipro outfits, the Hornets had to cut costs anywhere and any way they could. George Pretash, for example, doubled as the team's starting fullback and team president.

The Hornets were coached by Jim McCoy and played most of their home games at the Clearfield Driving Park, the same venue the Bucks would use at times in the '70s. But after the Hornets folded, the area lacked for any kind of local semipro team, and fans had to satisfy their thirst for Sunday football by rooting for the Steelers or Eagles.

Then a young man with local ties by the name of Mike McNeish came along. He had a vision of a semipro football team playing in the area.

McNeish had graduated from Philipsburg-Osceola Area High in 1967. He was an undersized but tough lineman for two varsity seasons, Bill Haushalter's last and Raymond "Bud" O'Brien's first as Mountie head coaches.

After high school, McNeish played offensive guard and defensive tackle at Columbia University.

"If you're familiar at all with Ivy League football," recalled McNeish in a recent interview, "you'll know the Columbia Lions are the traditional doormat of the Ivies, at least in football. I think in four years we maybe won 4 games."

He received his degree in 1971 and then became assistant director of student activities. That's when he got involved in semipro football.

"When I graduated," McNeish remembers, "I remained in New York City and worked at Columbia in the Student Activities Department. I still wanted to play and happened to hear about a team in Harlem, at 137th and Lex, I think. I don't remember the name but I played a year with them. The league was primarily black and Hispanic teams.

"After that year, I heard about another team, the New York Rams, a bit of a step up in the semipro world. My wife used to call our brand of football 'semi-football.' The Rams had a lot of very good players, mostly ex-college players, a couple who ended up with free agent tryouts with the Jets; one made it to the last cut. I played with them for that year [1972], primarily at offensive guard though I did play some defensive tackle from time to time.

"The owner and coach of the team was the cover editor for Newsweek magazine. The quarterback was a guy by the name of Bob Oates, a freelance sports writer with hair down to the middle of his back and a full beard. He was an excellent quarterback though, I've played with none better. He had a friendship with Joe Namath who was still with the Jets. Oates had an extensive article about the team published in the NFL magazine that was the weekly program."

In 1973, McNeish returned to Philipsburg to start graduate work at Penn State. But his appetite for football had not been sated.

"Anyway," McNeish continues, "I had decided to go to graduate school at Penn State which meant I would not be able to play for the Rams, or so I thought. The team owner said he would fly both me and my fiancé up to New York on Fridays where we would stay in the *Newsweek* floor of the Waldorf-Astoria Hotel. We had room service, as much as we wanted, and I'd get $125 'walking around money.' We'd play Sunday afternoon and then fly back late Sunday afternoon or evening. We would fly from Black Moshannon Airport on Friday evening to Newark or LaGuardia. One weekend the airline lost my equipment though they had it back to me by Saturday evening in time to play Sunday's game."

McNeish played well enough for the Rams to warrant a tryout with the New York Jets during the NFL Players' Association strike in the summer of 1974.

While he did enjoy playing for the Rams, McNeish wanted to play closer to home, however.

"Playing for the Rams lasted for a season but it became apparent I couldn't be in graduate school in Pennsylvania and also play football in New York City," McNeish recalls, "I concentrated on academics through the Spring of 1975 then figured out that if all my cohorts in graduate school all got our PhDs, we'd fill all the jobs in Anthropology in the entire United States for the next 25 years. I took that as an omen to get a real job.

"So, we moved to Philipsburg, since I was originally from Osceola Mills. I played touch football Sundays in the high school stadium with a bunch of guys I played with in high school, Alg Jones and Craig Kyler [*who would both wind up with the Bucks*] among them. We talked a lot about wanting to play "real" football again but couldn't see a way to do it.

"My Dad, Jim McNeish, was the manager of the Wolf's Furniture store in town. He had played football in high school and had a scholarship to play at Holy Cross but turned it down, that was during the Depression and he felt he could not leave his family.

"Anyway, there was a team in Osceola, the Osceola Indies, which I'm not sure if that was short for 'Independents' or 'Indians'; when Osceola High School was a separate school from Philipsburg, the school's mascot was Chief Osceola and they were known as the Indians.

"That gave me the spark to maybe start an independent team that played 'real' football."

McNeish's persistence and determination helped make his dream a reality. Spurred by the interest of several football buffs in the Philipsburg area, McNeish organized a team he called the Central Pennsylvania Miners in the Spring of 1975.

Confident of his efforts, McNeish even went one step further and entered the Miners in the Mid-Atlantic Semipro League based in East Palestine, Ohio.

As acting general manager and assistant coach, two jobs he said he was more than ready to give up to anyone who was interested and/or qualified, since he really wanted to play, McNeish checked out the league as soon as he could.

"I heard about the league around Pittsburgh, so I started investigating," he said at the time. "I contacted one league, although that's not the one we're in. When we really got the ball rolling here, I called some people in Pittsburgh and found out they had changed the league.

"There are eight teams in the Mid-Atlantic League. They are the Pittsburgh Ironmen, Latrobe Laurel Leopards, Washington Generals, Beaver County Cougars and us in Pennsylvania and the East Palestine Red Devils, Leetonia All-Stars and Eastern Ohio Dukes in Ohio. There is a possibility that one more team from each state may be added."

Like many semipro and minor league outfits, the MAFL played a rough brand of football that was not for the faint of heart.

"It was a tough league," remembers linebacker Tom Marlett.

"Some of those guys on the other teams thought they were in the Super Bowl," relates Darrel Rutter, who played several positions for the Bucks, "It could get vicious and mean. It was without a doubt the toughest semipro conference in the country, and was the roughest ball I ever played, even more so than service ball."

"It was rough," remembers wide receiver Ken Rutter, "They would push in on my eyes in the pileup. In one game they ripped my lip off!"

"Teams were made up of guys who had been cut by the pros and were sent down to play semipro ball to keep in shape," recalls defensive and offensive lineman Joe Wales, "My brother Albe had a big full beard and he shaved it off. I asked him why and he said, 'They kept pulling it in the pileup!'"

The Mid-Atlantic League opened play in late July and early August, and its season ran through Saturday October 25th. This was because many of the teams played on local high school fields, and scheduling games became more difficult as the calendar moved deeper into Fall.

"We could only get the fields before the high school seasons started," says Joe Wales, "We played in the dead of summer."

This led to players finding relief from the hot, humid Pennsylvania summers any way they could.

"It was 100 degrees in Glendale for a game," recalls Darrel Rutter, who wound up playing all four years with the club, "I was sweating, hot as hell. At halftime, I went out behind the stadium and there was a creek back there. I laid down in the creek in full uniform and let the cool water run over me. A couple kids came along and they thought I had drowned."

McNeish stated that each team played 10 games, and that the league had two divisions, with the Miners booked into the same group as Beaver County, Leetonia and Pittsburgh.

McNeish told reporters at the time that he hoped to draw players from all over Central Pennsylvania, from DuBois to State College, from Clearfield to Altoona. He added that he was shooting for June 23rd as the first day of preseason practice.

There was one roadblock. The team needed money.

"We're negotiating with a backer right now," McNeish said at the time. "The person is very interested but we've hit a snag.

"Things are getting down to the wire, and we need money," McNeish continued. "We have to order equipment soon and get an agreement with the school board for the field. We would like to have a substantial amount in reserve so we can get a lot of initial bills paid up.

"We would have to incorporate, pay for the insurance of the players as well as liability insurance. We need money for lights, stadium costs and transportation."

McNeish urged anybody and everybody in the area who was interested in investing with the Miners to contact him. To get an idea of what it was like back in those days in small-town America, the newspaper article in which McNeish asked people to contact him included his home phone number.

McNeish stressed that the Miners were a semipro operation, and that the players would not be paid. They would instead be reimbursed for their transportation expenses only.

"They told us we were an independent league," remembers Joe Wales, "that's why they couldn't pay us for games; we only got paid for practice."

"I've had this idea on my mind for two years," McNeish continued. "It's taken me this long to talk to the right people, who'd be at least interested in backing something like this.

"It gets in your blood, I guess. I thought about it long enough, and I feel it's something that would work here."

McNeish did it all for the Bucks, and to get his idea off the ground. He raised capital, organized practices, and served as both an assistant coach and as general manager for the club.

Thanks to McNeish's exhaustive efforts, by late May the team had become less a pipe dream and more of a reality, and it did indeed look like Central Pennsylvania would have its very own semipro football team in 1975.

The team's home base had shifted to Clearfield, and the nickname had been changed from the Miners to the Whitetail Bucks.

The name change was appropriate due to the fact that white-tailed deer—known in the area as "whitetails"—were, and are, Pennsylvania's best known wildlife species and only big game animal. It also gave the team what might be one of the longest names in the history of sports—the Central Pennsylvania Whitetail Bucks.

"I'm not entirely sure how the word got out but I believe I made contact with the sports editor of the *Clearfield Progress* who published an article about the idea," says McNeish now, "He gave us some press and we were able to get some backing as well as get the word out in central Pennsylvania about tryouts."

John W. Dixon of the *Philipsburg Daily Journal* also put out articles in support of the venture, saying due to the amount of football fans in Philipsburg as well as the 50,000 or so potential fans in State College, the idea of a semipro team in the area did not seem like much of a gamble.

McNeish had encountered a major stumbling block when it came to financial backing. But like his approach to all other areas of the operation, he persisted and it paid off in the form of a man who would be a vital part of the Bucks' franchise.

"I made contact with Al Siegel," remembers McNeish.

"Now there was a character," lineman and kicker Bill Luther recalls, "He had that thick New York accent."

"When he walked into a room, you knew he was there," running back Wayne Rockmore remembers of Siegel, "Everybody knew him and was glad they did. I learned a lot from him. He had a good head on his shoulders. He really helped me become a little more outgoing."

Siegel was born November 9th, 1937, in Brooklyn, New York, the son of Philip and Ray (Fleisher) Siegel.

In 1959, he married Brenda Rosen in Brooklyn, and they had two sons, Hal and Jay. Al then played minor league football for many years, bouncing from one team, and one league, to another, logging time with teams such as the Brooklyn Knights and New York Cardinals.

His experience playing in New York City, and the connections he made while there, would be an invaluable help in scheduling games with various teams from the Big Apple.

Siegel finally settled in Clearfield, and was president of the Clearfield Recreation Board and also served on the board of the Clearfield Chamber of Commerce and the Good Samaritans. He was a member of the Benevolent and Protective Order of Elks, Clearfield Lodge No. 540, the Fraternal Order of Police in Clearfield and the Loyal Order of Moose, Curwensville Lodge No. 268.

He also was a Boy Scout training chairman and leader, and was a member of the Beth Shalom Temple in Clearfield where he served as president for over 15 years. He was very active in civic endeavors in Clearfield through both his Temple and with Catholic Charities.

"Al was a great guy, a typical New Yorker—assuming there is a typical New Yorker—with a strong Brooklyn accent," recalled McNeish in a recent interview, "He was very gregarious and outgoing. He had played in New York City for the Brooklyn Knights in the same league I had played in with the Rams. I'm not sure if we ever played against each other though."

"Al was a real businessman," Darrel Rutter stated in a recent interview, "He got stuff done. If he told you he'd do something he did it. He was a good family man, no nonsense guy."

Basically Siegel was what is referred to as a "stand-up" guy.

"He was interested enough to put the idea before some people he thought might be interested in backing a team," says McNeish.

Through Siegel's efforts, the Whitetail Bucks were able to obtain the financial support to begin operations immediately. Siegel described the backing as "a lot of money" and added that a corporation would be set up in a few days to handle the team's monetary affairs.

"The financial backers were Jim Naddeo, an attorney in Clearfield and Al, I believe his name was, Johnson of the Johnson Coal Company down the line around Snow Shoe," remembers McNeish, "I do not know if Al approached anyone else. It's possible he did but at least for the years I was involved, the financial backing came from Jim Naddeo and Johnson."

With funds in the bank, the Bucks announced they would begin tryouts on May 27th at the Clearfield Driving Park.

On the subject of the Driving Park, on the same day that the Bucks held their first tryout at the aged facility, the Kamtro Company of Osceola Mills was awarded a contract for repairing and renovating the grandstand at the Park.

The company, with a bid of $19,725.70, was the low bidder among the four companies that submitted bids to the Clearfield Park Authority. The bids were received at a special meeting on May 21st, and were under study until the authority's special meeting on the 27th. The contract included patching of the concrete work and the application of a protective coating and a color coating over the entire grandstand exterior.

Work on the project was scheduled to start by the beginning of the following week so that it could be completed before the 1975 Clearfield County Fair, traditionally held during the end of July and beginning of August. The authority members said it was necessary to carry out the project because the grandstand was rapidly deteriorating. Pieces of concrete had chipped and dropped off, causing a safety hazard.

But would the Whitetail Bucks be able to use the renovated facility? In addition to awarding the contract, another order of business on the agenda was discussing use of the field at the Driving Park. The authority discussed this matter with Fred Neiswender, athletic director for the Clearfield Area Schools, and McNeish and Siegel, representing the Bucks. Authority Chairman Nick Biviano said that since the field was rented by the school district, it would be up to the schools to decide the extent to which it could be used by the Bucks.

Mr. Neiswender stated that he had no objection to the field being used for games, provided it was not during rainy weather or at times when it would be needed by scholastic teams. He added that he was opposed, however, to the field being used for practice sessions. He suggested that the section of the infield used as a practice field by the schools be used instead.

McNeish then spoke and reassured the authority that the Bucks had already obtained a practice field at Philipsburg and added that some of the games would be played at Philipsburg rather than at Clearfield anyway. Siegel said that probably only one or two games would be played at Clearfield, but insisted that these would have to go on, rain or shine. Since the Bucks' schedule had to be set by June 10th, the authority suggested that McNeish and Siegel meet with the authority members and Mr. Neiswender again sometime after that.

Siegel explained to the authority that as semipros none of the players would be paid and that sponsors would pay for the teams' uniforms, equipment and transportation. Siegel added that admission would be charged for all games.

"I have been trying for three years to get this started as a type of recreation which adults can enjoy, either as players or spectators," Big Al told the authority.

"This was a dream of Mike's and mine," Siegel said at the time, "We had both played semipro ball in New York and wanted to see it here. We got several backers who basically loaned us the money to get started and they're willing to take a tax loss or regard it as an investment. We will have our corporation set up within a week.

"We think this is the hottest thing to happen to football in central Pennsylvania since Joe Paterno," Siegel continued, "We would love to show people what we have and, if we can get enough people to show up at the gate, we could break even financially.

"Our expenses will run right around $12,000 and hopefully, we'll have a little more than that when all our backers send their checks in," Siegel went on, "We have backers from all over the area. We've bought our equipment, the players are all insured and when we go to away games we'll be going by bus."

In a later meeting, the Bucks were given permission to use the Driving Park for games. Rain or shine. Just as Darrel Rutter recalls, Siegel got stuff done.

So far, however, the team didn't have a head coach, and still needed people like managers, trainers and other helpers. Despite this, the team soldiered on.

"I knew Al Siegel because I worked in a gas station that he stopped at," says Mike Leone, who served as team manager in 1975, "and I remember talking to him about the startup of the team. They held practices in Philipsburg at the practice field near the football field. I remember Mike McNeish as being one of the leaders pushing to get the team started too. I didn't make it to too many of the games, but I was usually there on Sundays when they practiced to help out where I could. Sometimes I hauled all the extra equipment around and stored it in our garage until we got permanent storage."

Lacking a head coach, McNeish and Siegel put themselves in charge of the workouts. Siegel was also serving as the team's temporary general manger, but still hoped to play, even though at the age of 38 he would be the team's oldest player, and old enough to be the father to many of his teammates.

When the time came for the tryouts, however, the turnout was to say the least disappointing. Few local players showed up, and McNeish and Siegel were worried. There was real concern that the dream would die before it had a chance to live.

"I was going up to Clearfield for a racing pigeons meeting," says Darrel Rutter, "I was interested in them at the time. They told us about a team starting up. Had no idea there was a football team starting up when we went up there.

"Siegel and McNeish started the team," Rutter continues, "At the first tryout there was hardly anyone there."

"Very early in the tryouts we did not get many players," McNeish recalls.

Siegel and McNeish told those few who had shown up that if they didn't get any more interest they'd have to fold the team. Rutter says, "I told them, 'Don't worry,' and I went back to Altoona and got a few players to agree to come up and tryout."

Rutter got his brother Ken, who had played service ball in the Navy, running back Tom Hipp who had played for Bishop Guilfoyle High School and Memphis State University, and John Withers, who had played linebacker and quarterback for Altoona High and at West Virginia University, to go with him up to Clearfield for the tryouts. The players thought it would be a waste of time. "We didn't know if we'd make it but we decided to try out," says Rutter.

Soon other players were being recruited to join Siegel and McNeish's merry band, mostly through word-of-mouth.

"We started bringing in guys from the Altoona/State College area, all over Central Pa.," offers Darrel Rutter, "Al Siegel told me, 'If it wasn't for the Altoona kids, the Bucks would have never made it.'"

"Word spread quickly," says McNeish.

"I was painting my house, up on a ladder," says offensive tackle Ron Roefaro, another Altoona native, "Tom Hipp pulled up and yelled up to me, 'Hey you wanna play some football?' I said I didn't think so; I was kind of out of shape. Hipp said, 'C'mon with us.' So I went. Wound up playing almost three years!"

"I read an article in the paper, so I went up to Clearfield to try out," recalls linebacker Paul "Bam-Bam" Kanagy from State College, "When I got to the tryout everyone was taller than me but that didn't mean a thing to me. Never thought I'd make it, but I ran a 4.3 40 and they about shit. Coach Baumgardner talked to me, told me what I needed to bring, so I went to my high school and got my old equipment. Couldn't believe they let me have it."

"Al (Siegel) told me, 'Hey Wayne, why don't you come over to the field and try out?'" remembers running back Wayne Rockmore from Clearfield.

"I had just graduated from Penn State in the spring of '75," says Bellefonte's Bill Luther, who would place-kick and play on the offensive and defensive lines for the Bucks, "I was 22 years old. One of the guys from State College told me about the team so I tried out."

"In 1975 I was a sophomore at Penn State," recalls Pat Little, who played wide receiver for the Bucks that first season, "I called the Penn State football office to see about walking on and I spoke with Jerry Sandusky. He told me to come up and run a 40. Well, I knew that was the end right there. I wasn't fast but I could catch. So, I never went. Then the Bucks opportunity presented itself. My best friend Allen Potter and I played a lot of football with the college kids on Sunday afternoons and, usually, ran over them. We both played for State High and were in very good shape. So, we gave it a shot."

Thanks to the word finally getting out, more than 40 players from Clearfield, Curwensville, Philipsburg, Osceola Mills, Coalport, Tyrone and State College wound up reporting for tryouts. "We ended up with 35-40 total on the roster," says McNeish.

The Central Pennsylvania Whitetail Bucks were still alive.

"Semi-Happy Valley—Central Pa.'s other football team!" Penn State grad Darrel Rutter likes to call the Bucks, "We didn't take just anybody either. The team only kept the best. Some guys got cut. We didn't keep the hamburger, just the steak!"

At first the players felt a bit uncomfortable around their new teammates.

"It was a little weird at first," says Pat Little, "We played with some of the players we played against in high school and some were much older than us. The guys from Tyrone would rag us [the players from State College] that first year. They destroyed our undefeated season at the end of 1971 and they never let us forget it. It was good natured, but it was always a sore spot with us.

"However, we all had one thing in common: we all loved the game. We all became good friends in the end. The respect was always mutual, no matter where you came from. The league was tough and you could see that in the faces of our team in every game. My teammates were one rough group of football players who didn't play for glory, but loved to hit and play the game."

The team had players, but now it needed a head coach and some assistants. Practice was set to start in early June, and the team still had no one at the helm. McNeish and Siegel continued to stress that they preferred playing to coaching, but were still running things just to keep the team going.

"Big Al was the guy that talked us into playing for the Bucks," remembers Pat Little, "He told us, from the start, that we were not going to be paid, but he added with his laugh, 'This will be something you can tell your grandkids.' I really remember him and McNeish. They were both older and played because they loved it. I had a lot of respect for that."

Then, on May 28th, the Bucks announced they had hired their head coach.

Gary Baumgardner, a former assistant coach at Philipsburg-Osceola Area High under Steve Prisuta, and at Clearfield Area High under Bob Bonn, was named head coach of the Whitetail Bucks.

"Baumgardner—we called him Bummy—he was a good guy," remembers wide receiver Hugh Gibbons.

"My hat is off to this gentle teacher," Darrel Rutter recalls when asked about Baumgardner, "He took on the team first, and set the standard."

Baumgardner and his two acting assistants, McNeish and Siegel, continued to hold tryouts at the Driving Park in the hope of finding more able bodies for the team.

The team then hired Dave Paganetti from State College as an assistant coach, and asked quarterback Tom Miller from Tyrone to double as the offensive coordinator.

"I remember them being old-school coaches, where toughness dominated," recalls linebacker Tom Marlett.

"Baumgardner pretty much let the guys do what they wanted," says lineman Bill Luther, "We had plays, but most of the time we wound up just winging it.

"McNeish kind of coached the linemen," continues Luther. "Al [*Siegel*] thought he was in charge but we didn't really listen to him. We'd just think, "Right Al, whatever."

"I viewed and interacted with the Bucks coaches differently than the previous coaches that I had in high school and college," recalls Ron Roefaro, "I respected them and liked them but they weren't our mentors or motivators like the coaches at the other levels were. They put structure and stability to what we were trying to accomplish. We didn't have any films or scouting reports to review. No tendencies to study and prepare for. We just went out and played football the best way that we knew how.

"The coaches added some offensive and defensive structure and stability to what we were trying to accomplish . . . that was trying to win football games. At practice there wasn't a lot of drills or practicing of techniques. Our practices were centered around knowing our offensive and defensive plays and schemes. Many times we weren't sure who was going to show up for the games, so we had to know what to do at different positions. I think we had more interaction and trust with our leaders on the field, like the quarterback. The coaches added structure and some stability to a somewhat wild and woolly bunch of players."

The addition of Paganetti to the Bucks staff was one of the more positive moves the team made that first season.

"When Paganetti came in he changed our offense," recounts quarterback Tom Miller, "I was running the offense from the Harrisburg Capitols, the farm club of the Baltimore Colts, which was the same as the Colts' pro offense. Paganetti put the Veer in, which Oklahoma was using at the time. I really liked it, I liked the blocking schemes. It just took reading the tackles and calling a dive or a pitch."

"He was a master mind of football," says Pat Little of Paganetti, "He had concepts that are used today and people call genius. He knew the rules inside and out and used them."

"He was in grad school and was just getting established," adds Darrel Rutter when asked about Paganetti, "In my opinion he was born to coach. He was an X's and O's technician. He was fundamentally sound, a real solid coach and the guys liked him."

Since semipro teams could afford only so many coaches because of budget restraints, Paganetti worked with the offense and defense.

"Paganetti did a lot for the defense," says Hugh Gibbons, "He was a good coach."

"Coach Paganetti was there two plus years and was really into it," remembers wide receiver Ken Rutter, "He was very motivated and fully understood the game. I liked his style of football. He implemented the flea flicker pass or half back pass and we usually used it once a game and occasionally scored on it."

The reason Rutter liked Paganetti and the flea flicker was because he was the one who made the play work.

"The halfback option pass, or flea-flicker, was our bread-and-butter play," remembers Rutter, "I would take the handoff and start around end. I really had that ball tucked away to make it look like I was gonna run with it. Meanwhile, Alge Jones would be playing end. He would do a roll block to fool the defense, but would then get up and take off and he would be all alone."

Rutter's name is still listed prominently in the semipro football record book thanks to his success with the flea flicker.

"He could fire that thing 70 yards," offers his brother Darrel, "Should have been our quarterback." Then with a smile, Darrel adds, "The balls were deflated, of course. He mentored (Tom) Brady on that."

Miller's promotion and the hiring of Paganetti allowed McNeish and Siegel to concentrate on playing. They did, however, continue to act as the team's co-General Managers in an effort to both maintain some sense of continuity as well as save money.

The Bucks announced they were going to play an 11-game schedule, including two exhibitions and nine games against Mid-Atlantic League opponents. Their inaugural season would open August 9th with an exhibition against the Brooklyn Golden Knights in State College. A week later the team would play on the road against the Beaver County Cougars. Then it was back home to face the Washington Generals in Philipsburg, followed by another exhibition with the New York City Tigers at a site to be determined. Two weeks later the Bucks would host the formidable Pittsburgh Ironmen, again at Philipsburg. Then it was on the road again for contests at Latrobe and East Palestine, Ohio. On October 4th, the Bucks would play the Dayton Steelers at a site to be determined, then a week later journey to Washington, Pa. for a return match with the Generals. The Whitetail Bucks would host Latrobe at Clearfield, and then finish the season on the road at Pittsburgh.

The team announced that season tickets for the six home games would set a person back $12.50. The cost of admission at the gate would be $2.50 per game, but that ticket would admit one adult and one child under 12.

A semiprofessional athlete is defined as one who is paid to play and is not an amateur, but for whom their sport is not a full-time occupation, generally because the level of pay is too low to make a reasonable living based solely upon that source, making the athlete not a full professional athlete. As the team's roster began to take shape, this description fit the Bucks to a 'tee.' Like so many semipro outfits, the Bucks were composed of guys who wanted to give the sport one more try, to score one more touchdown, make one more big catch, tackle one more runner.

"This is football for football's sake. Central Pennsylvania produces a lot of good athletes who are never utilized after college," Mike McNeish told Leslie Kruk in an article for Penn State's *Daily Collegian*.

But, unlike pro ball, where the players work at the game full-time, the Bucks' squad was made up of guys who had day jobs to pay the bills. There were coal miners, accountants, teachers, salesmen, construction workers, supervisors, students, skilled laborers, and truck drivers. One player drove 70 miles one way to make it to practice. Ken Rutter and Joe Wales both worked for the railroad. Wayne Rockmore says he worked at various jobs while playing for the Bucks, including carpentry, construction and with the railroad. Tom Miller taught school at Tyrone High School, Ron Roefaro at Penn Cambria High. Darrel Rutter worked as a school teacher, in the mill and with the railroad during the day to make ends meet while he played for the Bucks.

"Most semipro players never got the cure from playing football," offers Darrel Rutter, "Their motivation came from within. The game was its own reward. It's not the NFL, but it's still football. Pride played a big part. Plus the personal satisfaction of being able to stay in shape."

The players ranged in age from 18 to 38 with an average age of around 24 or 25. And although they were technically "semipros," the team wasn't really getting paid.

"I'll tell you something," Al Siegel was quoted in an article by Ron Bracken in *The Centre Daily Times*, "These guys are here for only one reason: they want to play football. They're not getting a penny. We had two sessions last week and we had 36 guys at one and 39 at the other and of our 45-man roster 43 guys made one of the two sessions. And you're talking about guys who work, have families and vacations. They want to play. We want to do one thing and that's to play football. We would love to show the people what we have."

"We only played because we liked to play," remembers Joe Wales, "We just wanted to play football." And playing for the Bucks actually *cost* some of the players' money. "Playing actually took a lot of expense," adds Wales, "Had to drive to practice and to the games."

"Our pre-game meals usually consisted of stopping at McDonald's or Arby's on the way to the game," says Darrel Rutter.

"Sometimes it seems like we were playing for a hoagie and a beer," offers offensive tackle Ron Roefaro, "There were no contracts at all."

"We didn't really care if we got paid or not," relates Bill Luther, "We were young and having fun. Many times we got cold beer after the game, that was our pay."

The players didn't seem to mind getting paid in beer. "To this day it's the best beer I ever tasted," recalls Ken Rutter, "There was supposed to be a limit of one beer each but we never followed that."

The Bucks roster included a wide variety of players from all walks of life and backgrounds.

It included Darrel Rutter, a 30-year-old Vietnam Air Force veteran and a reserve back on Penn State's '68 and '69 Orange Bowl squads.

"I've always had an abiding love for the game," said Rutter at the time, who was returning to the game at a time when most players think of retirement. "It's more than just a game, more than satisfaction—it runs deeper than that. There's a whole psychological makeup, a feeling of self-worth.

"For me, football fulfills my desire for self-worth. I can express myself through football," Rutter told Leslie Kruk for an article in Penn State's *Daily Collegian*. He stated to Kruk that he felt football satisfied his determination to be creative. "I can't go to work from 8 to 3, come home and watch TV. I have to do something," he said.

Rutter had played service ball while serving a tour in Vietnam. "I didn't agree with the war, but I served anyway. I did what I felt I should do," says Rutter. When he came home, he was a walk-on at Penn State, where Rutter in his words, "gave it all he had," and by spring term "I felt that I had found a home."

In the fall of 1968, the 5'10" 185 pounder was a member of the special teams. In his first game against Maryland, Rutter made almost every tackle and was promoted to the traveling squad. His dream was becoming a reality.

"Dreams are the ceiling of reality," Rutter said at the time, "Playing in the Orange Bowl was the highlight of my career."

He then went to Chambersburg to teach and coach both football and wrestling. A new journey had begun. "I felt this was one of my more creative times," Rutter told Kruk.

After that, he returned to Altoona. Unable to secure a teaching position—he described his status at the time as "teacher-coach currently between jobs and self-employed philosopher"—Rutter felt his football career was over until he heard about the Whitetail Bucks.

"It's a new dimension for us," Rutter said then, "I don't feel man can be complete without mind, body and soul. The body is more than a home for the spirit to live in. This is another chance to be complete.

"I did a lot," Rutter recalls in a recent interview, "I guess you could say I was pretty versatile. Offense, defense, returned kicks. I was going to be the punter until Siegel rolled the snap back to me and I got killed. I told Bummy (Gary Baumgardner) to look for a new kicker. I played with reckless abandon. Guys called me 'Mad Dog' and 'Animal.' Those young guys, they were out to prove themselves, they wanted to kill you. I just wanted to enjoy the game and have fun."

Besides working full-time and playing for the Bucks, Rutter also found time after practices to help his wife Barb with her Master's paper.

John Withers had played linebacker for West Virginia University from 1971 to 1973 and was trying to make the team as a third string quarterback.

"Withers was a tremendous athlete," offers Ken Rutter.

"He could have played pro," adds Joe Wales.

There was quarterback and offensive assistant coach Tom Miller from Tyrone who headed the Colorado State teams in the mid-60s, and then played minor league ball for the Omaha Mustangs and the Harrisburg Capitols. Miller was a solid signal caller, but his obligations as Tyrone High School's head coach curtailed both his practice and playing time as the season progressed.

"Miller used to wear one of those flak jackets. He liked to get all armored up," states Hugh Gibbons, "He always talked about this 'skip pass' that he used to beat Oklahoma one time in college. He'd throw it beautifully. He threw it so it just skipped on the ground before you caught it. When everybody would stand there thinking it was incomplete, you could take off with it."

"Miller would get mad at some of the kids. He was a great guy but he had a temper," offers Darrel Rutter.

Wayne Rockmore was a running back who had starred for the Clearfield High School Bisons from 1967 to 1971. "He was a good, tough running back," recalls Tom Marlett.

"Great individual." Darrel Rutter says when asked about Rockmore, "Hard working man. He out-worked everybody. Unbelievable. He wasn't big, but he was strong and shifty. Smart, tough, good inside runner. A good leader on the field. Would have made a decent coach if he'd had the chance. Very personable guy, very easy to get along with. Tough kid, but a nice kid."

"He was a pretty good player," adds Ken Rutter, "Tough kid."

Sportswriter Vic Sellers would describe Rockmore in an article for *The Daily Collegian* as a running back "who could put moves on a leopard, and then outrun him."

But Rockmore's 1975 season would be a lost one for him.

"At the beginning of the '75 season, I was taking jiu-jitsu, which was fun and a very good disciplinary thing," says Rock now, "I was one of 5 students, and it helped get me in really good shape. I was not a starter for the team, however. I did a forward roll in practice, and my back just locked up. I was on my back for a week and a half and the season was pretty much a wash."

Still Rockmore would come back from his 1975 season and gain the respect of his teammates.

"I liked blocking for him," remembers offensive tackle Ron Roefaro, "He only needed a small opening, just a little space, to get through."

Roefaro was another Altoona native who had joined the team. He graduated from Bishop Guilfoyle in 1965 and then went to Mansfield State College [*now University*] where he played three years in the late '60s. He was teaching and coaching at Penn Cambria High School when he decided to join the Bucks and give football another try. Despite his relatively small size—5'10", 245 pounds—Roefaro would be a solid performer on both the offensive and defensive lines.

"Everybody I blocked was bigger than me," Roefaro states now with more than a little pride.

"Roefaro, he sewed up that offensive line," offers fellow lineman George Walker.

"Ron was a good guy," Bill Luther recalls, "We got fairly close, palled around a lot."

McNeish remembers Bill Luther's contributions to the team. "In particular, I recall Bill Luther, he was a big guy but quiet. Bill generally played tackle on my right. He was smart, quick, strong, and dependable. He worked hard and was a great asset."

"A gentle giant," is how Pat Little remembers Luther.

There was the aforementioned Al Siegel, still strapping on the pads at 38 after playing for years with several semipro teams in New York City.

"Siegel was old but he was tough," recounts George Walker, "Used to play for the Brooklyn Knights and New York Cardinals. He held us together."

"He was not the cleanest player," remembers Bill Luther, "He liked to start things. Many times we'd have to drag him away and say, 'What the hell are you doing man?'"

"He did like to get into some skirmishes," offers Darrel Rutter, "He was really an 'old man' for football. He didn't have the tools at that age. Not a great caliber athlete, but he was big and worked hard. He really loved to play ball."

Charvi Skillings had been an All-Central Counties League player for the Tyrone High Golden Eagles in 1970. He could run, catch, and kick.

"Charvi Skillings was our feature back," says Bill Luther. "A lot of times we just gave it to Charvi and got out of the way and let him do his thing. He was quick and strong. He was quite a character, but a good man. He was a couple years younger than me. He had grown up without a Dad and my Dad helped him out a lot."

Alge Jones was a wide receiver from Philipsburg-Osceola High and North Carolina State.

"One of the most memorable players," says Mike McNeish, "I had played with Alg in high school at Philipsburg-Osceola; he was a year or two behind me. He went to college and played a year, I think, then dropped out. We were always friends and hunted and fished together frequently. Alg was not the fastest guy on two feet but he had the best hands of any receiver we had while I played."

"Most of time I was just a decoy for our star receiver Alge Jones" remembers Pat Little, "He played at North Carolina State. Man, he was really good. I used to tell the defensive backs covering me that they were wasting their time because we were throwing to Alge."

"Great ballplayer," Darrel Rutter says of Jones, "Not fast, but shifty and hard to tackle. He was lanky, and ran kind of lanky but that was deceptive. You had to 'keep your eye on his belt buckle,' as the old saying goes. He was hard to get hold of. Had to keep an eye on him. He seemed lazy but he was good. He got a lot of his yards after the catch. Quiet guy, nothing abrasive about him."

Wide receiver/linebacker Gary Pheasant from Altoona had played for Purdue.

"He was probably our biggest name player," says Bill Luther, "but he didn't stay for the whole season."

"If he would have applied himself, he could've played anywhere," adds Hugh Gibbons.

"Super athlete, but honestly was not real smart," observes Darrel Rutter, "He was overwhelmed when he got to college. It's too bad, he could've made the NFL. But he was a battler, never cracked a smile."

Quarterback Larry Rydbom had played high school football locally with Glendale, and his college ball at Slippery Rock State.

He played for two years—1971 and 72—at Slippery Rock before getting a cup of coffee with the Washington Redskins and the New York Giants, plus the Toronto Argonauts of the Canadian Football League.

"You always have the big dream of playing pro football," Rydbom said. "Unfortunately, I was always the slow white guy."

Unable to catch on with a pro team, Rydbom decided to play semipro ball to keep his skills sharp. He joined the minor-league Latrobe Laurel Leopards and had to wonder what he was getting himself into as he carried his Leopards' uniform in his arms, walking through the Western Penitentiary in Pittsburgh.

Rydbom was there to play a minor league football game against the prison team and The House, a 6-foot-10, 485-pound inmate who was in prison for murder.

"He's the biggest man I ever saw that was physically fit," said Rydbom.

Rydbom was contacted in 1974 by the Philadelphia Eagles, and attended free agent camp, but felt he "wasn't up to par," and that he needed time to ready himself. For the 6'4" 195 pound passer, semipro ball was a chance to stay in shape in hopes of another pro tryout.

"Big tall blonde-haired guy," is how Bill Luther describes Rydbom, "He was our fearless leader."

"Rydbom could really throw the ball," offers Wayne Rockmore.

"When I caught a pass from him, you could see the impression of the seams of the ball on my arm," remembers Hugh Gibbons, ""Rydbom had all the physical tools, a cannon for an arm, size . . . but he didn't have anybody to work with him to help make him better."

"He was a 'professional wanna-be,'" is how Darrel Rutter describes Rydbom, "He was aiming for the NFL. He was tall, 6'4" and had a cannon for an arm. He was a good leader. But he was not controlled, not consistent with his passes. He could be erratic. He could also get emotional, a little fiery. We had words a few times during games. He deserved a shot at the NFL, but was he NFL caliber? I don't know. But he was a great guy, nice personality."

Offensive guard and middle linebacker Albe Wales was "quite a character" according to Bill Luther. "He was a 'piece of work,'" Luther remembers, "He liked to wear a lot of pads—arm pads, whatever. He liked to look the part of a football player."

Teammate Darrel Rutter remembers Wales for another attribute.

"He was always yakkin.'" Rutter said in a recent interview, "Couldn't get a word in edgewise in the huddle. He was always yelling at the other team. Not big, kind of a fireplug. But he was a good hitter and good blocker."

Paul "Bam-Bam" Kanagy was an undersized but fearless player who certainly didn't let his lack of size hinder him.

"Small but tough," is how Darrel Rutter describes him.

"Wayne [*Rockmore*] and I had the same problem," Kanagy says today, "We were always looking up at everybody! But that didn't make a difference. Once I had a guy 6'7" across from me, but he couldn't catch a thing."

"He did enjoy playing," Hugh Gibbons says of Kanagy, "Paul would be going all out as usual, and Coach Baumgardner would say, 'Don't you just love it!'"

"Kanagy was nicknamed 'Bam-Bam,' and we knew why," recalls George Walker, "He hit me once and took a chunk out of my shoulder. He hit like a truck."

"I was the youngest guy on the team," Bam-Bam remembers, "I didn't get drunk until I met them."

The Whitetail Bucks certainly had their share of what you might call unique individuals.

"Ed Peters. 'Crazy Ed,'" Darrel Rutter says now, "He killed a sheriff. Said the sheriff was harassing him and pulled the trigger on him. He did his time, but he was not sane. He and Charvi Skillings would talk all the time on the bus, never stop the whole trip. They'd call each other names. Peters used to call Charvi the 'N-word' all the time. We got used to it after a while. But he was not afraid of anything."

"I remember Ed showing up to practice driving his Clearfield Cheese Truck," says Mike Leone, "and wearing his cowboy boots. He wore a jersey that had the number 747 on the back, because at that time they had just started flying the Boeing 747 jets!"

The team made arrangements with Philipsburg to use a local field next to the football stadium for practice. The players left their day jobs and had to travel from all over the area for practice, and, while it might have been inconvenient, they made the best of the situation.

"We would pile into Dirk Grissinger's van and drive over to Philipsburg for practice" remembers Pat Little, "The tryouts and the practices started off in Philipsburg beside the football stadium. We would always drink on the way home. No seats in the back of the van. We would just sprawl across the floor."

The team now had coaches, players, and money. And although the team would lead a somewhat nomadic life in the Fall of '75 and play games in State College, Tyrone, Philipsburg and Clearfield—"We tried to play our games in towns where the players were from," states Bill Luther—they at least had fields available to play on. What could possibly go wrong now?

Well, on July 26th, team officials headed out to Mid-State Airport to pick up their equipment that was being shipped in by plane. Airline officials sheepishly told the club that they had lost the whole thing, kit and caboodle. The airline promised it would locate the equipment as soon as possible.

The team took it all in stride. They simply continued to practice without most of their equipment and team officials would check every day with the airline until the shipment was finally located.

"We thought we'd have the pads for today," said Siegel on July 27th, "and you should have seen the dejection on the faces of these guys when I told them we didn't have them yet. They are ready to hit."

Because the shipment was delayed and there were no pads available, the team was only able to get one hitting scrimmage under their belts before the season started.

A couple other teams in the Mid-Atlantic Football League were experiencing their share of problems. The Latrobe Laurel Leopards were now the Johnstown Miners, and would play their home games at Point Stadium.

The Dayton, Ohio, Steelers, who were slated to play the Bucks on October 4th, had folded up their tents after their General Manager had suddenly disappeared—along with $20,000 of the team's money.

Welcome to the world of semipro football.

# CHAPTER

# 2

"Well guys, welcome to the big time!"
—DARREL RUTTER TO HIS TEAMMATES
BEFORE THE BUCKS' VERY FIRST GAME

Once they recovered their lost equipment from the airline, the Central Pennsylvania Whitetail Bucks were ready to play some real football. So far they had impressed their coaches.

"For being our first year, the athletes of Central Pennsylvania have responded well from most towns in the area," said Gary Baumgardner, "All of them have made many individual sacrifices so that the area can be represented by a semipro football team.

"On the whole, I am more satisfied than dissatisfied with the progress of the team thus far," the head coach went on, "Our people have come a long way since June, and have shown improvements to a man. The starting lineups printed in the paper don't really mean much for this game; we have a lot of good people who are going to see action, and none of the starters are really secure in their positions.

"Our linebackers are perhaps the most solid aspect of our defensive game," Baumgardner concluded, "Our secondary has responded well in practice and has shown a lot of improvement."

"Our line is quick and consistent and gets off the ball," Dave Paganetti added, "Holes have been opening up in practice and with the quickness of our backs, we should be able to move the ball on the ground. Our receivers are coming into their own, and Alge Jones of Philipsburg has been particularly impressive."

But a knee injury to Bill Luther, who was slated to start at offensive tackle, made it necessary for the Bucks to shuffle their offensive line. Doug Hrenko from Philipsburg would move to tackle and Clearfield's Scott Bowes was inserted at guard.

The Whitetail Bucks officially opened their inaugural season on August 9th, 1975 in State College, hosting an exhibition game against the Brooklyn Golden Knights, a club that finished second in the New York Semipro Conference in 1974 and had been in existence for 15 years. The Knights arrived in State College with a traveling squad of 62 players, six coaches, the team owner, the team general manager, two press box scouts, and what seemed like a battalion of managers and equipment people. The Bucks were beginning to learn that there were semipros, and then there were *semipros*.

"The very first game we ever played was in State College against the Brooklyn Golden Knights," remembers wide receiver Pat Little, "Since Allen Potter and I lived in State College we were assigned to meet the bus when it arrived in State College at the High School. Well, when the bus doors opened two of the largest men I have ever seen stepped off the bus. I mean they were both 450–500 pounds. Allen and I looked at each other and were thinking, 'What the hell did we get in to?'

"We tried to tell our team what we saw, but they thought we were exaggerating. We weren't," adds Little.

The Golden Knights' roster featured running back Charlie Smith, who had been the last cut of the New England Patriots in 1974, Earl Belgrave, who played at Ohio State and with the WFL's Chicago Fire, 6'5" 310 pound tackle Howard Bryant, and Bob Pugh, Jethro Pugh's little brother (although being 6'6" and 250 pounds hardly made anyone a *little* brother).

"The pre-game hype was that Jethro Pugh's brother was playing for the Knights," recalls team manager Mike Leone.

"On the field they looked like they were stuffed into their uniforms," says Pat Little, "Their helmets looked too small for them!"

"Their tight end is Argyle Whitfield, a 6'4" 250 pounder who played with the Dallas Cowboys," observed Al Siegel, "Their fullback, Claude Grayson, played with the Jets."

On top of all that, the Knights already had two games under their belts. But none of this seemed to deter the upstart Bucks.

In the locker room before the game, Darrel Rutter looked around at his teammates and said, "Well guys, welcome to the big time!"

"Our people have come a long way since June," said Gary Baumgardner on the day before the game, "I feel that tomorrow's game will be good, competitive football, and that the Bucks will perform to the best of their abilities."

"The players have sacrificed a great deal, driving after work to practices from such places as Osceola Mills and Altoona," Mike McNeish added, "I think we'll show people a lot."

They didn't show the 1,000 or so fans who paid $2.50 a head much of anything at the outset, however.

The Bucks got their season off to an auspicious start when they were hit with a penalty on their very first play from scrimmage. It went downhill from there. On second down, starting quarterback Tom Miller was sacked, and two plays later the Knights had the ball thanks to a Bucks' fumble.

Unfortunately, that first drive was just a glimpse of what was in store for the Bucks for the rest of the game as their first-game jitters and mistakes outweighed a fine effort by their defensive unit. Fortunately, this was only an exhibition game for the team, and that's what exhibition games have always been for, to work out problems and see who can do what. After the game, Baumgardner said he was "discouraged with the score but not the performance.

"They had already played two games this year and this was our first and that playing experience always helps. I'm just amazed how far we've come in five weeks of workouts," Baumgardner went on to say, "and, in fact, we even got better tonight as the game went on. Considering the limited hitting in practice we had because of lack of depth and the late arrival of pads we were very successful."

Baumgardner added that "we made the usual first-game mistakes but we found out what we had as far as individual abilities go, so we can work from there."

The Bucks shuttled all three of their quarterbacks into the lineup, using Miller, Larry Rydbom and John Withers, and, although the trio spent most of their time running from the Knights' strong pass rush, they threw for 170 yards worth of offense, completing 13 of 31 passes.

Things, however, were a little grimmer as far as the Bucks' ground attack was concerned. The team could manage a total of only a minus 72 yards on the ground. But assistant coach Dave Paganetti felt that "the offensive line will get better with experience and when we get some depth to spell time. We showed we can move the ball, especially in the second half, but like everyone says, it was just too many mistakes that hurt us."

With the help of numerous illegal procedure penalties and punting problems the Bucks and Knights battled scoreless through most of the first period until Brooklyn quarterback Mike Bonham capped off an 11-play, 39-yard scoring drive by sneaking around the left end for a one-yard touchdown with just 16 seconds to go in the opening quarter.

Team Manager Mike Leone quickly learned that in the semipro game, he would have his share of unique tasks to perform.

"My fondest memory was from that first game we played in 1975," Leone remembers, "I remember part way through the first quarter, Ed Peters, who was playing linebacker, ran off the field and gave me his false teeth! He asked me to give them to his mother who was sitting up in the bleachers! He ran back in and finished the game, while I dutifully gave his teeth to his mother, much to her surprise, and mine as well!"

Midway through the second quarter the Bucks yanked Miller and inserted Rydbom at the offensive helm. Rydbom was harassed on almost every play and was hurried into tossing a couple quick interceptions. The Knights took advantage of the second of these turnovers when second-string quarterback Tom Green led his team on an 11-play drive that was halted on the Buck seven. That set up kicker Bob Jamison for a 27-yard field goal, making it 10-0 at the half.

Brooklyn wasted little time lengthening their lead in the second half, and this time it was their defense that put the points on the board. The Knights fumbled the ball away and linebacker Paul "Bam-Bam" Kanagy, the Bucks' youngest player at 18, pounced on it at Brooklyn's 30-yard line. This despite the fact that he was basically playing the game one-handed.

"I broke three bones on my hand, behind my knuckles on the opening kickoff," Kanagy remembered in a recent interview, "Played the whole game."

Kanagy's recovery put the Bucks over the 50 and in Brooklyn territory for only the second time in the game. But one play later, linebacker Len Meyers scooped up a Rydbom fumble and raced 55 yards for a touchdown three minutes into the quarter, putting the Knights 16 points in front. Jamison missed the extra-point attempt.

Brooklyn continued to control the ball throughout most of the third quarter, putting together two long, time-consuming drives. The second march resulted in a touchdown when Bonham snuck around the left end again for his second score with a minute to go. The Bucks now trailed 23-0.

Central Pennsylvania opened the fourth quarter with the ball and with Withers now at quarterback, but their initial drive with him at the helm stalled on their own 28. The Bucks, looking desperately for some kind of spark, attempted a fake punt that was stopped short of the first down. It then took the Knights just four plays to raise their advantage to 30-0. Green provided the capper to the short drive with a perfect pass between two Buck defenders to Jim Phillips in the end zone.

To their credit, the Bucks, down by 30, didn't just fold up their tents and slink away with their whitetails tucked between their legs. "The individuals played a good game taking into account the problems we have," Baumgardner said afterward.

The Bucks suddenly and finally caught fire offensively, starting with a 34-yard kickoff return by Tom Hipp to his own 49. Withers, still at quarterback, went to the air or ran it himself on six of the next seven plays. The key plays in the drive were a 28-yard pass to Ken Rutter, a five-yard sneak by Withers, and a desperation fourth-down pass to Alge Jones, all of which resulted in big first downs. The eighth and final play of the drive was a pitchout to Hipp around the left side for a one-yard touchdown. The Bucks missed the extra point when confusion on the sidelines left kicker Charvi Skillings and his holder, Jim Slabon, without a kicking tee.

The Bucks' offense continued to play more efficiently and effectively. When a fumble recovery gave the Bucks the ball on the Brooklyn 41, Miller was reinserted into the lineup, and the veteran signal caller went to the air on all seven plays in the march. A 14-yard aerial to running back Craig Kyler circling out of the backfield put the points on the scoreboard. Kyler, who had attended Lenoir-Rhyne College in North Carolina, made a fine second effort to get into the end zone as he carried two defenders the last four yards and over the goal line. The snap on the extra point was high but Slabon grabbed the ball, jumped to his feet and hit Ken Rutter for the conversion. That made the final a little more respectable at 30-13.

At several points, the contest was halted due to some "extracurricular activities" by both teams. With a minute remaining, Baumgardner, fed up with the rough play, threatened to pull his team off the field and take them to the showers, but he was persuaded to finish the game. Tony LoVerdi, one of the Knights' offensive guards, screamed toward Baumgardner, "This isn't touch football we're playin' ya know!"

Offensively the Bucks had look ragged, but that was to be expected from 11 men from various backgrounds who hadn't been together, and probably for the most part didn't even know each other, just five weeks before. But defensively they did manage to more than hold their own against the more experienced

Knights. Slabon had an interception and a fumble recovery. Their small but more-than-willing defense led by "Bam-Bam" Kanagy, Tim Irvin, 270-pound defensive tackle Terry Graham and John Sommer put in a fine effort and helped the Bucks prove they were there to play some football.

"Our defense really hung in there despite bad field position 95 per cent of the time," Baumgardner said, "They got a little fatigued at the end because of being in there so much, but it usually takes the offense a little longer to get organized and working as a unit."

"I'm amazed at how far these guys have come," the head coach added.

The feeling in the locker room after the game was not one of defeat and despair, but of a sense of accomplishment. "Their experience definitely hurt us," Baumgardner said, "but the improvement made by both our offense and defense throughout the game amazed me."

The Bucks had also impressed their opponents. "For a first-year team, these guys hit hard and showed they can become a fine organization," said a Knights' coach.

Several days after the opener, an article appeared in a Harrisburg newspaper saying that Bucks' coach Gary Baumgardner had accepted the head coaching job at Newport High School. Baumgardner denied the report to the press on the 13th, saying that "coaching has never been more enjoyable for me.

"I've never been more relaxed in any coaching position I've ever held," Baumgardner went on, "It's a completely different atmosphere then I've been in before in that there is no pressure whatsoever. The total environment, both at practices and at the games, is an enjoyable experience. The players are more mature and coachable and you can apply a broader scope of football knowledge to the game.

"This is the first year for the Bucks," the head coach concluded, "and the atmosphere is just great. And things are getting better as we go along."

With their first game under their belts, and their head coach still their head coach, the Bucks then traveled to Beaver Falls for their league opener against the Beaver County Cougars. The Cougars had finished with a record of 7-3-1 in 1974, but had experienced difficulty in finding players for '75 and had only a 29-man roster.

They had picked up quarterback Dave Palkowoski from Pittsburgh, and Dave Paganetti had scouted the Cougars and reported that they were a run-oriented team that also played a basic 4-4 or 4-3 defense.

When the Whitetail Bucks arrived for the game, they found the facility, the Brady's Run Sports Complex on Route 51 near Beaver Falls, to be poor, to say the least. It had no running water, no showers, and the field was strewn with rocks. "In Beaver County we played on a dirt field and it was hot," remembers Pat Little.

After the season, the Cougars, represented by Joseph Petrella, would approach the Beaver County Commissioners asking if the complex would be provided with showers. Petrella was told that installation of the showers—as well as a septic system—would depend on the 1976 budget for the county recreation department.

The Cougars were yet another example of a semipro team struggling to make a go of it. In the July 24th, 1975 edition of the *Beaver County Times*, a letter to the editor from Denny Minnitti of Beaver Falls stated that the Cougars were still looking for sponsors to help meet expenses. Mr. Minnitti added that the team's coaches were all working for no pay.

Beaver County had always found it difficult to find a home. In 1972, the Hopewell Area School District refused to allow the team to use its junior high school field. In 1976, the Beaver Falls School Board denied a request by the team to use the high school field for six games, but did authorize their athletic director, Lyle Peluso, to work out arrangements to let the team use the field for one game.

The Bucks, "who reduced their offensive mistakes by 90 per cent since last week" in the words of coach Baumgardner, controlled the tempo of the game as Tom Miller, who played the first three quarters, completed 12-of-23 passes for 172 yards, and the defense held strong whenever the Cougars made any offensive penetrations inside the 25.

"Our entire offense was executing better than last week, the line was giving Miller more time, the receivers were running better patterns and the backs were hitting the holes," Baumgardner told reporters after the game, "and defensively, well, I could tell I had no worries from the first practice."

The offense improved tremendously over their efforts of the previous week against Brooklyn. The Bucks ran for 123 yards, led by Hipp's 45 yards in 12 carries, which greatly helped Miller's passing attack and took some of the heat off the veteran signal caller.

Another thing that helped the Bucks was the fact that the Cougars were playing their first game of the season, something the Bucks knew all too well could hurt a team.

"Beaver County looked disorganized," Baumgardner said, "and defensively they never did play us right, and we took advantage of every hole they gave us."

The Cougars didn't look very disorganized when they took the opening kick-off and put together a strong drive that carried them to the Bucks' 16. But it was there that newcomer Dirk Grissinger, a linebacker from State College, sacked quarterback Palkowoski for a 10-yard loss. Grissinger had been a 1972 All-Pennsylvania selection at offensive tackle, and had graduated from State College High in 1973. He then played at Slippery Rock State [*now University*].

"Helluva football player, probably the best linebacker we had." recalls Darrel Rutter, who hurt his shoulder on the third play of the game but kept playing, "When he teamed with 'Bam-Bam' Kanagy they were a great duo. No one got past them. All-State, Big 33 pick from State College. You could really depend on him, he didn't make mistakes. Absolute best at his position. He could've played at Penn State."

Coach Tom Miller called Grissinger "the best defensive ball player I've ever played with."

One play after Grissinger's sack, running back Leon Tisdale, a speedy track star from Beaver Falls, fumbled a fourth-down play 10 yards behind the line of scrimmage, giving Central Pennsylvania its first offensive chance on its own 31.

The Bucks struck quickly as Miller unleashed a 40-yard pass to Alge Jones on the first play from scrimmage and then carried the ball himself around the right side for a 29-yard touchdown run, making it 6-0. Charvi Skillings' extra-point attempt drifted wide.

Beaver County took over but soon gave the Bucks the ball back on another fumble. Miller, however, returned the favor by firing an interception over the middle at the Cougars' 30.

The Cougars then proceeded to open it up offensively and a 13-play drive put the ball on the Bucks' 14. On the next play, fullback Greg Braund went around right end and into the end zone, but the touchdown was nullified by a motion penalty. The Buck defense jumped on the break and on the very next play defensive back Bill Gordon, who hailed from Curwensville and had played service ball with the Army, picked off an errant pass to kill Beaver County's scoring threat.

The Bucks' offense went three-and-out, and Allen Potter from State College punted the ball out to midfield. Eight plays later the Cougars were knocking on the door again with a fourth-and-goal on the three. Their big fullback Braund tried to take it up the middle, but was met by a host of Buck defenders, led by Grissinger and Ed Peters, and stopped cold.

The defensive stand energized the Bucks and the tempo of the game quickly changed. The Bucks controlled the ball for most of the remaining four minutes of the half, and even when Beaver County did get the ball, their drive was cut short by another Gordon interception. The Whitetail Bucks' slim lead of 6-0 was intact.

The second half then belonged to the Bucks. Their offense kept the ball in good field position most of the time, and the defense allowed the Cougars inside the 25 only twice.

The Bucks took the second-half kick and made it 13-0 as Miller engineered another fine drive by mixing passes and the running skills of Tom Hipp. The running back from Memphis State capped the drive with a 16-yard gallop up the middle. Skillings made good on the conversion and the Whitetail Bucks had a little more breathing room.

The Cougars narrowed the margin when the Buck offense made one of its rare mistakes in the game. Larry Rydbom, in for Miller, fumbled the ball away while scrambling. Two plays later, Beaver County's Palkowoski tossed to Tisdale for the touchdown. "Bam-Bam" Kanagy batted down the extra-point kick, however, and that kept the margin at seven points.

The Bucks then put the game out of reach on their next possession, when Rydbom, who completed 2-of-2 passes for 46 yards and also ran for 28 more on eight carries, snuck around the left side for a four-yard touchdown.

A beautiful 42-yard punt by Charvi Skillings, which came late in the game and rolled out of bounds at the Cougars' 10 yard line, also helped keep Beaver County at bay.

Since the facility had no showers, the Bucks piled into their bus and drove home, but made a quick stop at a local state park.

"After the game we went to a State Park and my friend [*lineman*] Ken Grove ran off the bus and into the lake with his entire uniform on," says Pat Little.

"They chased us out of the park," says Darrel Rutter.

The Bucks were now 1-and-1 on the season and 1-and-0 in the Eastern Division of the league. They would be returning home to face their next opponents, the Washington Generals, in Philipsburg.

Philipsburg was a typical small town in Central Pennsylvania, a borough located in the mountainous region of Rush Township, on the banks of Moshannon Creek in Centre County with a population of around 2,500 people and covering a total area of less than one square mile.

The town's business interests, like most of the region, had long been in lumbering and coal. Named for an Englishman named Philips who first decided to build a settlement on the location in 1794, the town was first settled by hardy immigrants who journeyed there along a foot-path leading from Bellefonte.

Many of the modern-day roads in the region are referred to as "cow-paths" as it sometimes seemed as if the winding thoroughfares had been built from the paths taken by farm cattle as they wandered over the area.

Because the borough had been the hometown of United States Congressman Charles Hedding Rowland, two of its landmarks were the Rowland Theater and the Rowland Mansion. Halehurst, a house located off Presqueisle Street near Ninth Street, was rumored to be a stop on the Underground Railroad, although no evidence had been unearthed to support this claim.

The Generals were coming off a 20-7 loss to the Pittsburgh Ironmen. They played a 4-4-3 defense anchored by 6'4" 285 pound defensive tackle Jim Dunn, who had been cut by the Baltimore Colts in 1973, and a pair of brothers at linebacker, Ray and Don Newhouse. On offense, the Generals featured quarterback/punter Tom Karpinski from Waynesburg College, who had a tryout with the Cardinals, and placekicker Bill Hughes, who had gone to camp with the Eagles, Cardinals and WFL Philadelphia Bell.

Co-General Manager Al Siegel hoped for a large turnout, and had to be pleased when 1,100 fans passed through the gates of Memorial Stadium for the contest against the Generals.

The fans watched as the Buck defense, anchored by John Sommer, "Bam-Bam" Kanagy, and Dirk Grissinger, continue to play a solid, hard-hitting type of game that was starting to make both their opponents and their fans take notice. The defense held the Generals to a total offensive output of four yards, including minus five on the ground, scored two touchdowns, set up another score, intercepted three passes, and allowed Washington to advance past the Bucks' 40-yard line only twice, both times late in the game when coach Baumgardner was substituting freely.

Offensively the Bucks, quarterbacked by Larry Rydbom throughout most of the contest, rolled up 391 total yards, 257 of those by the aerial route, and treated the fans to some big-play passes in key situations. Rydbom saw most of the action because Tom Miller's obligations as Tyrone High School coach had begun to limit his practice time.

"I just can't say enough about how improved we become each week," said coach Baumgardner after the game. "I'm just glad to see the players are going all-out and they're happy playing and that the fans, especially tonight, are beginning to get excited."

Baumgardner went on to say, "I can't single out any one player tonight, it was just a great team effort again. We've picked up a few new players, giving us more depth and balance, and I'll tell you right now that no team we're scheduled to play can be any better defensively than us, especially our linebackers."

Although the Bucks led by only a touchdown, 13-6, at halftime, there was never much doubt about who was in control of the game.

The Bucks took the opening kick-off and drove 65 yards in eight plays. Rydbom, who rushed for a game-high 97 yards on 17 carries, capped the opening drive by plowing up the middle for four yards and the score with less than five minutes gone in the game. Charvi Skillings converted to make it 7-0.

Neither team could generate much offense. Washington got its only touchdown in what would be a long and frustrating game for them when Frank Bucci, a speedy defensive back who had broken a league record the previous week with a 103-yard punt return against the Ironmen, grabbed a misguided Rydbom pass and ran it back 69 yards for the six-pointer. The Generals failed to even the score, however, when Jim Slabon and company got a hand on Bill Hughes' extra point kick.

The remaining 48-and-a-half minutes belonged to the Whitetail Bucks. The upstart team was looking more and more like a squad that had played together for six years instead of six weeks. The defense continued to shine, as a two-play General possession was cut short by an interception by John Sommer.

"He was from BG [*Bishop Guilfoyle*], and was one tough boy," says Darrel Rutter of Sommer, "Smart kid, did a good job. All those BG players were tough and smart. Sommer did great on special teams with guys like Kanagy and Withers."

The Bucks then held the ball for over eight minutes and 54 yards on a drive that reached the Washington 10 before an illegal procedure penalty, two incomplete passes and a five-yard loss by Rydbom halted the threat.

It didn't take long for the Bucks to get the ball back, however, as Dirk Grissinger picked off a Tom Karpinski pass and ran it back 28 yards to set up his teammates at the Washington 42. Following a big second-and-11 pass which covered 35 yards from Rydbom to Alge Jones, who yanked the ball out of defender Ron Hinish's arms, Craig Kyler bulled his way over from the four. Skilling's kick was batted down by Rick Visconti but the Bucks owned a 13-6 lead with 4:24 left in the half.

Tom Miller, who had an outstanding game in the 19-6 win over Beaver County, was the signal caller on the scoring play. He had been inserted after Rydbom had connected on the long pass to Jones. It seemed like an odd decision given the circumstances, and Baumgardner was asked to clarify the quarterbacking situation after the game. The coach explained that "they both [*Miller and Rydbom*] are so close in talent that it doesn't matter who's in there. Each has a little edge over the other in one category or another but it's so little that, since they're both great athletes and they both work hard at practice, I like to let them both play. We also have John Withers at quarterback, giving us a fine trio at the position."

Despite the head coach's explanation, the Bucks seemed to have a quarterback controversy brewing.

The Bucks continued to dominate play as they scored on their first two possessions of the second half to grab a commanding 26-6 lead.

The first drive got kick-started by a 60-yard bomb to Alge Jones. It took only four more plays for Rydbom to find Ken Rutter all alone in the corner of the end zone for a three-yard scoring pass. In a bit of trickeration, Skillings then faked the extra point kick and holder Jim Slabon threw to Jones in the end zone for the conversion.

The next time the Bucks had the ball, after a fine 21-yard punt return by Darrel Rutter, Rydbom took it in himself on a bootleg to the right from the eight-yard line. Skillings' try at the extra point was partially blocked, sending it off to the side.

Washington's next possession was stalled on its own 40, forcing Karpinski to punt. Darrel Rutter hauled in the kick on the Buck 24 and breaking several tackles along the way, took it all the way back, 76 yards, to paydirt. That raised the Central Pennsylvania margin to 33-6 after Skillings' extra point kick split the uprights.

Late in the game sub running back Jerry White fumbled the ball away on the General seven yard line. After Washington failed to move the sticks, Karpinski punted from the end zone, but the Generals' offense was given another chance when the overzealous Bucks were charged with roughing the kicker. The Generals could not take advantage of the mistake, however, as they again went three-and-out. Karpinski went back to kick again, but this time he never got the punt off. Bishop Guilfoyle grad Jim Steinbugl rushed in hard and blocked the kick. John Sommer then quickly pounced on the ball in the end zone for a touchdown.

The Bucks once again tried the fake on the conversion, and Slabon was once again successful, this time connecting with wide receiver Pat Little.

"We had trick plays where players faked injuries, flea flickers, and some that bordered on assault," recalls Little.

The Generals, who had made a 150-mile trip to Philipsburg for the game, controlled the ball for most of the last five minutes but their offense was unable to score. Hughes' 43-yard field goal attempt on the last play of the game fell way short.

The Bucks once again had played rugged defense and had seen their offense continue to improve. The fans in attendance chanted "Bring on the Ironmen" after the game, obviously impressed with the play of their hometown team and in anticipation of their September 13th match-up against Pittsburgh in Philipsburg.

But according to several players, after the game the locals did not seem too impressed with the home team.

"We were in Philipsburg and the Bucks were supposed to be their team," recalls Darrel Rutter, "A bunch of them ganged up on the team in a bar. Albe Wales liked to fight. He never backed away from a fight. After Vietnam, I wasn't too keen about starting trouble. But we all supported each other so I joined the fray.

"Ken (Rutter) wound up pouring beers on drunks. Then a drunk pulled a knife on Albe and Ken kicked the knife out of his hand. Ken wound up even pouring a beer on John Withers' head.

"Withers left the team after the fight in Philipsburg. Never came back."

The Pittsburgh Ironmen, who "had been around longer than almost any Pennsylvania team," according to Ron Roefaro, were the most respected and feared team in the league and were considered by many the team to beat. But with the win over Washington, the Bucks were tied for the Eastern Division lead with Pittsburgh, with each club sporting a 2-0 record.

"Three months ago this team was just an idea," Al Siegel remarked after the game, "but look at us now, it's just fantastic."

The Bucks prepared in anticipation of their next game, a non-league show-down with the New York City Tigers at Curwensville.

Curwensville, located about 45 miles north of Altoona in Clearfield County, had been named for John Curwen in 1799. On December 10th, 1798, Curwen, of Montgomery County, Pennsylvania, obtained from the Commonwealth a patent for three hundred and fifty-one acres of land on the banks of the Susquehanna River, at the mouth of Anderson Creek, in what was at that time part of Lycoming County. On this property Curwen laid out a town, consisting of forty-eight lots, lying between what are now known as Thompson and Locust streets, which he named Curwensville.

Curwensville likes to boast that it's the most thriving and progressive, as well as one of the most beautiful, towns in Clearfield County. Like many of the boroughs and towns in the region, Curwensville is a small community, with a population of around 2,500 people. The principal industries have always been two large tanneries, the largest fire brick plant in the county—which the locals like to call "The Brick Yard"—two stone quarries, as well as other smaller industries.

The game would be played in Riverside Stadium, a facility that was not a favorite of the Buck players.

"Curwensville was a bad field," recalls linebacker Tom Marlett, "The lights there looked like flashlights. We had to piss in a big bowl in the locker room."

The conditions for the fans weren't much better on August 31st, 1975, as rain showers soaked the 400 or so fans who attended the game. But although the weather hurt attendance, it didn't slow the ever-improving Bucks as they made it a surprising three wins in a row by routing the Tigers, who had scored wins over the Adirondack Wings and Bay Side Lions, and who featured a pair of defensive tackle who tipped the scales at 280 and 290 pounds. They were a team that liked to do a little trash talking, too.

"We played a team, the New York City Tigers," remembers Wayne Rockmore, "One of our captains, Dirk Grissinger, went out for the coin toss. They were talking all kinds of stuff, and they told Dirk, 'we're gonna bury you.'"

"They talked so much shit ... that lasted about five minutes," adds "Bam-Bam" Kanagy.

The Whitetail Bucks used a combination of their rugged defense along with a wide-open offense that rolled up season-highs with 465 yards in total offense and seven touchdowns.

But as good as the offense was, the Bucks' defense was better. Headed by a superb front-four featuring Bellefonte's Tom Arnelle, who'd had a tryout in 1974 with the WFL's Philadelphia Bell, John White from West Branch High, Stanley Paul "Stash" Yastro, a 6'5" 235 pounder from Osceola Mills and Lycoming College, and Ed Peters from Philipsburg, the Bucks held the Tigers to minus-four yards on the ground and 119 yards in total offense. Almost half of those 119 came on a 57-yard scoring play from Tyrone Jackson to Marshall Newkirk, only the second touchdown scored against the Bucks' defensive unit in three games. It was the second straight week that the Bucks managed to hold the opposition to minus rushing yards.

"The defense we had was great." Darrel Rutter recalled in a recent interview. "We had some real ballplayers. It was a privilege to play with some of those guys. We played some formidable teams, but they got their ears pinned back by our defense. We may not have beat them but we certainly played 'em tough.

When asked about Yastro, Rutter states, "He looked like a stork, kinda like Ted Hendricks. You couldn't get around him. Had long legs and arms. He was quiet but played big. Had long hair and a long beard. Very reliable. Good at containing an offense and plugging things up inside."

The Jackson-to-Newkirk touchdown pass, which was set up by a Buck fumble, earned New York a 6-0 first quarter edge, but once the Central Pennsylvania crew got it in gear the Tigers failed to threaten again.

After turning the ball over on their first two possessions, the Bucks then mounted a 56-yard drive. With Larry Rydbom, who got the start because Tom Miller was limping on a pulled groin suffered against Washington, mixing runs and passes perfectly, the Bucks marched downfield with little in the way of opposition from the Tigers. Rydbom hit Alg Jones with a beauty of a pass, and then capped the impressive drive himself by carrying it over from the one. The Bucks went ahead 7-6 when they once again used the old trickeroo on the extra point. Charvi Skillings faked the kick and holder Jim Slabon connected with Jones for the conversion.

The Tigers' next possession was cut short by a fumble, and the Bucks took over on their own 35. In just four plays the team had struck again. The scoring play came on Ken Rutter's "bread and butter play," the flea flicker. Rydbom pitched out to Rutter, who started running and then stopped short and lofted a pass to Jones, who outran Roy Clements for 76 yards and his first touchdown of the season.

After Glendale High's Ron Kimberly and John White from West Branch batted down a pair of Jackson passes, the Tigers were forced to punt. The Bucks then proceeded to make it three consecutive scoring drives as Rydbom found Skillings with a 28-yard toss and the slotback hurdled three New York defenders on his way to the end zone. That gave the Bucks a 20-6 halftime lead.

Central Pennsylvania didn't let up on the gas pedal in the third quarter. The defense was an immovable object, as they held the Tigers to a minus 12 yards in six offensive plays, and recovered two fumbles and picked off an interception. Meanwhile, the Bucks played a ball control offense that ate time off the clock and kept the pigskin away from New York.

The team was even able to overcome its own rare bad plays. After Allen Potter of State College got off a miserable punt, Buck linebacker and another former Little Lion Dirk Grissinger came up with a fumble, one of 15 on the rain-soaked field, that set up another Rydbom-to-Skillings scoring aerial, this one covering 13 yards.

Safety Bill Gordon stopped the Tigers' next drive with his fourth interception of the year. Rydbom then turned that bit of good fortune into another touchdown. Running back Wayne Rockmore raced 14 yards to the five on the backend of a faked double reverse, and then Rydbom scored on a keeper.

Charvi Skillings, who converted four of six extra points in the game, then watched as his ensuing line drive kickoff bounced off a Tiger and rolled to the Bucks' 44 where it was recovered by the Bucks' Ed Peters. That drive was halted by a penalty and an unsuccessful fake punt try by Jim Slabon, but the Bucks quickly regained possession when on the Tigers' first play from scrimmage John White recovered another fumble.

Three plays later it was John's brother Jerry White joining the scoring parade as he drove eight yards through a big hole opened up in the Tiger line to give the Bucks a 40-6 edge with 14:16 to go in the game.

The huge deficit had finally silenced the Tigers' trash talking about "burying" the Bucks, who started talking a little smack of their own.

"When we got so far ahead," Wayne Rockmore remembers, "Dirk Grissinger yelled at them, 'What's wrong, did you guys forget your shovels?'"

With Baumgardner substituting freely the Bucks scored their final touchdown when Jerry White broke three tackles and raced 21 yards for his second six-pointer of the evening.

"Like I keep saying, it was just another great team effort," commented Baumgardner after the 47-6 trouncing. "I just can't give enough credit to Dave [*Paganetti*] for developing our offense, he really has them cooking."

While Paganetti, who was the type of coach who always saw room for improvement, said the Bucks' offense "still has a long way to go," Baumgardner pointed out that the offensive success of the team so far was due to the fact that "the other teams just haven't been defensing us correctly and we've been taking advantage of every opening presented to us."

The head coach also had praise for his defense. "Our defense is just dominating everyone," lauded Baumgardner, "and they're going to continue that way with the added depth we've acquired in the past few weeks."

Since their opening 30-13 setback to Brooklyn, the Bucks had been working like a well-oiled machine, amassing 106 points on offense while surrendering just 18. The first-year team, now a surprising 3-and-1 on the season, seemed to be in high gear in anticipation of their September 13th showdown with Pittsburgh, which was coming off a 33-31 loss to Wheeling in a non-league contest.

The team was in a mood to celebrate, and held a team party at the St. Charles Café in Clearfield after the game. The Tigers, who because of a lack of transportation back to New York City had to stay over in the area, joined the Bucks and partied with the home team.

But this being semipro ball, there always seemed to be a fly or two in the ointment. Tom Miller told the squad that he was considering leaving the team due to his increasing obligations as a coach and teacher at Tyrone High School. Co-General Managers Al Siegel and Mike McNeish had to report that the date of the Pittsburgh game might have to be changed because the Philipsburg-Osceola High School Mounties were to play at Curwensville the same evening. Siegel also reported that the October 4th game, originally slated for DuBois, had been changed to Altoona.

Never a dull moment in the semipro game, which resembled the early days of the NFL, where fluid schedules, folding teams, and rough-and-tumble play were the norm.

Sure enough, to avoid a conflict with the Philipsburg-Osceola/Curwensville game, the Bucks game was moved from Saturday the 13th to Sunday the 14th. Even though the Bucks were semipros, and seemingly a rung above the high schoolers, they weren't about to lock horns with high school football in Central Pennsylvania. The fans of the area did, and still do, take their local high school sports very seriously.

So the Bucks squared off with the Ironmen a day later than planned. The extra day did nothing to help the Bucks against one of semipro football's most feared teams.

"The Ironmen are noted for their defense," said Pittsburgh running back Ed Farmer, a Villanova graduate who was working as a trainee with Merrill Lynch, "I like to call it street fighting. Our middle linebacker likes to eat beer glasses. Our outside linebacker, known for a notorious use of forearms in the game, likes to practice hitting cars and walls."

"They were the best team in the league," recalls lineman Bill Luther, "We shouldn't even have been playing them. They always seemed to hammer us. I know the guy I played across from kicked my butt pretty good."

Pittsburgh linebacker Pete Naputano, who had played his high school ball at Altoona's Bishop Guilfoyle and sold insurance during the day to make ends meet, called the Ironmen, "the poor man's Steelers."

Naputano, who would eventually be inducted into the Semipro Football Hall of Fame, was a member of the 1970 Marshall University football team that lost 37 players and eight coaches in a plane crash that has been called the worst sports air disaster in history. Naputano was not on the team flight that fateful night of November 14th, 1970 due to an arm injury. That's why it shook him when he saw his name in *The Pittsburgh Press* the day after the tragedy, November 15th, counted among the dead.

"You know what, some papers grabbed a team roster and actually listed me as dead," said Naputano at the time, "It's still very uncomfortable to talk about. After all these years, you still get a lump in your throat."

The Ironmen roster also included All-Semipro defensive end Jim Chapas, nicknamed "Dr. Sack" for his specialty of sacking the opponents' quarterback despite the fact that at 214 pounds he was the smallest defensive end in the league. Wide receiver Dennis Koch was a 29-year-old plumber-welder from Murrysville, Pa., who had been playing semipro ball for 10 years. He didn't go to college because as he said, he "kinda screwed around too much." Small and slow, Koch liked to tell people, "I just get open and catch the ball." In 1976, he would catch 60 passes for 986 yards and would be named All-Semipro.

The Bucks did get some good news when veteran quarterback Tom Miller decided to remain with the squad despite coaching and teaching conflicts at Tyrone.

The Bucks gave it their best shot against the best, but the Ironmen always seemed to come up with a big play when they needed it. Central Pennsylvania punted and one play later Pittsburgh's Eddie Fullum was striding into the end zone on the tail end of a 43-yard scoring pass from Don Folden. The Whitetail Bucks then fumbled on their own 30 and on the very next play Fullum and Folden hooked up for another touchdown. Pittsburgh's Bob Allen then picked off a Central Pennsylvania pass and the Ironmen need only one play again for a six-pointer, this time a 10-yard run up the middle by Dean Smith. Pittsburgh's quick-striking offense, combined with nine Buck turnovers, were more than enough to help the Ironmen temporarily ground the high-flying Central Pennsylvania squad 27-18 in Philipsburg's Memorial Stadium.

Although the Bucks lost they proved one very important thing to themselves and the 1,300 fans who looked on: they could play football with the league's best.

Coach Baumgardner emphasized this by saying after the game, "We played a real good game with a real good team. A couple of turnovers, a few bad calls on my part and those big plays are all that kept us from winning this game."

"I guess we should've kept them on their side of the 50," Baumgardner remarked, "because they couldn't sustain a drive. We gave them good field positon for every one of their touchdowns."

The loss dropped the Bucks from the league's unbeaten ranks and lowered their record to 2-1, putting them a game-and-a-half behind Pittsburgh in the Eastern Division.

The Bucks showed off their own fast-score offense in the first quarter and it was good enough for a 6-0 lead. Central Pennsylvania, which usually liked to use a trick-play to start every game, opened its first offensive series with the old "flea flicker" and as usual it went from Larry Rydbom to Ken Rutter on the overhand lateral and from Rutter to Alge Jones, who was wide open downfield, for 80 yards and the touchdown seven minutes into the game. It was the second time in two games that the Rutter-to-Jones combo paid off. Jones, although not an exceptionally fast receiver, had used quick moves and good open field running to catch 19 passes so far on the year for 540 yards, an average of 28.4-yards-per-catch.

The ensuing Pittsburgh drive was halted by the stubborn Buck defense on the 10 and for the second time the Ironmen failed to score thanks to a missed field goal by Pete Ross. Central Pennsylvania had trouble moving the ball and finally, early in the second period, the Bucks were forced into a punting situation from their own 40. But instead of kicking, the fake punt, another favorite play of the team, was on. Allen Potter tried to pass from punt formation but his toss went right into the hands of Ironman Jack Brumbaugh at the Pittsburgh 30.

The Ironmen took the ball and began marching downfield, reaching the Buck 39 before Melvin McMillan was hit for a three-yard loss on a sweep and Folden tossed an incomplete pass. Facing a third-and-thirteen situation, Folden decided to try to go deep to Fullum. The pass wasn't on target but the Central Pennsylvania defenders lost sight of the ball and they bumped Fullum to keep him from getting his hands on it. That gave Pittsburgh a first-and-goal on the one. Sonny Richardson then got the call and he powered his way behind left guard to even the score with a little over three minutes left in the first quarter. Ross then put the Bucks behind to stay with his extra point.

Central Pennsylvania took over on its own 41 on Tom Hipp's 20-yard kickoff return. A four-yard keeper by Rydbom moved it to the 45, but an incomplete pass and a sack brought in the Buck punter again. Once again Potter was instructed to fake the kick. Once again it was unsuccessful, this time with the pass falling far short of its intended receiver.

"It's easy to second guess when it's over," Baumgardner said of the two plays, "but at the time I thought we were doing the right thing."

An exchange of punts gave Pittsburgh control on the Buck 43. Folden then found Fullum along the sidelines for touchdown number two for the Ironmen.

Fullum hauled the ball in on the 25 and raced untouched into the end zone to make it 14-6 when Ross converted.

Later in the quarter the Bucks drove to the Ironmen 23, but with a little less than two minutes left in the half, a fumble by Hipp ended the drive.

The Bucks had to be buoyed by the fact that they came out for the second half trailing by just eight points. But the roof proceeded to cave in during the next two-and-a-half minutes.

On the first play after the kickoff Rydbom scrambled around left end for three yards, but then fumbled the ball into the hands of Pittsburgh's Chapas on the 30. Folden then connected with Fullum again on the sideline pass and the receiver ran over Jim Slabon and into the end zone near the end of the third quarter.

Following the ensuing kickoff, Rydbom decided to go to the air but his pass was hauled in by Bob Allen, an ex-Cleveland Brown, who was wearing the wrong color shirt and returned the interception 10-yards to the Bucks' 10. That set up Smith's gallop up the middle. Pittsburgh now led, 26-6.

The Bucks were reeling and didn't seem to know what hit them. Baumgardner decided a change at quarterback was needed and the veteran from Tyrone, Tom Miller, got the call. Trailing by 20 points, Central Pennsylvania had to pass and Pittsburgh knew it and were ready for it. The next three Buck drives were halted by interceptions.

The Buck quarterbacks wound up throwing a season high 41 passes. "Our scouting report showed that their defense was set to stop our running attack so we thought we could throw the way their linebackers and secondary positioned themselves," Baumgardner said to explain the change in strategy, "It's just that Larry and Tom just couldn't connect and sometimes when they did we'd drop the ball."

Still, despite throwing seven interceptions, the Bucks wound up with 225 yards through the air. A lot of those yards, however, came in the final period when Miller began tossing to Jones, who hauled in six of his passes in the last frame.

The Bucks' first possession in the fourth period ended in six points when Miller hit Jones cutting across the end zone from the seven. But the drive took 15 plays and seven valuable minutes off the clock.

Slabon then smothered his own on-side kick and Miller hit Jones and Skillings for a total of 30 yards. His fifth pass of the drive, however, was grabbed by Pittsburgh's Naputano and he raced 32 yards with it before being stopped on the Central Pennsylvania 46.

The ball-hawking Bill Gordon got into the interception picture by hauling in one of Gary Shope's passes, his fifth steal of the year. It took Miller three passes to Jones to get the touchdown, the score coming from 18-yards out. The Ironmen took over with 1:40 left in the game and time ran out on the Bucks, this despite Slabon's late interception which he ran back 62 yards behind a wall of blockers to the Pittsburgh 26 with four seconds on the clock.

The win left Pittsburgh undefeated in the league standings. The loss had snapped Central Pennsylvania's three game winning streak, but the Bucks had made a good showing of themselves. They proved they weren't going to back down from anyone.

"We played a lot of good teams that first season," recalls Darrel Rutter, "We played a tough schedule for basically a start-up team."

# CHAPTER

# 3

"My Dad wound up taping a lot of the guys before
the games—ankles, knees, shoulders."
—BUCKS' KICKER AND LINEMAN BILL LUTHER

The Bucks were back in action six days after their loss to Pittsburgh when they traveled to Johnstown for a non-league tilt with the Miners. Johnstown was paced on offense by the Gunby brothers, Nelson and Cordy, who had both starred for the Johnstown High Trojans in the late 1960s and early '70s, and on defense by Wesley Harris, who had recorded five sacks in a game for the Miners on August 23rd.

The Bucks had been playing well in recent weeks, but this time the showing the Bucks put on was anything but good.

"We were flat," says Darrel Rutter.

Jay Siegel put it a little more succinctly: "I remember that one. They kicked our asses."

One player had a reason for the Bucks' performance.

"In Johnstown Coach Paganetti was late for the game," says Pat Little today, "He was traveling and got held up somewhere and we played without him."

What turned into a fiasco started on the Bucks' very first play from scrimmage. Once again the Bucks tried a little trickeration. Rydbom passed to Alge Jones who then tried to lateral to Wayne Rockmore. The running back from Clearfield fumbled the ball and Johnstown recovered. The Miners did not capitalize on that break, but the 250 or so fans in Point Stadium had witnessed just the beginning of the visitors' problems. All in all, the Bucks would fumble 13 times and have two passes intercepted on a long night in the Flood City for the first-year club.

The Miners showed why they were 4-1 on the year on their second possession. Keith Hall broke loose on the first play for 53 yards and three plays later Cordy Gunby raced into the end zone from the Bucks' 17 to give Johnstown a 6-0 edge.

Central Pennsylvania got a break when Charvi Skillings smothered a fumbled punt on the Miners' 41. But on the very next play Rydbom's pass for the end zone was picked off by Cordy Gunby, who fell out of bounds on the two yard line. That's when the usually tough Buck defense flexed its muscles for the only time of the game. Four plays after the interception, three Bucks' defensive linemen, John White, Tom Arnelle and Les McCoy, teamed up to chase quarterback Chuck McCabe into the end zone for a safety.

A fake punt that gained 15 yards kept the Bucks' ensuing drive alive. But the march was stopped when Rydbom misfired on a fourth down pass at the 17. Johnstown then widened its lead to 13-2 midway through the period on a four-yard drive up the middle by Nelson Gunby and Bob Layo's extra point kick.

Although their offense hadn't generated much in the way of yards or points yet, the Bucks were managing to stay in the game due to their rugged defense. A case in point came when the Bucks had a great chance to narrow the gap as they set up with a first-and-goal on the 10 yard line. But Rydbom then proceeded to commit one of his eight fumbles on the night at the 17, and Johnstown's Chuck Wyatt quickly scooped up the ball and raced 83 yards for the score and a 19-2 Johnstown lead.

"Larry [*Rydbom*] had a tendency to get rattled," remembers Ken Rutter.

The Bucks would not quit, however. They marched 65 yards in 12 plays and Rydbom capped the drive with a one yard plunge with 18 seconds left in the half. Central Pennsylvania had cut the halftime deficit to 19-8.

But that was as close as the error-prone Bucks could get. The Miners scored four second half touchdowns, three of them set up by Buck turnovers.

Thanks to the miscues, the Buck defense found itself on the field more than usual, which gradually wore down the defenders. They managed to hold the score at 19-8, however, until Johnstown's big-play offense struck again. This time a 26-yard pass from McCabe to Nelson Gunby put the ball on the Central Pennsylvania 13. McCabe then went to Cordy Gunby for the touchdown late in the third period.

The problems continued for the visitors in the last quarter. Two plays after Jerry White fumbled, McCabe connected with Keith Hall for a 26-yard scoring pass. On their next series, which was set up by another Rydbom fumble, Johnstown scored again when Cordy Gunby ran six yards for another score.

The final Johnstown touchdown came off an interception that gave the Miners the ball on the Buck 42. Three plays and one penalty later Nelson Gunby broke loose for 21 yards and his second score.

The 13 fumbles and two interceptions, combined with an over-worked defense that surrendered a season-high 408 yards in total offense, left coach Gary Baumgardner with just one word of explanation. "Unbelievable," he muttered after the debacle had ended with the score 45-8 in favor of Johnstown. "We blew assignments everywhere and I'm just shocked at how we've slipped instead of progressing over the past two weeks."

Fortunately, the weekend wasn't a total loss for the Central Pennsylvania bunch. They were awarded a win-by-forfeit over the defunct Latrobe Laurel Leopards to raise their record to 4-3 on the season. The forfeit also gave them a 3-1 record in the Mid-Atlantic League's Eastern Division.

But this news did little to soothe the wounds of the drubbing the Bucks received at the hands of Johnstown.

"It was just one of those games," says Wayne Rockmore, "We just did some of the dumbest things. It seemed like the team was infected by a virus. They beat us bad."

Their performance a week later against East Palestine (from Ohio, not the Middle East) in Curwensville did little to help their outlook either.

This game was originally scheduled as a road game in Ohio. But a few days before the game, Al Siegel announced that the game was being played on Sunday the 28th at 2pm in Curwensville. Both the teams were 3-1 in the MAFL standings, the Bucks second in the East and the Red Devils in first place in the West.

Over the course of a football season, some losses are hard for teams to swallow. But there are those defeats, like the Bucks' loss to the Red Devils that are a lot tougher to stomach than others.

Such was the case on Sunday, September 28th, 1975. Four times the Bucks had first downs at or inside the Red Devils' 10-yard line. Still another time they had first and 10 at the East Palestine 26. These five possessions, however, produced only one touchdown. Ultimately the Bucks lost a heartbreaker, 9-8, their third setback in a row on the field of play. Afterward, the disappointed team didn't even want to talk about it. And who could blame them?

The Bucks' lone threat in the first half came in the final two minutes when Larry Rydbom connected on long passes to Pat Little and Alge Jones to put the ball on the Devils' 10. However, the next four passes fell incomplete to kill that chance as time ran out in the half.

Early in the third quarter Terry Rydbom, Larry's brother, who played a solid game in his debut at defensive end for the Bucks, recovered a Red Devil fumble at the East Palestine 26. The hosts then scored in four plays, with Jerry White's 16-yard scamper the big play. The payoff was a six-yard pass from Larry Rydbom to Charvi Skillings at the goal line. Bill Luther's extra point kick was blocked by Tom Olive, a 260-pound defensive tackle who had been cut by the Cleveland Browns and would be a thorn in the side of the Bucks all afternoon. For one of the Bucks,' however, Olive was literally a pain in the neck, and fortunately, as it turned out, not something worse.

"I was severely injured during the game in Curwensville against East Palestine," remembers Pat Little, "They had this defensive end, ex-NFL player, Olive, who was a monster of a player. He beat up a bunch of our players.

"Well, I was a wide out—all 180 pounds of me—and we ran an end around on my side of the field. My job was to block the defensive end and blind side him to knock him off the play. Like I said this guy was killing us and I thought this was my opportunity to get a good hit on him. So, I came down the line and just as he turned around I dove into his knees with everything I had at the fastest speed I could muster. I heard this very loud crack and I immediately thought that I broke his leg and how pissed he was going to be.

"Then, as I lay face down on the ground, I realized I couldn't move," Little continues, "Arms and legs did nothing, then they began to tingle and I *slowly* got to my knees and then barely got to my feet and then off the field. After a few minutes I was okay.

"Ten years later I fell on some ice and injured my back. I had to have a radiation X-Ray of my skeletal system and the doctor said, 'Everything looks good except you have a cracked vertebrae in your neck that must have happened some time ago because it is healed over now.' I told him, 'Makes sense, I can tell you the time and place that happened.' The crack I heard on that play, in Curwensville, was my vertebrae being broken. I am so thankful that I wasn't paralyzed from that hit. I was lucky and I know it.

"Later I remember returning to the game and I caught up with Olive after a play and asked him how his knee was and he asked me what I was talking about," recalls Little, "He didn't even remember the hit. The ultimate insult!"

Little wasn't the only Bucks' player who Olive made life miserable for. The man assigned to block Olive for the Bucks was Ken Grove, a tough but small offensive lineman from State College who stood 5'9" and weighed all of 195 pounds.

"Ken Grove got his ass handed to him by that Olive character and quit the team after that game," says Little, "Ken was a great undersized lineman and Olive beat him viciously."

"He was smart to quit after getting beat so bad," remembers Darrel Rutter, "he was smart enough to know when he was licked."

Central Pennsylvania had two chances to increase its 6-3 lead as John White and then Tom Arnelle recovered fumbles at the visitors' 45 and 39, respectively. In both cases, however, the Bucks very obligingly turned the ball right back over to the Red Devils. On the first possession, Larry Rydbom fumbled the ball away to Olive, and then on the second the ex-Glendale signal caller threw an interception that John Coleman returned 27 yards to the East Palestine 38.

The Red Devils then marched to their lone touchdown as quarterback Larry Jordan hit Bennett Bruno for a 15-yard gain, and then scrambled for another 21 yards. Jordan capped the 10-play drive by bootlegging around left end from the two. Jim Slabon broke through to block the conversion try by Kirk Andrews, a former Geneva, New York, College placekicker whose 43-yard field goal had accounted for the only first half points.

Although outplayed, the Bucks still had two golden opportunities to pull out a victory. Immediately after Jordan's touchdown, the Bucks pushed to the Devils' 8 on a 13-yard pass from Larry Rydbom to Robbie Miles and a 35-yard gain on a bootleg by Rydbom. However, the drive stalled there as Jerry White was stopped for a yard-loss, Rydbom gained just three around left end and two passes fell incomplete.

A little later, the Bucks' defense forced the Devils to punt and Bill Gordon caught it at the East Palestine 48. Rydbom quickly hit Jones twice for 12-yard gains, and then went to him deep. The pass was incomplete, but a pass interference call in the end zone gave the Bucks the ball and a first and goal at the one.

Victory looked imminent for the Bucks. But Rydbom was twice stacked up at the goal line, as was White on third down. On fourth down, the Bucks were called for a procedure penalty, moving the ball back to the six. At this point, Baumgardner might have gone for a field goal that would have tied the game at 9. Instead he decided to go for broke and the touchdown. Rydbom rolled right and elected to run instead of pass, and he was tackled at the five to kill that threat.

East Palestine held the ball for most of the last two minutes, and on fourth down at the three, reserve quarterback Jack Dugan simply took the snap and ran back into and out of his end zone. An over-anxious and probably more than a little frustrated Buck was called for hitting Dugan after he was out of the end zone. The Devils could then free kick from their 35 instead of the 20, and the Bucks could return it only to their 37. Rydbom's last gasp desperation pass was intercepted.

Baumgardner had to deal with the second-guessers after the game. They grilled him about his use of a one-back offense at the goal line and his option of going for the touchdown rather than a field goal that might have forced overtime. Explaining his choice of the run over the placekick, the coach said, "In the past several weeks, we just haven't been that consistent in our kicking. It's not that I don't have faith in Bill Luther's kicking, but the way they caved us in on the extra point try, I just couldn't see us doing it.

"The situation where we got down to the one-foot line was just inconceivable to me that we wouldn't score," the coach continued, "We talked about going for the field goal on the sidelines, but I made the decision to go for six. I just couldn't believe we couldn't get it in."

As for the goal line offense, he said, "Our primary problem installing a two-back offense is that we don't get all the backs together at one practice. We might have one there Tuesday and the other Wednesday.

"We worked on that type of offense some last week and, hopefully, we'll have it ready for the next game."

Baumgardner cited Jerry White for his running—he managed 50 yards on 17 carries—and Terry Rydbom for his defensive play.

"White has been an asset all year," the head coach stated, "He is a good back. He has good balance, but we've got to get holes for the kid. East Palestine's interior was the biggest we've played against. Even the Ironmen weren't that big.

"Olive was excellent, and double zero [*Bill Greenawalt*] was tough, too. We just couldn't handle them. Our interior linemen aren't big enough."

Olive was all over the field for the Red Devils, but mostly he spent a lot of time in the Bucks' backfield forcing Larry Rydbom to hurry his passes.

"I thought we played well enough to win," Baumgardner went on to say. "Defensively, we bent at times, but you can't expect to hold teams every down. Although I think we improved from last week on offense, we just lacked that consistency again. We'd get a drive going and then we'd make a mistake, like fumbling or dropping a pass or jumping offsides."

Their lack of offense now had the Bucks on a three-game losing streak, and at 3-2 in the league's Eastern Division, two games behind Pittsburgh.

The Bucks were next scheduled to play the East Ohio Dukes from Wellington, Ohio. As stated before, the game, originally scheduled for DuBois, was moved to Altoona.

Altoona, located in Blair County at the base of Brush Mountain within Logan Valley and Pleasant Valley, was founded by the Pennsylvania Railroad in 1849 as the site for a shop and maintenance complex. Some say the name Altoona comes from the Latin word "altus," which means high, a theory supported by the fact that Altoona's nickname is the "Mountain City." Others say the name derives from Colonel Beverly Mayer, a civil engineer who laid out the tracks for the railroad and named the place Altoona after the city of Altona in Holstein, Germany.

Altoona soon grew into a major and important railway and manufacturing center with a population of around 200,000. The nearby Horseshoe Curve, now a National Historic Landmark, was built as a method of getting trains to a sufficient elevation to cross the Allegheny Ridge to the west. Because the Curve quickly became an industrial link to the western United States, it was the target of a Nazi sabotage plot during World War II.

Like many of the towns and cities in the Northeast that relied on the steel, coal and railroad industries, Altoona suffered a slow but steady decline starting in the late 1940s. This economic downturn, so prevalent in "Rust Belt" cities, resulted in the closing of many of the downtown's landmark stores and industries. People left the city and moved to the suburbs where much of the commercial development had shifted. Altoona did remain a hub of the area's railroad industry, evidenced by the fact that many of the Bucks worked in the various shops in the area while playing football on weekends.

On Friday, October, 3rd, the Bucks lived by the old adage, "desperate times call for desperate measures." Unable to secure a practice facility during the week before the game, the Bucks, minus their uniforms and decked out in sweat shirts and sweat pants, snuck onto the intramural field behind Beaver Stadium at Penn State and held an impromptu practice session in the rain.

"We practiced at the Penn State intramural fields," recalls Hugh Gibbons, "The lights wouldn't work but one of the guys climbed the light tower to get the mercury lamps lit to get the lights to work."

"Some college guys watched us and said, 'hey you're pretty good, what team are you?'" remembers Darrel Rutter.

"I think they were hoping we weren't a team that would play them," adds Wayne Rockmore.

The contest the next night, which was the first pro game ever held at Mansion Park, drew 600 or so people, and the fans saw the local team, led by their opportunistic defensive secondary, regain their winning form as they outslugged the Dukes 13-0.

The defense, solid all season, did the job once again, keeping the Dukes from penetrating any farther than the Central Pennsylvania 30, while picking off five passes in the process. In fact, the last five times the Dukes had possession of the ball the Buck defense managed to come up with an interception.

The offense had its moments too, however, and one of those bright spots came on the very first play from scrimmage. The Bucks, who were making a habit of running a trick play to open every game, came through with their version of the "flea flicker" and for the third time it paid off in a touchdown. Rydbom started the play by tossing an overhand lateral to wide receiver Ken Rutter, which pulled the defense in. Rutter then fired downfield to a wide-open Alge Jones, who raced 57 yards to the end zone. Bill Luther added the extra point and the Bucks led 7-0 with less than a minute gone in the game.

So far, Rutter had thrown five passes and he had completed four of them for 242 yards and three touchdowns.

With the Buck offense performing inconsistently, the defense, as always, was keeping things under control, beginning on the first Duke play when defensive end Jim Steinbugl broke through for a 14-yard sack on Hubler.

"Another tough smart Bishop Guilfoyle guy," Darrel Rutter says when asked about Steinbugl. "You just didn't get around him."

East Ohio was forced to punt the first five times it had the ball but each time the Bucks had to give it right back, either because they were forced to punt or they turned the ball over.

Late in the half the Dukes tried to convert a fourth-and-six on the Buck 31, but linebacker Lee Baughman from State College was there to bat down Hubler's pass.

Central Pennsylvania's offense finally showed signs of life again as Rydbom went to the air eight straight times trying to beat the clock. The drive stalled on the Ohio 15, however, when three straight passes fell incomplete.

The Bucks got a break early in the second half when Duke punter Joe Thompson got a bad snap from center and out of desperation tried to kick the ball anyhow. The ill-advised kick was partially blocked and went only five yards before Terry Graham jumped on it at the Bucks 41.

Rydbom, using the air attack, then moved the ball to the Duke 17, but Luther's field goal try of 34 yards was wide right and the ball went back to East Ohio.

The first of the five Bucks' pass interceptions came early in the fourth quarter when they were still clinging to that narrow 7-0 lead. Once again it was Bill Gordon who was the culprit, picking off the pass and returning it 25 yards to his own 32. Three plays later Larry Rydbom connected with Charvi Skillings for the touchdown and a 13-0 Buck edge. Skillings did a lot of it on his own as he tight-roped down the sidelines for the last 10 of the 34 yards.

With the Dukes now forced to go to the air in an effort to catch up, the Whitetail Bucks set up their defense to defend against the pass, and took advantage of the fact that quarterback Mark Hubler was a bit off target with his throws.

Lee Baughman stole the first Hubler toss after the touchdown. But the Bucks lost the ball and then let East Ohio move to the Central Pennsylvania 33. Jim Slabon, however, then got into the interception act by picking off a tipped pass.

"He was a good guy, a solid football player." Darrel Rutter says of Slabon, "Good leader on defense. Called the signals for the secondary. He was a good cover guy, if the ball was in the air, he felt it was his. Also a solid tackler. You didn't fool him. Had a real nose for the football. But he liked his interceptions a bit too much and could be a bit of a ball-hawk. He'd go for the ball sometimes and you'd have to cover for him."

In the final two minutes with the Dukes desperately going to the airways, Altoona's Gary Griffith, who went to Bloomsburg State [now University] grabbed two misdirected passes and showed some fine running by returning the picks 71 yards.

"Our defense was just great," Baumgardner proudly said, "and they kept giving us good field position all night. The offense, however, didn't do as well once they got the ball, we just couldn't seem to get moving consistently."

Assistant Dave Paganetti also felt "we couldn't get our offense going at times. We just didn't seem able to come up with the big play when we needed it."

Rydbom completed 11 of 25 passes for 178 yards. He had two passes picked off but did register the touchdown toss to Skillings in the fourth quarter.

Elsewhere on offense the Bucks found a new running back in 22-year-old Steve Robinson, a 5'11" 180 pounder from Tyrone who rushed for 42 of the teams' 45 yards, causing Baumgardner to compliment that "he is a very good runner that follows his blocks well and hits the holes hard."

Alge Jones continued his fine season, as he hauled in six more passes for 153 yards, raising his season stats to 31 catches for a whopping 853 yards. His mixture of speed and moves that could get him into the clear made him the Bucks' biggest offensive threat.

"Alg made quite a number of absolutely circus catches for us," states Mike McNeish, "Good tight end with great hands. If we would have had game films, they would have made the highlight reel. These were laid out flat fingertip grabs."

The fourth period turned into a slugfest as fights broke out left and right, twice emptying both benches. "It's bad but a lot of the blame goes to the refs," Baumgardner said of the circumstances, which seemed to plague the semipro game, "They should take better control of the game. East Ohio has a good team but they could have done better if they'd kept their cool.

"It could have been better but it's still good to win," Baumgardner went on to say afterwards. "This is just our first year and we're still trying to get things straightened around. Our practice conditions aren't the greatest and we've had some key injuries, but our people are playing well under the circumstances and that's all we can ask."

The Bucks were next scheduled to travel the 150-plus miles to Washington, Pa. to take on the hapless Generals, a team they had whipped 40-6 in the third game of the season. During the week the Bucks added two defensive players, picking up Gary Pheasant from Altoona, who had played wide receiver at Purdue but was penciled in as a linebacker for the Bucks, and Jeff McCartney, a 250-pound defensive tackle from Penn State.

McCartney had decided to give up his career at Penn State to join the Bucks. When asked why he did so, he said he'd had it with books and studying and he just wanted to play football.

"He was very good," says Darrel Rutter when asked about McCartney, "actually better than Brad Benson from Altoona, who went on to be an All-American at Penn State and an All-Pro with the Giants. He could wreck an offense real quick. Good size, one of our biggest players. He was intelligent, had a high IQ, and was a nice kid. But he didn't like to study. He just liked to play ball."

The pitiful Generals, 1-4 and in last place in the Eastern Division, managed to draw only 50 or so people to the game.

Because of similar poor attendance figures, the Generals had always struggled financially, operating for the most part on a shoestring budget just to try and get by. The area was never a hotbed for semipro football, despite several attempts to place a team there. Besides the Generals, the Pennsylvania Mustangs, headquartered in Washington, played in the North American Football League in 1965, the only year of the league's existence. Despite some real talent, such as former New York Giant Glynn Griffing, ex-Steeler and future Browns running back Charley Leigh, and wide receiver Jerry Simmons, who went on to play for the Falcons and Broncos, as well as a working agreement with the Steelers that gave the Mustangs first chance at any player Pittsburgh released as well the opportunity to use any players from the Steelers taxi squad, the Mustangs, like the Generals, barely scraped by, playing before small crowds at Charleroi and then

Wash High School. After the season, director of player personnel Bob Dahlgren resigned, claiming the team owed him his $5,000 salary and $1,375 in expenses. On his way out the door, Dahlgren also said the players had not received any pay for their last three games. The Mustangs folded with the rest of the league before they could play a second season.

"It was good football but there were a lot of problems involved," Phil Ahwesh, the Mustangs' coach, told Fred Sigler of the *Washington Observer-Reporter* in November of 1985, "Finances were always a problem. Playing at two different sites didn't help either."

In the late 1960s, another team tried to make a go of it in the area, but the Washington County Miners didn't last very long, either.

The small crowd did little to inspire the hometown club on October 11th. Washington's first offensive drive was an indication of what the evening held for the Generals when Gary Pheasant quickly made his presence felt by picking off an errant pass and racing 45 yards untouched into the end zone. Bill Luther added the extra point to give the Bucks a 7-0 edge.

The other new Buck, Jeff McCartney, nicknamed "Mother" by his teammates, was virtually unstoppable on the pass rush, recording two sacks and recovering a fumble and otherwise punishing the Generals' offense with numerous hard hits. "He is very quick." Baumgardner said proudly of his new found defensive hero, "and he reads keys well. He uses good slip blocks like they teach at Penn State."

He also, according to Rod Ullein, hated, and still hates, the nickname "Mother."

"He hates that name 'Mother.'" Ullein said recently, "He got that name from one of our Junior High School coaches, the late Milford Pittman. Before every practice, Jeff's Mom showed up in the Caddy and they sat in the A.C. as he gobbled a Big Mac, fries and a milkshake, every practice, through high school, six years. She also laundered his practice uniform every day. The rest of us stunk to high heaven, never laundering the entire season."

Led by Pheasant and McCartney, the entire defensive unit overpowered Washington throughout the game and their dominance showed in the final stats. The Generals were held to 32 yards in total offense, which included a net rushing total of a minus 52 yards.

The Bucks also picked off four interceptions. Pheasant, with his pick-six, and Bill Gordon, who hijacked his seventh toss of the season, both intercepted a pass, while linebacker Jeff Best from Glendale added two more interceptions.

It was a good thing for the Bucks that the defense was so strong, as the offense struggled for both yards and points. Central Pennsylvania managed only 191 yards in total offense, and although they spent most of the game in Washington's end of the field, they managed only three touchdowns.

Three times the Bucks saw offensive drives stalled inside the 20 when Larry Rydbom turned the ball over on interceptions. Adding to the Whitetail Bucks' problems was the fact that they were whistled for 14 penalties for 126 yards. More than a couple of the infractions killed any momentum the Bucks may have had at the time.

Despite the problems, the Bucks moved out to a 13-0 lead, thanks to a one-yard plunge by Steve Robinson late in the first half.

With less than two minutes to go in the half, Central Pennsylvania was on the move but saw their march grind to a halt at the Washington 12. Baumgardner and Paganetti decided to go for the field goal, which would be a 29-yard try by Bill Luther.

Jim Slabon was the holder and waited to set the ball on the 19, but the snap from center was muffed. The Bucks' "mayday" play, as Baumgardner called it, went into action. Slabon got to his feet and spotted wide receiver Doug Kritzer, who had drifted to the goal line unnoticed. Slabon's looping pass found the mark, and Luther's extra point made the score at intermission 20-0.

"Kritzer was a cop from Clearfield." remembers Darrel Rutter, "He was a running back, would get 2 or 3 or 4 yards when you needed it. Not flashy, just got the job done . . . kinda like a cop."

The Bucks' last score came on another "flea flicker," this one a 24-yarder from Ken Rutter to Alge Jones. It was the fourth time the two had hooked up for a touchdown. Luther's point after set the final at 27-0.

The Bucks defense completely throttled the Generals offense, holding them to seven first downs—three of those by way of penalties—and two yards in total offense. You read that right, two yards. The Generals had 54 yards passing but lost 52 yards on the ground.

By now, Central Pennsylvania had a surprising 6-4 record for their inaugural season, an impressive mark for a relatively inexperienced team. The Bucks were winning despite the fact that they were basically an "expansion team." The squad's showing so far had surprised a lot of people. Their defense was one of the best in the league, and their offense seemed able to score when they needed to.

Rydbom had thrown for 986 yards so far, while Ken Rutter had completed five of eight "flea flicker" passes for 286 more yards and four TDs. Alge Jones had pulled down 34 receptions and scored six touchdowns.

"We did pretty well in 1975, won quite a few games," remembers Bill Luther.

Luther also remembers his Dad, Bill, Sr., helping out the financially-strapped team.

"I wound up missing the first few games in '75, I had hurt my knee," recalls Luther, "I wanted to play so I went to an orthopedic surgeon and said I wanted to play. He said if you're stupid enough to play, go ahead. My Dad, who had played at Penn State and was a coach, wound up taping my knee before the games in the locker room. The other guys would see this and say, 'He looks like he knows what he's doing.' So my Dad wound up taping a lot of the guys before the games—ankles, knees, shoulders."

Another newcomer joined the Bucks after the Washington game. Ritchie Shoop, a running back from Hollidaysburg who could also place-kick as well as kick-off, joined Baumgardner's merry band.

"Shoop was a very good kicker." says Darrel Rutter, "He could get those kickoffs nice and high so the team could cover them. As a running back, he was nothing fancy, but could get you 2 or 3 yards when you needed it."

Next up on the schedule for the Bucks was a rematch with the Johnstown Miners. A few weeks before the Bucks had played probably their worst game of the season as they lost 45-8 to the Miners, and to rub salt in the Bucks' wounds, Johnstown had started a few fights and even added a few unnecessary touchdowns by passing late in the game while holding an already safe lead. Needless to say the Bucks wanted some payback.

"We remembered that when we played them in Clearfield," says Wayne Rockmore, "we came together and killed them."

Approximately 300 fans came out to the Driving Park in Clearfield to watch the game. They saw the Buck defense shut down an opponent again, while the offense did its job with five touchdowns and four extra points.

Baumgardner, who responded to a reporters' question about the win with one word, "Revenge," pointed out that "the defense was ready for them, and we stopped the reverse that hurt us in that first meeting. The whole squad played well but Jeff McCartney, Gary Pheasant, Terry Graham, Albe Wales and Al Siegel all looked especially good on defense."

Baumgardner added, "it was the first time in a while that we got our passing and running games working well in the same game and our line played a lot better than it has."

The Bucks scored on their very first possession, as Larry Rydbom hit Alge Jones with a touchdown pass, the first of two the duo would hook up on. The Bucks were off and running—or was it passing?—to their third straight win.

The Bucks' offense continue to fire on all cylinders. Rydbom tossed a scoring pass to Ritchie Shoop and also ran for one himself. Shoop added a 20-yard touchdown run and converted four out of four extra points. Larry Rydbom's brother, Terry, added another touchdown by recovering a fumble and returning it to the end zone.

The Bucks' revenge was complete. "It was really sweet," recalls Darrel Rutter.

Although Johnstown broke Central Pennsylvania's two-game shutout streak, technically, the Bucks defense shut out the Miners, as their only score came when punter Allen Potter got a bad snap from center and, instead of eating the ball or letting the Miners jump on it for six, he booted the ball out of his own end zone for a safety.

The Buck defense was so formidable that only once did the Miners threaten, with a first-and-goal on the three. But Albe Wales forced a fumble that Ed Peters recovered to end that drive.

Wales also combined with Darrel Rutter on a sack of the Johnstown quarterback that knocked him from the game.

Central Pennsylvania raised its record to 7-4 with the win, and celebrated with another party at Al Siegel's house. "I went, but my wife got mad and I wound up sleeping on the couch," says Darrel Rutter.

The Bucks were now a solid 5-2 in league competition. Regardless of what happened in their season ender with Pittsburgh, the Bucks would have a winning record in their first season, quite an accomplishment for a team that only existed on paper five months before.

The Bucks faced the Ironmen at Pittsburgh North Park's Stone Field on Sunday night October 26th. The Ironmen had already clinched the Middle Atlantic Eastern Division championship, and showed why they were the league's best team.

The Bucks ran into a tough Ironmen defense that forced a lot of mistakes which Pittsburgh's offense was able to take advantage of. Central Pennsylvania managed only a minus 96 yards rushing, most of those negative yards coming because of Pittsburgh's numerous sacks of quarterback Larry Rydbom.

Rydbom had an inconsistent night due to a combination of cold-handed receivers, a porous offensive line and four passes that ended up in the hands of Pittsburgh defenders. The former Glendale passer did manage to complete 19 of 50 attempts for 191 yards but his performance was hampered by the four picks and a nonexistent ground game.

Pittsburgh quickly showed the Bucks why they were league royalty by cashing in on some of the Whitetail Bucks' early mistakes with good field position. This led to field goal kicker Pete Ross splitting the uprights from 33, 24 and 31 yards out.

The Bucks did get the first break of the game when Pittsburgh punter Ray Weir got a bad snap from center and had to eat the ball. Bill Gordon and Terry Rydbom tackled Weir on the Pittsburgh one.

From there Ritchie Shoop was knocked for a one yard loss. Then the Bucks were sent back to the six when they were whistled for an illegal procedure penalty. Central Pennsylvania finally got it over, however, when Rydbom connected with former Glendale High School teammate Gary Kizina on second-and-goal for the touchdown. Shoop lined up to kick the extra point but the referee noticed that Shoop was wearing an illegal shoe. Shoop was waved off the field, and Bill Luther had to come in for the try which was batted down, keeping the score at 6-0.

The Bucks forced another Pittsburgh turnover later in the opening quarter when Jim Slabon picked off a Gary Shope aerial in the end zone. On the next play, however, Rydbom and Shoop had a mix-up in the backfield, and the quarterback's misdirected pitch out was jumped on by the Ironmen at the nine.

The Bucks defense managed to hold Pittsburgh, thanks in part to a seven-yard sack by Lee Baughman. Pittsburgh had to settle for three points on Ross' 33-yard kick.

Central Pennsylvania proceeded to give the ball away again, this time on an interception toss by Rydbom. Five plays later fullback Joe Jancosko plunged over from the five yard line early in the second frame. Ross' extra point made it 10-6.

Midway through the second quarter the Bucks got themselves into a hole from which they never recovered. Allen Potter, back to punt, had his kick batted down by Ramsey Simmons, who had been to training camp with the Steelers and would prove to be a thorn in the Bucks' side for the next several years. The blocked kick was recovered by Ironman Rich McCord. The Central Pennsylvania defense, anchored by their line of Baughman, Al Siegel, Jeff "Mother" McCartney and Terry Rydbom, refused to yield, however. They stopped the Ironmen on the two yard line.

But the offense couldn't get them out of the hole. They went three plays and out. Potter dropped back into his own end zone to punt. But a fierce rush shook the kicker, and his hurried kick only reached the 19. Spud Jenkins gathered it in there and returned it to the five.

It was there that the Central Pennsylvania defense held once again. Pittsburgh had to settle for another field goal by Ross to up the margin to 13-6.

After that it was all Ironmen. On their first possession in the second half, Pittsburgh scored on a 41-yard pass from Shope to Jack Brumbaugh. Ross' kick made it 20-6.

The next time they got their hands on the ball, the Ironmen scored again. This time the score came on a 31-yard field goal by Ross just five minutes after the Brumbaugh touchdown.

The Buck defense continued to bend but not break, and remained solid in the red zone. Pittsburgh had a first-and-goal at the seven but the stubborn, persistent Bucks halted the Ironmen drive.

The Bucks' offense, meanwhile, continued to have its problems throughout the game. They did finally manage to get six more points early in the final period. Rydbom's aerials to Charvi Skillings, Alge Jones, and Pat Little moved the ball from the Pittsburgh 49 to the Ironmen 2. Ritchie Shoop then ran it in from there. Holder Jim Slabon tried to pass for the conversion, but his toss was off-target and fell to the ground, leaving the score 23-12.

Central Pennsylvania never threatened again, but their defense managed to stop the Ironmen twice after giving up the ball on a bad snap on a punt and another Rydbom pick-off. Both times Pittsburgh missed field goal tries.

The end of the game brought the usual semipro football chaos, including fisticuffs, referee baiting and penalties. The commotion resulted in two more Ironmen touchdowns, the first coming when Spud Jenkins, apparently stopped cold at the 20, broke loose when no one blew the whistle and raced for a 22-yard touchdown.

Pittsburgh managed to tally one more six-pointer when Jim Sanders stole a Rydbom pass on the first play after the kickoff and ran it back 25 yards for the score. Ross added the extra point with just 51 seconds to go and the Ironmen had upped their advantage to 36-12, the final score.

Despite the loss, the Bucks had finished the season with a 5-3 record in the Mid-Atlantic League and 7-5 overall, very good for a first year club and much better than a lot of people had expected. But the mood after the final game was anything but euphoric. Already there was talk of the team folding.

Darrel Rutter remembers, "The lights had been turned off, maybe forever. The crowd left, and friends, family and hangers-on milled around, all wondering the same thing—'would there be another season of semipro ball for the Bucks in 1976?'"

# CHAPTER

# 4

"Win or lose, we had fun. We played like champions."
—BUCKS OFFENSIVE TACKLE GEORGE WALKER

The Bucks' success in their first season did not guarantee there'd be a second season. Like all semipro teams, the Bucks existed with one foot in the grave and the other on a banana peel. Money troubles were the team's constant companion.

This was especially true in a mostly rural area like Central Pennsylvania. According to the players, there was always talk making the rounds concerning the team folding.

"We were always worried about the team folding," recalls Wayne Rockmore, "If we'd had some stability we could have had a great organization."

"There were always rumors of the team folding." adds Darrel Rutter, "All winter long the Bucks' players in Altoona wondered about the possibility of one more season. The gate net was not that great. We didn't have enough money after the first year. We didn't know if the owners would put up the money for another season."

"There were always rumors about the team folding all the time," remembers Ron Roefaro, "but we didn't pay attention to that talk. We just kept playing and showing up until they locked the doors on us."

"I do remember talk of dismantling the Bucks," adds Tom Marlett, "but I never did pay too much attention to rumor, I just wanted to play ball and have a great time doing so."

Also, there seemed to be some personnel trouble as well. Team founder, assistant coach and offensive guard Mike McNeish had left the team and resigned as Co-General Manager.

"The beginning of the second season was not an easy one for me," McNeish stated in a recent interview, "There was a lot of infighting among the players and some stuff was said that did not sit well with me. I left the team and stayed away for the first time."

Not only was there uncertainty regarding the Bucks, but also the Mid-Atlantic Semipro League itself, as well.

Only two clubs that had competed in the league in 1975, the Pittsburgh Ironmen and the Beaver County Cougars, indicated they'd be back in the fold for 1976. Even if the Bucks would join them, and there was no guarantee they would, three teams could not make a league.

Then the Bucks' listing ship was righted.

"Ziff bailed us out," says Ken Rutter.

Herman "Hymie" Ziff was a clothing manufacturer who was born in Philipsburg on January 25th, 1926, the son of Simon and Lena Ziff. Herman had four brothers, Saul, Albert, Philip and Sidney. Herman's father founded what would become a local institution, Ziff's Clothing Store, in 1914 when he opened his first store in Philipsburg in the Clarkson Building on Front Street, just north of Laurel. A year after Herman was born, Simon moved the store in to a location between Pine and Spruce, and three years later, in 1930, it was expanded into both ladies and men's wear stores.

Herman graduated from Philipsburg High School in 1942, and then served with the Navy in World War II. When he returned from the war, he married SaraBelle Sealfon of Tyrone, and they had two children, a daughter Susan and a son Julian. Herman had joined the family business, and he helped run the company until his father passed away on March 23rd, 1962. Under Herman's guidance and with the help of his brothers, the business continued to expand and flourish. Ziff's Youngland store was opened in an adjacent site in the early 1960s, a Tot-to-Teens store was opened in Clearfield shortly thereafter, and a Young World store was opened in 1964 in Tyrone.

It was truly a family business. Herman's brother Saul was put in charge of the men's store and his brother Albert ran the ladies' clothing store. Sidney Ziff spent his time between the Youngland and the Tyrone stores, while Herman divided his time overseeing both the Clearfield and Tyrone stores.

Herman was a long-time official for the Congregation Sons of Israel in Philipsburg, and in early 1976, he invested in the team, ensuring there would be a second season for the Bucks.

"My Dad LOVED his team," says Julian Ziff, "every player, every coach . . . everyone."

Thanks to Ziff, the Whitetail Bucks were represented when the Mid-Atlantic Semipro Football League held a reorganizational meeting on Monday April 19th, 1976.

Besides the now-refinanced Bucks, Pittsburgh and Beaver County were the only 1975 league members present at the meeting. But fortunately, five teams who had been in the Eastern Semipro Football League in 1975, had representatives present saying that they planned to switch to the Mid-Atlantic League. These five were the Sharon Old Express, the Erie Panthers, the Dayton, Ohio, Metros, the Lima, Ohio, Astros and the Washington Generals.

League members present at the meeting vowed to make the league as strong as possible in 1976, so they decided on a $1,000 good faith fee for teams planning to join the circuit. It was discussed that the fee would possibly be used as a forfeit fee, and any new members had until the end of April to make their final payment on it.

It was decided that league play would start the weekend of Aug. 14th and 15th, and it was hoped that the league would be able to secure referees from a central location in Pittsburgh.

The meeting also resolved the fact that no teams would be admitted after April in order for the existing teams to finalize their schedules. Members also voiced approval for a league commissioner who would not be affiliated with any league team. This came about because in 1975 Joey Bowker was president of the East Palestine, Ohio, Red Devils franchise *and* the commissioner of the Mid-Atlantic League. This situation naturally caused some major problems as far as fair rule enforcement was concerned, not the least of which was when Bowker's Red Devils, who were rumored to have recruited "ringers" from around the league for the game, upset Pittsburgh in the '75 championship title match, a contest Pittsburgh protested vehemently about.

In order to help publicize the league, the commissioner would be required to publish a weekly newsletter containing standings, the previous weekend's scores, the week's schedule and any disciplinary action to be taken by the league against any team or player. In the opinion of some of the Bucks, the lack of publicity hurt their team.

"The team wasn't advertised too well," says Bill Luther, "We really didn't get very good crowds because of it."

"It was tough competing against Penn State for space in the newspapers," recalls Hugh Gibbons.

Others thought the idea of a regional team hurt the club, especially when the towns in that region were small and widely scattered.

"The difference between us and the other teams was that it was Pittsburgh, Chambersburg, and Erie," Wayne Rockmore said in a recent interview, "Those teams were associated with a specific city. We were Central Pennsylvania, more of a regional team. It was a rural area, and it was tough to draw fans. The concept was good, but we had to try to pull it off in a rural area like Central Pennsylvania. We just did not have the consistency we needed. But we did the best we could with what we had."

"It was a great idea, having a team made up of all local players." offers Darrel Rutter, "But it should have been centered in one town. Philipsburg or Altoona would have made a good base of operations."

"People didn't seem to know who we were," remembers George Walker, "I remember going to functions, and we'd be introduced as the 'Whitetail Bucks,' and people thinking we were a hunting club. I'd have to tell them, 'No we're a football team.'"

Then a story concerning the Bucks made the papers—a change at the top spot for the team.

"I was one of the quarterbacks," says Tom Miller, "I went to a team meeting and somehow came out the head coach and offensive coordinator! I said to myself 'What the hell did I just do?' Here I am teaching and coaching high school football. I said to myself, "I can't be doing this kind of stuff!!""

But despite his reservations, Miller was now not only in charge of the team, he was also responsible for the offense and expected to battle Larry Rydbom for the quarterback spot. Gary Baumgardner, the head coach in 1975, was named an assistant coach. He was put in charge of the kicking game and the defensive secondary.

"It was unfortunate for him that he did not remain as coach," Darrel Rutter recalls of Baumgardner, "But on the other hand it was good for the team in that it took us in another direction. Tom Miller was a no-nonsense coach and a good guy. He was a good coach, very sound X's and O's guy. He was a straight-arrow and a family man. He is still very well-respected in Tyrone and is considered a football icon there."

Dave Paganetti was still on board, slated to coach the defensive line, and the Bucks added another assistant in Don DeSantis from DuBois, who would be in charge of the offensive line. The Bucks took the coaching changes in stride.

"We were used to that because we didn't know who was going to be our coaches or players from practice to practice or game to game," recalls Ron Roefaro.

Miller's promotion to head coach was not the only change in the Bucks' ranks. McNeish's resignation as Co-General Manager made Al Siegel the full-time GM. Also, like many semipro teams, the Bucks had seen—and would continue to see—quite a few changes to their roster. Many players would come and go constantly.

"A lot of guys came and went," says Darrel Rutter, "A lot of the younger ones had no income, and they couldn't afford to get hurt. They'd play a couple games, get beat up and quit."

"Some guys lasted only for one game and that was it," offers Ron Roefaro.

"I only attended two practices . . . and I was gone," says Scott Yocum.

"The only guys that stayed had decent jobs," adds Ken Rutter.

The Bucks would end up losing a few players from their 1975 team.

"I got married in May of '76," recalls Bill Luther, who decided to call it a career during the off-season, "and I had started teaching at Huntingdon Area High School that January. The injuries I sustained in '75 also were a factor."

"Jerry White was an All-American wrestler who was a pretty good running back for us," says Hugh Gibbons, "But his wrestling coach got wind that Jerry was playing football and that was it. He didn't want Jerry to lose his wrestling eligibility."

"I played just 1975," remembers "Bam-Bam" Kanagy, "I was 18, youngest player on the team. I turned 19 that fall. After the Bucks I spent three years in the military, two of them in Germany."

Alge Jones, one of the team's best receivers in 1975, left the team to operate his farm. Others, for one reason or another, would leave during the '76 season.

"I only played a few games in 1976," states Pat Little, "When they informed us that they could no longer cover us with insurance, that was it for me."

Because of the roster attrition, the Bucks held tryouts for veterans and new players on June 5th and 6th. Miller announced that any and all candidates had to supply their own workout gear—spikes and sweat suit. He also emphasized that all positions were open.

"We are especially looking for interior linemen, both offensive and defensive," stated Miller at the time, "but are also looking for anyone who can help us at any position. The veterans have been informed that they will have to work for their position and that being on the starting lineup or even making the team will not be automatic for them. Everyone who comes to the tryout will receive a meal."

Besides the free lunch, the team promised it would supply all players with equipment and transportation to and from games by bus.

"We traveled well, we used the Penn State Fullington buses," remembers Darrel Rutter, "If Paterno would have known what went on in those buses . . ."

"Our bus was fairly normal in the front," adds Hugh Gibbons, "It did get crazier as you moved toward the back."

Once again the Bucks would play an 11-game schedule, and once again they would open the campaign with a home game in State College against the Brooklyn Knights. Three more home games would follow: August 8th against the Boonton Bears in Philipsburg, August 14th in Altoona hosting the Brooklyn Mariners, and August 22nd against the Washington Generals at Glendale. After travelling to Pittsburgh to face the Ironmen, the Bucks would return home to host Beaver County in Curwensville. Then it would be time to hit the road for games in Sharon and Washington. The Bucks would then host Pittsburgh in Philipsburg, and after journeying to Beaver County, the team would end its season with a game against Sharon in Clearfield.

Tom Miller said he was encouraged by the turnout for the June tryouts, which brought an influx of new players to the team. More than two dozen newcomers worked out, including a big contingent from one area.

"We got a big group in from Altoona in 1976," says Ron Roefaro.

"My brother Ken, Joe Wales and I recruited players all winter," adds Darrel Rutter, "We were the most flamboyant and outspoken of the Altoona gang."

"We kept in touch with Al Siegel, letting him know we were poised for another season and that we had some great talent coming."

That talent included defensive lineman Rod Ullein, linebackers Kurt Kessler and Tom Marlett, running backs Guy Houghtaling and Dave Belfield, wide receiver Elton Futrell, defensive back Glen Brandimarte, offensive guard Hyland Jeffries, and defensive end Joe Wales, who all joined the team for the 1976 season.

"I started at defensive end and defensive tackle for the Bucks," recalls Rod Ullein, "We had some high quality players, particularly on defense. Gary Pheasant and I were both Letterman Magazine All Americans in high school. He went to Purdue and I went to the Naval Academy. We were personally recruited by Joe Paterno along with Jeff McCartney who did go to Penn State. I went to the Academy as a result of some intense recruiting by Joe Bugel who later became a well-respected pro football offensive coordinator for Houston, Washington, and ultimately head coach at Arizona."

"First in his class and went to the Naval Academy," remembers Darrel Rutter when asked about Ullein, "Didn't like the discipline so he quit. He was intelligent, smart and savvy. A solid player, tough kid, top-notch player. Good kid but liked to party too much."

Wide receiver Elton Futrell was a hero both on and off the gridiron. After a solid career at Altoona High, Elton attended Indiana University of Pennsylvania.

On November 11th, 1974, he showed that his strength of character and resolve reached far beyond the football field.

Futrell and his younger brother, Kenneth, who everyone called "Candy," were on their way to work that day, when Candy noticed the house of a neighbor, the Cordova family, was on fire.

Candy summoned Elton, who raced to the scene, and instructed Candy to pull the fire alarm, which in those days hung on neighborhood telephone poles.

In the meantime, Elton heard Cora Cordova, who had jumped out the second-floor window, "hollering for help." Candy quickly secured a blanket, and Elton hustled to the front of the house, "and that's when I heard the kids hollering from the window."

Futrell started to go through the front door, but it was too hot, so he somehow climbed onto the roof above the porch. Amy Cordova, 6-years-old, was handed out the window to him. Two other sisters, Gina and Dolores, "were going to jump," but Elton kept them calm "because I could hear the fire trucks coming."

Thanks to Futrell's quick thinking and swift, sure actions, seven of the nine people in the house survived.

"He was good on coverage." Darrel Rutter recalls when asked about Futrell, "Gifted athlete and a ball-hawk. He was fast, maybe the fastest kid on the team."

Tom Marlett, a 5'11" 190-pound linebacker from Shippensburg State College (*now Shippensburg University*), was in the words of Darrel Rutter a "pretty good player. He was undersized but tough, tough as nails. He played two years then joined the Army. Wound up being a career man in intelligence. He was a smart player, stayed in his area, you could rely on him. Called defenses in the huddle."

Not all of the Altoona players lasted very long. "Belfield only played a couple games, he was just a kid, 17 or 18," says Joe Wales.

But they all made an impression in one way or another.

"The Altoona guys were good at starting rumbles," says George Walker today, "We had to stop them some times. But they were tough kids, guys like the Wales brothers."

Joe Wales was a graduate of Altoona High school, Class of 1969. He then joined the Marine Corps, and after being stationed in Okinawa, he served in Vietnam from 1970 to 1973. He was working for the railroad during the day and taking classes at Penn State (and would graduate in 1977 and then take some grad courses at St. Francis College) when he joined the Whitetail Bucks.

"My brother Albe told me about the Bucks," says Joe Wales, "I was working for the railroad at the Samuel Rea Shops in Hollidaysburg, the night shift, with

Glen Brandimarte, who also wound up with the Bucks. Albe said, 'Why don't you go up and play?,' so I did."

Going to college brought about one unusual drawback for Wales.

"I never made the team picture 'cause they took it while I was still in college," says Joe now, "I would have to wait to play until after school left out."

When asked why he continued playing football nearly a decade after graduating from high school and having served several tours in Vietnam, Wales shrugs his shoulders and replies simply, "I just wanted to play football."

Players from other local towns joined the fun. Alex Anto from DuBois was another member of the offensive line who was added to the roster in 1976.

"Alex was tough as nails," recalls Wayne Rockmore, "Once we came back to the huddle, and he told me, 'don't worry I'll get that guy.' I was wondering who he was talking about. After the next play, he came up to me again and said, 'I got him for you.' I said to him, 'Who?' and Alex said, 'That guy that was twisting your ankle.' I said, 'That wasn't my ankle, but thanks.'"

Anto was from DuBois who had gone to Slippery Rock State College [*now University*] and was an All-Pennsylvania Honorable Mention selection in 1970. After he graduated from "The Rock" in 1973, he taught in the Fort Pierce, Florida school system, but then, like many people, moved back to the area. He got married to a local girl and was hired as the assistant director of the DuBois Area Youth Activities Association in November of 1975.

The Whitetail Bucks had made arrangements with the small town of Madera to be the site of the Bucks' workouts in '76, and the team was given permission to use the field located behind the elementary school.

Tom Miller remembers that the method of choosing Madera as a practice facility was quite unique.

"Big Al [*Siegel*] just put his finger on a map and it landed right in the middle of nowhere, on Madera," relates Tom Miller, "He said, 'this is where we're gonna practice.'"

Siegel explained at the time that Madera was centrally located and most convenient for the Bucks' players, who were driving from communities all over the area, such as DuBois, State College, and Hollidaysburg.

The Bucks players certainly thought otherwise, however.

"That place was really in the middle of nowhere," remembers Ron Roefaro. "There was no easy way to get up there."

"That was just a haul up there," recalls Joe Wales.

If the players had to drive to "the middle of nowhere," at least some of them wanted to do it style.

"I remember Baumgardner asking us when we arrived at practice in Madera why all the Altoona guys had nice cars," says Tom Marlett, "I had just purchased a brand new Chevy Monte Carlo in 1976, Joey Wales had a Monte Carlo; I said 'we live in a city and not the country, and girls like the nice cars.'"

In an effort to boost attendance, the Bucks offered the area fans a limited time deal, reducing the price of a season ticket to just $10—yes, you read that right, $10—for seven home games. They said this discount would remain in effect through June 16th.

The Bucks had a lot of new players in uniform as preseason drills continued. But no one made an impression quite like their new offensive tackle, one of the more memorable players the team ever had.

George Walker.

"He was the real deal," explains Hugh Gibbons, "If he'd had different circumstances growing up and opportunities I am sure could have played at the highest level. I am not saying a super star, but he did and does deserve more. He was also a top weightlifter, and," he adds with a smile, "he kept me alive more than once by protecting me, an average size person, in a big man's game."

George was a 6', 255-pound offensive tackle from State College High who had bulked up thanks to the Bucks' General Manager. "I got into powerlifting with Al Siegel, and that made me bigger," says Walker today. Siegel was a strong advocate of drug free weightlifting, and Walker took to this philosophy like a fish to water.

"I worked as a meat cutter for Weis Markets and in my free time lifted weights," recalls Walker, who adds that he found out about the Bucks from two teammates from high school. "Allen Potter and Tom Arnelle told me about it," says Walker, "I had the chance to play another year of football."

And play he did, as he helped anchor the Bucks offensive line, and like so many other semipro players, did his share of work on the defensive side of the ball as well.

"Although I was usually the offensive tackle," Walker recalls, "I went in as the nose tackle on defense when the other team got inside the 10-yard line."

Walker's play impressed his teammates.

"He played the offensive tackle on the right side, I played the left side tackle," remembers Ron Roefaro, "George was strong as an ox. He was a big muscled power lifter that hit like a mule. I liked George because he didn't play with his mouth, he did his job and blocked with intensity."

"George had good speed, just not sideways," says Hugh Gibbons.

"He was a fun loving beast," says Ken Rutter, "He seemed very intense in the huddle. No nonsense. He'd kick your butt in a heartbeat. George was pretty fast for his size. He was very likable."

"I remember George as a funny guy," offers Tom Marlett, "he was also heavy into weightlifting back then and coincidentally, had the body of a weightlifter, big arms, shoulders. A pretty decent player."

"He was fast as a running back when going straight ahead, but didn't have much lateral movement," offers Joe Wales, "He was strong, though, could bench press 500 pounds."

"George was strong as an ox," recalls Rod Ullein. "I was rushing the punter one game and DR [*Darrel Rutter*] landed on me and sprained my ankle. George ran out on the field and snatched me up like a bag of potatoes and started running with me to the sidelines yelling, 'Rod's hurt, Rod's hurt' and I was yelling, 'Put me down dammit, put me down.'"

"Good guy who liked jokes, but when he was on the field, there was no joking around," says Darrel Rutter, "he was all business. Just wanted to win. He never gave an inch. Not too many could move him. He would go into the gym and out-lift Penn State guys like Bruce Clark and Matt Millen. Had a great personality."

Then Rutter adds, "He was an animal."

Of course, there's a good reason Rutter describes Walker that way.

"I used to whomp on Darrel Rutter all the time in practice, but he could take it; he was tough as shit," recalled Walker in a recent interview.

But Darrel would have his day in the sun against George.

"I remember Darrel, my brother, arm wrestling him and Darrel beat him and George wasn't happy at all," recalls Ken Rutter, "Darrel had technique and had beaten formidable foes in the past though."

"I beat him in arm wrestling at a party at Siegel's house." remembers Darrel, "He couldn't believe I beat him, he just kept shaking his head."

Like NFL players such as Fred Biletnikoff, George had a unique pre-game ritual.

"George used to throw up before games," recalls Wayne Rockmore.

"I got nervous," George says with a shrug now, ""I'd show up an hour early for the game just to get ready."

His ex-teammates contend that Walker was often ready more than an hour before the game.

"[*Wide receiver*] Phil Flipse and I were driving to the game and we were going to pick up George," remembers Gibbons, "We get to Atherton Street, and there's George standing there on the street corner in full uniform. He was always ready to play."

Walker made an impression on his teammates in other ways too.

"You haven't seen anything until you've seen George Walker in the locker room buck naked singing The Supremes at the top of his lungs," recalls Wayne Rockmore.

"Martha Reeves and the Vandellas too," Walker is quick to add.

"When we drove to practice, George would just tell jokes non-stop in the car," says Hugh Gibbons, then adds, "My car was never the same after George sat in it."

"I remember one game at Philipsburg," says Pat Little, "when George took white athletic tape and wrapped his head in it like a head band. He just wrapped the tape around his head and hair. I just thought that was going to be painful when he took it off."

Walker smiles and shrugs at memories like this. "I did some crazy things," he says.

"But I was never a dirty player," George remembers, "I just liked to hit hard. I did the best I could. We'd just show up and play the game. We'd play everybody tough. Put our heart and soul into it. Most fun playing football that I ever had.

"Win or lose, we had fun. We played like champions," says George.

George continued to make an impact on people from the area for many years after he hung up his cleats.

"George Walker played for the Bucks," says Mike Leone, the team manager in 1975, "I didn't know him at the time, but many years later he coached my son in weight training from Junior High through High School and he had him power lifting. Thanks to George, when my son was in high school he also lifted in several meets that Al Siegel hosted in Clearfield.

"I don't remember how we got on the subject of the Bucks, but George gave my son one of his jerseys with the number 76 on it and it too had purple numbers on white. That's when I got out my jacket to show to George and then gave it to my son. My son went on to attend West Point where he lifted competitively all four years and even qualified for national competition his last two years."

Walker still commands respect among his former teammates.

"My kids still call him 'Uncle George,'" recalls Rockmore.

In late June, Darrel Rutter went to Pleasantville, New York for a tryout with the NFL Giants.

"I ran a 4.68 40 and they told me I had good speed," Rutter remembers, "Also told me I had punted well and had a great skill set.

"They also told me I was too old. That was it." Rutter rejoined the Bucks.

Just before the season started, the Bucks received their new uniforms, which were purple, gold and white.

"That's because the supplier said 'if you take this color (purple) we'll give you 10% off,'" recalls Darrel Rutter.

Once again, the Bucks would play home games at various locations around the area, in order to spotlight the local talent. State College, Clearfield, Philipsburg, Curwensville and Glendale once again were slated to host games.

And once again, the Bucks opened their season with a contest at home, in State College to be exact, with the Brooklyn Golden Knights, the same team they had played in their 1975 opener.

"The reason we played the New York/New Jersey teams every year was that Dad played for the Cardinals in Brooklyn, New York and still had contacts," recalls Jay Siegel, "Those guys really liked coming to 'the sticks' to play."

"They have most of their starters returning from last year's team," said Tom Miller, "They did lose a few players from their roster, but no one who's going to hurt them.

"They've had a game already, so they should be really tough," the Bucks' mentor went on, "This is their 16th year in existence and they have the same coaching staff, so their system is not new to them, as is ours.

"Their line will outweigh us for sure," Miller concluded, "They have a pair of really big tackles on offense and have a super player in Charlie Smith."

But Miller added that he was not conceding a thing to the Knights or the rest of the teams on the Bucks' schedule.

"These guys are winners," Miller said optimistically, "They come from good high school programs with winning backgrounds. We are averaging 35 to 45 players per practice session this year and are much further ahead at this point than we were last season. The men's attitude is much better."

Torrential rains before and during the game held the crowd to only 350 diehards at Memorial Stadium, and made life rough for the players.

"The end zone was under water," Darrel Rutter remembers now, "I thought I was gonna drown. I was a former lifeguard but 12 inches of water with 10 guys on top of you is not good for anyone."

The fans saw a tough, hard-fought contest. The Bucks showed their fans that they appeared to have the ability to repeat their surprising success of 1975, as they displayed a very tenacious defense that kept the Knights bottled up for most of the night.

The Bucks showed off their new offense as well, having scrapped the some-what predictable Veer option they used in '75 to a more diversified straight pro offense. Still not back yet, however, was Mike McNeish, who had not re-turned to the team. In McNeish's absence, the offensive line was shuffled to compensate. George Walker was moved to guard, and Allen Pletcher, a 6'1" 245 pounder from Bellefonte, was inserted at tackle.

Walker was going to have to face one of his toughest opponents.

"Earl Belgrave was a guy who gave me trouble," George says today of the Knights' 6'5" 255 pound tackle who was considered one of the top linemen in minor league football, "You just couldn't move him."

The Knights still had Charlie Smith and quarterback Tom Green at their dis-posal. But the Bucks' ferocious defense stifled the few serious threats Brooklyn was able to put together. Central Pennsylvania was able to come up with three timely fumble recoveries as well as two interceptions. Led by Jeff "Mother" McCartney, Dirk Grissinger, Albe Wales and Jim Slabon, all holdovers from the '75 unit, the Bucks defense showed just how good they could be.

Neither team was able to mount any early threats until just over midway in the first quarter when a fumble recovery by the Bucks set them up at Brooklyn's 34-yard line. After Wayne Rockmore was stopped for no gain on first down, Dave Belfield skirted the left side for 14 yards and a first down at the Knights' 20.

Larry Rydbom was sacked for a seven-yard loss, but on the next play, Rockmore took the handoff on a draw play and raced up the middle for 27 yards and a touchdown. Rich Skillings, brother of running back Charvi Skillings, split the uprights for a 7-0 lead with 6:46 to play in the first stanza. It had looked so easy, but as it turned out, those were the only points the Bucks would get against a tough Brooklyn defense.

Following the ensuing kickoff, the Knights drove 75 yards in a time-consuming 19-play drive. A 13-yard pass from quarterback Green to end Vin Shook on a third-and-nine situation at the Bucks' 36 was one of the key plays in the march. Green bootlegged the final seven yards for the touchdown. Charlie Waters' extra point was perfect and the game was tied 7-7 with 12:47 left in the second quarter.

The Bucks put together a solid drive late in the first half starting at their own 18. Rushes by Rockmore and Rydbom gave the Bucks a first down, then Rydbom connected with Rockmore on a screen pass and Allen Pletcher made a superb block to spring Rockmore loose. "The Rock" drove for 21 yards to the Central Pennsylvania 48.

Several plays later, on a fourth-down-and-five, Rydbom connected with his former Glendale High School teammate, Gary Kizina, with a 21-yard pass to pick up another crucial first down.

On first-and-10 with 30 seconds to play in the half, Rydbom hit Belfield in the flat, and the halfback from Altoona High gained six yards before he went out-of-bounds with 28 seconds to play. Rydbom then just missed connections with Kizina in the end zone, but a penalty on Brooklyn gave the Bucks a first down at the 14. On the next play, Brooklyn's Laverne Johnson was called for pass interference when he mugged Penn State's Phil Flipse. That moved the ball to the five for first-and-goal. The Bucks gave it to Rockmore, but Rock was hit hard and the ball was jarred loose and a Knight recovered it at the four yard line to end the half.

Because of the occasional downpour, the sloppy field conditions worsened, making both the field and football slippery and hard to handle, and led to eleven turnovers—four interceptions and seven fumbles—in the second half. This, combined with the ferocious defensive play by both sides, led to a half where neither team could mount a serious scoring threat. Central Pennsylvania drove to Brooklyn's 29-yard line late in the game, but Rich Skillings missed on what could have been a game-winning 36 yard field goal with 4:52 left in the 4th quarter.

Regulation time ended with the game still tied, 7-7.

Mid-Atlantic League rules then called for sudden death overtime. There was no "kissing your sister" in this league. The Knights won the overtime toss and chose to receive, with Irving Manigault returning Rich Skillings' kick to his own 19. From there on, it was all Brooklyn. The drive seemed to have stalled at the Brooklyn 22, but a roughing-the-kicker penalty gave the Knights new life.

Charlie Smith, who would wind up rushing for 1,752 yards in 1976, third-highest total in semipro football history, and was the Bucks' main antagonist on the ground with 122 yards in 23 attempts, flew around right end for a 34 yard pick-up which turned out to be the longest play of the game. That set up the Knights at the Bucks' 38. A six-yard loss and an incomplete pass failed to deter Brooklyn, as Smith then gained 11 yards and Green drilled a 16-yarder to Jim Phillips for a first down at the Bucks' 17.

Two plays gained just three yards, but then Smith's nine-yard run gave Brooklyn another first down and kept the drive alive. After Jeff McCartney, at 6'4" and 265 pounds the biggest man on the team, nailed Smith for no gain, Green kept the ball himself and drove around left end, racing desperately for the flag. The only thing between Green and the end zone was defensive back Glen Brandimarte. Although Tom Marlett likes to remember that Brandimarte "was a great guy, but he had an awkward way of running," he was able to move up quickly enough from his defensive back position to drive Green out of bounds with a great stop just short of the goal line.

Green kept it again and tried to plow over, but McCartney once again led a wall of defenders who wouldn't budge. That made it fourth-and goal. Green gave it to Smith and Brooklyn's meal ticket gave it all he had and fell right on the goal line for the game-winning score. A fight erupted between two players after the touchdown but was quickly broken up. Brooklyn had won, but the Bucks had nothing to be ashamed of. They had played the Knights even all night.

Besides McCartney, fellow Bucks Allen Potter, Phil Flipse, George Walker (despite his move to guard), and Darrel Rutter all played well in the contest. Potter got off a 60-yard punt while Rutter contributed a 32-yard punt return.

A week later in Philipsburg, the Bucks hosted the Bears from Boonton, New Jersey. The game drew only 779 people to American Legion Memorial Field. Low attendance figures like this one that plagued the Bucks throughout their existence may have disappointed their investors, but didn't seem to faze some of the players.

"The crowds were more than we were used to anyway," says Joe Wales.

Those fans that didn't bother to show up missed another outstanding defensive performance by the Bucks. The defense hit hard and often. They had earned a well-deserved reputation as one of the league's toughest units.

"The defense we had was great," offers Darrel Rutter, who played his first game at defensive end against the Bears, "We had some real ballplayers. It was a privilege to play with some of those guys. We played some formidable teams, but they got their ears pinned back by our defense. We may not have beaten them but we certainly played 'em tough."

Their hard-nosed style of play seemed to make life difficult for everyone, even their own teammates.

"I hated to run against our defense in practice," remembers Wayne Rockmore, "Someone, I think it was [Gary] Pheasant, knocked me senseless in practice once."

"I remember one practice where it was getting very physical," recalls Tom Marlett, "and it was first team offense against the first team defense and I hit Wayne Rockmore very hard where we went helmet to helmet and pads clanked; I could hear everyone saying ooooooh, knowing it was a good hit, and the coaches came running in; 'Who was that? That's exactly what we need, Marlett, good hit,' and we were energized that night."

Boonton certainly seemed to hate to run against the Bucks defense, gaining just 57 yards on the ground. They didn't have much luck passing either, as the Bucks gave up just 107 yards through the air.

The offense got a boost when Mike McNeish returned to the team. He moved back into his guard position while George Walker returned to his more familiar tackle spot.

"I stayed away for the first game but quite a few players contacted me to get me back so I returned for the remainder of the season," reported McNeish in a recent interview.

Neither team did much of anything on offense in a scoreless first quarter.

On the last play of the opening period, Miller hit Dave Belfield with a little swing pass to the right. Belfield picked up five yards but had the ball knocked from his hands, with the Bears' Bennet Thompson recovering on his own 36-yard line.

A 13-yard pass play, from Cunningham to Gene Hagen, and a 15-yard carry by Mike Bouroult moved the Bears to a first down at the Bucks' 33-yard line. The defense stiffened and three incomplete passes followed. A field goal attempt which fell short was downed on the Bucks' three, and the hosts seemed in trouble.

Three plays netted almost nothing and the Bucks punted to their own 48, giving the visitors good field position. Bouroult got one, a five-yard penalty against the Bucks followed and Cunningham then found Hagen for 19 yards a first down at the Bucks 23. Reilly was stopped at the line, an incomplete pass followed and the Bears were called for offensive pass interference in the end zone that put the ball back to the 38, the closest penetration the Bears were to obtain for the remainder of the game.

Following that defensive stand, the Bucks marched 87 yards to the winning score in just nine plays. Rydbom, in at quarterback, started the march with an 11-yard keeper, then after an incomplete pass kept it himself and ran for eight more yards. A screen to Rockmore was good for 18 yards and a first down at the Bucks 43. Belfield picked up one then Rockmore got 10 on two carries before Rydbom found Tyrone's Rick Skillings going against the grain for a 44-yard touchdown with 1:55 left to play in the first half. Skillings' attempt at the extra point was wide and the Bucks went into the locker room ahead 6-0.

After the intermission, the Bucks took the kickoff and marched from their own 41 to the Bears' seven yard line. A Rydbom to Phil Flipse 12-yard pass, and Jim Slabon's 12-yard strike to Flipse were the big plays in the drive. Rydbom, however, had a pass picked off by Bill Walker in the end zone to kill that march.

But after the interception, the Bears ran only three plays before the Bucks had the ball back. Cunningham's pass on the third play of the possession was intercepted by linebacker David Noel which gave the Bucks' possession on the Bears' 27.

Rockmore went for three, Belfield for six and then the Rock gained two more and a first down at the Bears 16. The "Rock" then went for the score on a trap sprung by great blocks by Mike McNeish and Jeff McCartney. The try for the extra point failed once again and the Bucks had a 12-0 lead with 4:32 to play in the third period.

After scoring the touchdown, Rockmore did what he always did: handed the ball to the referee.

"No celebrations," Rock says now, "I thought it was stupid. You celebrate when you win the championship. George Walker always tried to get me to do something in the end zone, but I didn't."

Rockmore, enjoying a good start to the season after his '75 campaign was cut short by injury, was the leading ground gainer on the afternoon with 15 carries for 66 yards while also grabbing a pass for 15 yards.

"I got hurt that first year but I worked hard to get back," Rock says now, "If they needed a running back I was there. If someone wanted to take my job his name had better be 'O.J. Simpson.'"

Leading tacklers for the Bucks defense were Marlett with seven, Albe Wales and McCartney with six and Dirk Grissinger and Gary Pheasant with five each. Slabon, Noel, and Allen Potter all came up with interceptions. Slabon's came on the last play of the game and was picked off at the six-yard line. He then lateraled to Glen Brandimarte who returned the ball to the Bears' 35-yard line.

Slabon also broke up four passes on the afternoon, managed five tackles and also tossed the 12-yard desperation pass off a bad field goal attempt snap which set up the Bucks' second score.

Central Pennsylvania walked off the field 12-0 winners. Their defense had so far yielded only 13 points in nine quarters of football.

Following the victory head coach and starting quarterback Tom Miller felt the 5-2 defense the Bears set up in the first half had thrown the Bucks off-stride. "We practice playing against the 5-3 defense which we scouted against the Bears and when they opened in the 5-2 we just couldn't pick up the men blitzing from their end positions," said Miller.

"Defensively, I feel we are more advanced at this stage of the game this year than at were last year," added assistant coach Gary Baumgardner, "We are changing players around all the time, and it just seems to work out easier on defense than on offense. Of course the defense is easier to learn and right now we are trying to get a few more plays and players into our offense. But our defense both last year and the first two games this season has looked really good."

The Whitetail Bucks had now evened their slate at 1-1 in anticipation of their next contest, a home game in Altoona against the Brooklyn Mariners, probably the toughest opponent the Bucks would face all season.

In an effort to help drum up interest in the game, Altoona Mayor William C. Stouffer received a plaque from the Bucks organization in appreciation for his continued support in promoting sports in the Altoona area. Al Siegel also presented the mayor with an official Bucks coaching staff cap and named him honorary coach.

So far the Bucks had been fortunate in the injury department, which was always a fear among semipro teams living on limited budgets and limited rosters. No starters had been injured, but the Bucks depth, thin to begin with, was being tested by several battle scars. Al Siegel had a banged-up knee, Ken Rutter had some major dental work done, defensive end Mitch Mancuso was limping on a sprained ankle although he had played against Boonton, and substitute running back Joe Good had a hip-pointer.

That week at practice, quite a few players were grumbling about not starting and lack of playing time. Others, like Darrel Rutter, tried to encourage the players to "hang in there."

The Mariners were a perennial contender for the New York City Gotham Division championship, and featured no less than four future Semipro Football Hall of Famers—quarterback Joe Gagliardi, center Mike Goodwin, and linebackers Bill Ahearn and Paul Carbonaro, who would play for the Mariners for an amazing 28 years until his retirement in 1992. The team was also made up of quite a few New York City policemen and firemen.

"Some of the New York teams we played were made up of policemen and firefighters from New York City," says Darrel Rutter wistfully, "A lot of those guys died in 9/11. They were a tough bunch. I can see them going in fearless that day just like they were when we played them. I get misty-eyed thinking about it now. God bless every one of them."

According to Tom Miller, the Mariners were a much better team than the Brooklyn Knights. He told reporters that he felt that a key to beating the Mariners would be the Bucks' passing attack.

"We have to improve our passing game," said the head coach, "Our offense is coming along and we've got to get something going against Brooklyn. It'll come, I feel. We have some good receivers."

So, for the second time in three weeks, the Whitetail Bucks had to play a tough New York Semipro Conference club. The game drew one of the team's best crowds ever, an estimated 2,250 fans, to Altoona's Mansion Park. But while the crowd was the biggest of the season so far, General Manager Al Siegel noted that most of the fans were children who got in on special, reduced prices.

"We still need to get more adults out," he said.

The fans, big and small, saw the Bucks play another strong opponent to a stand-off.

Central Pennsylvania withstood the Mariners' first possession, taking over on downs at their own two when Bucks' defensive back Gary Griffith swatted an apparent touchdown pass out of the arms of wide receiver Greg Rupp.

The first of two interceptions by Tom Marlett halted the next Mariner drive, but when the visitors gained possession again they proceeded to march 61 yards in 13 plays. Key plays in the drive were two passes on third-and-long from Joe Gagliardi to Don Curtin which gained 17- and 13-yards. Washie Sommers sprinted six yards around left end for the touchdown with 10:45 left in the half, and Mike Tarpey booted the extra point to put the Mariners up, 7-0.

Central Pennsylvania responded with its first decent drive, moving the sticks three times and eating up more than six minutes. But the drive stalled and Allen Potter boomed a punt to the Mariner 12.

Brooklyn then showed why they were so highly-regarded. Gagliardi, who had played brilliantly for the Mariners since 1969, engineered a solid march late in the half, pecking away with short sideline passes that stopped the clock. Finally, on fourth down at the six, Curtin circled left end for the touchdown. Tarpey, a soccer-style kicker, was perfect on the conversion to make 14-0 with 42 seconds to go before intermission.

The Mariners, the defending New York Football League Gotham Division champions, then evidently thought they'd be able to run up the score and came out throwing in the second half. However, Bucks linebacker Kurt Kessler stepped in front of Gagliardi's pass and returned it to the Mariner 21 yard line. On fourth-and-10, Larry Rydbom hit tight end Gary Pheasant and the ex-Altoona standout roared to the one. Ritchie Shoop powered over left tackle for the six-pointer, and then also kicked the extra point. The Whitetail Bucks were back in it at 14-7.

The now fired-up Buck defense stopped the Mariners and forced a punt, and the hosts proceeded to march 56 yards in 12 plays. Wayne Rockmore, continuing his fine comeback season from his injury-shortened '75 campaign, had a 30-yard run and then Shoop broke free for 11 yards. Guy Houghtaling popped over from the three with 2:59 left in the third period. A low snap from center stymied the extra point kick, but holder Jim Slabon alertly picked up the errant snap and raced around right end for the point that tied it at 14-all.

The Bucks had the only opportunity in the fourth quarter, as Marlett picked off a Mariner pass and returned it 21 yards to the Brooklyn 40. That chance went by the wayside, however, when Rich Skillings couldn't hold onto Rydbom's fourth down pass.

So, for the second time in three weeks, the Bucks were heading into overtime.

The Bucks won the toss and received but on their first possession Rydbom was sacked on second down and then there was a mix-up in the backfield the next play. Potter was forced to punt and his kick was gathered in by Rupp, who made a nice 15-yard run back to the Bucks' 43.

Central Pennsylvania held for three downs but on fourth down got a bad break when Kevin King, back to punt for Brooklyn, picked up the low snap and decided to run. There was nothing on his left side but green grass, and he rambled 17 yards to the Bucks' 25.

Seconds later, the Mariners moved the sticks to the two. The Bucks stiffened as Gagliardi missed a receiver wide open in the end zone and then King was stacked up at the one. But on third down, Rick Lucan blasted over right tackle for the game-winning touchdown.

Despite the loss, the Bucks and the Mariners partied together at an establishment called R-Place in Altoona after the game.

"'We played a good game against what really is the premier team in New York," Tom Miller said afterward. "The Mariners and the Pittsburgh Ironmen are the toughest teams we'll play this year.

"Our defense turned it around with that interception at the start of the second half. We needed a break or two like that to get the momentum going our way.

"I wasn't too happy with our offense, but I think it will pick up. Our passing game has got to come around. The potential is there. We're gonna work on pass protection this week.

"It's hard to iron things out when you practice only twice a week like we do, but the guys have good attitudes. We're gonna win some games."

Many former players felt that the Bucks' lack of practice time was the thing that hurt them the most in the long run.

"It was just a question of not being organized," says Hugh Gibbons, "Our coaches were not really organized. Miller came in with a good playbook, but we didn't have good, detailed practices. We never really had a system in place. We had a lot of talent on the team, but we just didn't have enough time to work together. We'd only have 2 or 3 practices a week, and many times we didn't have everybody at practice. Plus Miller was not a disciplinarian."

"We didn't get enough reps for people to get things down and get things straightened out," adds Paul Kanagy, "Usually the first quarter was just a warm up to get things working. Some of those teams we played, like Pittsburgh, were tough, but they were good teams that were just better organized."

"Practices were not necessarily about conditioning, rather the team knowing the offense as well as the defensive plays," observes Tom Marlett, "The coaches were not motivators, or in your face types. They were, out of necessity, the strategists, mainly to bring a group of guys from all over Central Pennsylvania to play for one common goal, and that was to win. For the most part, they were good coaches, and I think they did a good job with what they had."

"We just didn't practice a lot," remembers Darrel Rutter, "We'd only practice 1 or 2 hours a couple days a week. We had no game films to study, just photos. And that wasn't all the time."

"You had to go to work 8 or 10 hours a day then go to practice," says George Walker.

"We just didn't have the manpower or the reps needed to compete with teams like Pittsburgh," recalls Wayne Rockmore, ""We practiced at Madera, and we practiced at other places, wherever we could find a field. Never knew where we'd be practicing. If we'd had some stability we could have had a great organization. We had to do a lot on our own to get ready to play. How much better we could have been . . ."

Then George Walker finished Rockmore's sentence. "If we'd been on the same page."

# CHAPTER

# 5

"We were usually outmanned but never outplayed."

—RUNNING BACK WAYNE ROCKMORE

Aweek after their loss to Brooklyn, the Bucks prepared to host the Washington Generals and begin a five-team, round robin tournament for the Western Pennsylvania championship. The Generals were coming off a 20-9 loss to the Pittsburgh Ironmen, and were thoroughly whipped twice—40-6 and 27-0—by the Bucks in 1975, but head coach Tom Miller, impressed with the defensive improvement made by the Generals, urged the team not to take Washington lightly.

"They're a much-improved ballclub," Miller told reporters at the time. "They lost a very close game to the Pittsburgh Ironmen and were beaten by Sharon 3-0."

"Washington is a vastly improved ball club," echoed assistant coach Gary Baumgardner, "especially in the defensive line, in the linebacking and at quarterback."

The Bucks worked on their offense which had begun to show some improvement in the past few weeks.

"We've worked a lot on our pass protection," stated Miller, "I think we could have moved the ball better against the Brooklyn squad we played last week. We're looking for a better offensive showing this week. We're due to have a big night."

The Buck defense was still its foundation, and had allowed just five touchdowns in 14 quarters. The defense would continue its fine play as they hosted the Generals on August 22nd. But if the offense was due for a big night, this was not it. The hard-luck Bucks did not heed Miller's exhortations, took the Generals a bit too lightly and were caught napping. They were also done in by the play of a fellow named Jim Dingeldine.

Dingeldine was a 6'1" 230-pound rookie from West Virginia Wesleyan College, but he played like a battle-tested veteran against the Bucks. In the process, he tied a long-standing semipro football record and singlehandedly beat the Bucks.

As they would throughout their existence, the Bucks played the Generals on a local high school field to showcase their local talent. This time it was the Glendale High School field in Flinton, as the Bucks roster included no less than seven former Vikings—quarterback Larry Rydbom, wide receiver Gary Kizina, center Dale Keith, and linebackers Jeff Best, David Noel, George Dick, and Jon Morrison. But the game drew only 500 fans on a very hot day, most of whom had come out to cheer on their former high school heroes.

"We played home games all over Pennsylvania—State College, Philipsburg, all over the place," recounts Joe Wales, "But we always seemed to play Washington in Glendale for some reason."

Flinton, home of the Glendale School District, which also includes nearby communities such as Irvona, Glasgow, Coalport, Fallentimber and Hastings, is located in the northwest part of Reade Township on the east side of Clearfield Creek in Cambria County. Prince Gallitzin State Park, a favorite summertime picnicking, boating and swimming spot for the locals, lies just southeast of the town.

It was the smallest town the Bucks played in with a population of less than 1,000. Hoping to draw as many fans as possible, the team always included quite a few Glendale High graduates. This idea helped, but not enough to make a difference.

So far the 1976 season had been a struggle for the Whitetail Bucks, and the Washington game would prove to be no exception.

Quarterback John Smith, a 6'3" 215-pound southpaw cut by the CFL's Winnipeg Blue Bombers after four games north of the border, kept the Bucks' defense honest with some accurate passes and a little fancy footwork on the option play. Guard Blaine Popp, center Carl Hellmuth, and long-time semipro veteran tackle Tom Averell anchored the Generals offensive line. Bill Hughes was a solid placekicker, and running back Sam Willis would make the MAFL all-star team. Ends Jim Lacko and Bill Meyers and linebacker Ron Willis paced an improved defense.

But it was Dingeldine who was the real thorn in the side of the Bucks.

The Whitetail Bucks got the first break of the game and took advantage of it. Jim Slabon intercepted a Smith pass and returned it 16 yards to the Washington 49. Three running plays gave Central Pennsylvania one first down, but the drive stalled and the Bucks faced a third-and-15 situation at the Generals' 43.

That's when Rydbom and his old high school passing combination partner, Kizina, thrilled the 500 fans on hand by recreating some of the magic they had displayed during their days together with the hometown Vikings.

Rydbom took the snap and dropped back, looking for a receiver to his right. Flushed out of the pocket, Rydbom was chased back to his left. He looked up to find his old battery mate wide open. Rydbom put the ball right on the money for an easy six points with just 4:07 elapsed in the game. But on the extra point there was a portent of things to come.

Ritchie Shoop got a perfect snap and hold, but his kick was batted down by the hard-charging Dingeldine. At the time, there was no way of knowing how important—or how historic—that block would become.

Washington dominated the rest of the first half and did everything right except put the ball in the end zone. On their first series after the Bucks' touchdown, the Generals reached the Central Pennsylvania 5-yard line, but Smith overthrew Jerry Skocik on fourth down.

The Bucks' took over, and a 30-yard pass and run play from Rydbom to Kizina moved the Bucks out of the shadow of their own goal posts. Rydbom fumbled on his own 41 however, and John Pawlish recovered for Washington. That threat failed when Bill Hughes' 41-yard field goal attempt drifted wide to the left.

Rydbom was not happy about his play so far, and his temper was getting the best of him.

"We were playing in Glendale and it was very hot," recalls George Walker, "The ref came up to me and said, 'If your quarterback says the F-bomb one more time I'm gonna toss him.' I went to Rydbom and told him and he said, 'I can't help it.' I said, 'You'd better stop because Miller is limping around on the sidelines and we need you to play.'"

Washington marched deep into Central Pennsylvania territory but lost the ball on downs at the Bucks' 24 midway through the second quarter. Late in the half, the Generals tried to beat the clock on a drive, but Hughes had a 40-yard field goal kick fall short. The Bucks were whistled for offsides on the play, however, and the Generals had another chance.

This time, Washington tried a fake field goal with holder Jeff Massey taking the snap, jumping up and trying to pass for a touchdown. But Jim Slabon stood his ground, and was in the right spot to pick off the throw. The half ended with the Bucks still up, 6-0.

Despite trailing on the scoreboard, the Generals were full of confidence when they returned to the field for the second half. They proceeded to march 37 yards in eight plays. Keeping the ball on the ground, the Generals got to the one before Smith kept it himself and dove over the goal line with 7:50 left in the third quarter. Hughes booted the extra point that put the Generals up for the first time, 7-6.

A little later in the third quarter, defensive end Darrel Rutter recovered a General fumble at his own 47. Central Pennsylvania then staged its best march of the game by pushing from its 47 to the Generals' 11. But the drive came to a halt when Rydbom's blocking broke down on third down and he was sacked back to the Generals' 21. Ritchie Shoop came in to try a 38-yard field goal, but that man Dingeldine was there once again. He swatted the ball right back at Shoop to preserve Washington's one-point margin.

With 2:45 left, Gary Griffith's 21-yard punt return set up the Bucks at the Washington 31. The Bucks moved to the eight but on a third and inches play, the team was whistled for illegal procedure, a penalty that stalled the drive completely. Coach Tom Miller decided to go for the field goal. But the results were a carbon-copy of the last attempt. Dingeldine, who would wind up making the Mid-Atlantic League all-star team at the end of the season, crashed through the line and slapped down Shoop's 30-yard attempt.

The Generals then ran out the final minute and 11 seconds to win their first game of the season, and send the snake-bitten—or maybe it was Dingeldine-bitten—Bucks to their third loss in four games.

"I don't know how the guys are gonna come out of this," Miller said.

"We're not playing bad ball," added Gary Baumgardner, "We've lost three games that we could have won. I know the offense can do it and Shoop can kick field goals from anywhere, but I don't know what was going on up front. We had scoring opportunities but we had some mental mistakes. We have offense when the guys really put their minds to it. It's a matter of concentration. We had a little trouble handling their Veer on the one side. The other side was handling it well. We weren't reacting to the ball well today. I thought we were flat. It was hot, but that was only part of it."

Dingeldine's performance was definitely the difference in the game and was indeed of historical significance, as his three blocked kicks in one game tied a semipro football record set by Augie Fracazzi of the Niagara Falls Lumbermen in 1954.

The Bucks were now 1-3 on the season, a disappointing start following their winning record in 1975. In an effort to explain their struggles of 1976, some of the players believed that the team was a few players short of being a very good squad.

"We had some good guys, but we were about 5 or 6 guys short of being pretty good," says Tom Marlett.

"We just didn't have enough men," reasons Wayne Rockmore, "We were usually out-manned, but never outplayed."

The Bucks needed to get back on the right track. Their next game was a crucial one for the team in the five-team, round-robin chase for the mythical Western Pennsylvania championship. In the standings, the Pittsburgh Ironmen and the Sharon Old Express were 1-0, Washington was 1-2, Beaver County was 0-0 and Central Pennsylvania was 0-1.

Tom Miller was concerned that his offense was averaging only one touchdown per game. Halfback Wayne Rockmore, leading the team in rushing, and quarterback Larry Rydbom were having solid seasons. But the chances of a turnaround for the team did not look good.

Why? Because next on the schedule were the Ironmen from Pittsburgh, always one of the Bucks' tougher opponents. Pittsburgh looked to have yet another strong championship contender, as they had opened their season by crushing Dayton 57-6 while giving up just two first downs.

Their defense, nicknamed the "Iron Curtain," was one of the best in all of semipro football. They would shut out seven of their opponents in 1976, and lead the league with 51 quarterback sacks, 16 of them by defensive end Jim "Dr. Sack" Chapas.

Chapas' story was one of those tales so typical to semipro ball. He was discovered playing flag football in Millvale, when a coach for the semipro Millvale Indians approached him about signing up. That evening, Chapas played defensive end for the Indians—his first ever tackle football game. At 145 pounds, he had never played the game in either high school or college.

But at 215 pounds, he quickly built a reputation as one of semipro football's toughest and quickest defensive ends. He played five years with the Indians and then moved on the Ironmen, where he made all-conference his first three years.

At 30 years of age, and vice principal for Arsenal Middle School in Lawrenceville, Chapas was enjoying playing and told people he intended to play as long as he could.

"In my job as a vice principal, I face a lot of mental and emotional stress," Chapas told Steve Hecht of the *Pittsburgh Post-Gazette*, "Football for me is an outlet for that. I get a kick out of going up against guys bigger, stronger and younger than me. As a defensive end every play is a chess game."

Another factor working against the Bucks was the return of one of their old nemeses. During the week before the game, the Steelers made a number of player cuts. The Ironmen then announced that they had signed one of the players who had been released. It was none other than Ramsey Simmons, the 6'2", 245-pound defensive end who had given the Bucks fits in both their contests in 1975. He was ready to rejoin the team in time for the game against the Bucks.

The Bucks were not relishing the idea of facing Simmons again.

"The only guy I had trouble with was Simmons," says George Walker, "He wore the biggest helmet I ever saw. It was like a diving helmet. He hit me so hard once I was looking out of my earhole. He was the toughest guy I faced."

Walker would definitely have trouble with Simmons in this game.

The game was a road contest for the Bucks and would be played in Mount Lebanon, Pennsylvania. "It was the only time we played on Astro-Turf," remembers Tom Miller.

The Bucks did not enjoy the experience.

"That turf was hard on your feet and legs," says Hugh Gibbons.

"I've been on gym floors that were softer than that," adds Wayne Rockmore.

Traveling to the game, Rockmore was feeling under the weather. "I felt miserable on the bus," The Rock remembers, "Took some Tylenol, when I hit that turf I felt better."

Rockmore felt good enough to rush for over 100 yards, including touchdown runs of 70 and 21 yards, but he didn't get a lot of help from his teammates. The usual solid Bucks defense couldn't find a way to stop Pittsburgh's offense, the Central Pennsylvania offense lost five fumbles, and Pittsburgh rolled, 40-13. The Ironmen expertly mixed their running and passing plays to score six touchdowns, including two each by flanker Ron Graham and running back Ed Farmer.

Ramsey Simmons, always trouble for the Bucks, added insult to injury.

"Georgie was going against Simmons," recalls Joe Wales, "He was a big guy who had been drafted by the Steelers and always murdered us. Anyway, Simmons came up under Georgie's helmet and hit him in the chin and throat."

"I had a big lunch, he nailed me right under the chin in the throat," says Walker, "I just lost the whole lunch."

"I remember George getting hit in the throat and throwing up everywhere," recalls Pat Little, "He was gasping and choking. It was pretty scary."

"So, George is puking and has to come out of the game," adds Wales, "They brought in Mitch Mancuso, who was this little karate guy. Mancuso said to me we're gonna get Simmons. He said 'Just let him come through and when I get behind him I'll nail him.' I said, 'What if the play comes our way?' Mancuso looked at me and said, 'Who cares?'"

"Mancuso was a rough guy," recalls Darrel Rutter, "worked in a state prison and sent his boss through a plate glass window."

"Later, Georgie had to come back in the game," adds Wales, "and the poor guy couldn't even talk. More like a growl."

The whole team probably felt sick. The loss put the Bucks' record at 1-4 on the season. They needed a win over their next opponent, the Beaver County Cougars, at Curwensville to turn things around and hopefully salvage the year.

Beaver County was yet another minor league club that was struggling financially. In June the West Aliquippa Swimming Pool announced it was having a benefit pool party for the Cougars to help raise much-needed funds.

But although the Bucks hoped to turn things around against the Cougars, injuries had hit the club hard. Mike McNeish had hurt a shoulder and was out. Albe Wales and Ken Rutter were also both injured and out of the lineup. This being semipro ball, players had other lives that took them away from practices and games. Defensive back Glen Brandimarte was traveling with his family. Defensive tackle Jeff McCartney was also unavailable. Due to the manpower shortage, both Gary Pheasant and Guy Houghtaling would be asked to play both offense and defense against Beaver County.

But the Bucks overcame against the Cougars. They moved Gary Spizzirri into McCartney's spot on the defensive line, and the 6'2" 222 pound rookie from Redbank Valley High in New Bethlehem, Pennsylvania, spent most of the game in the Beaver County backfield. Spizzirri had help from Rod Ullein, and together the duo destroyed the Cougars' inside running game. Although the Cougars boasted two dangerous runners in Leon Tisdale from Slippery Rock State College [now University] and Denny Hightower, they couldn't move the ball thanks to Spizzirri and Ullein, and managed just 45 net yards rushing.

"I thought Ullein and Spizzirri did a pretty good job," said assistant coach Gary Baumgardner, "and Allen Potter has just made great strides at weakside cornerback. Gordie [defensive back Bill Gordon] has been playing hurt the last two games."

The Cougars didn't fare much better through the air. Central Pennsylvania's defense picked off two passes, and held Beaver County to just 115 aerial yards.

Jim Slabon and Gary Pheasant each picked off a pass, giving the team 15 picks in six games, a stat that pleased Baumgardner.

"Slabon has eight interceptions," Baumgardner told reporters, "He's been playing really good football this year at safety. He does a fine job back there in centerfield. We run an awful lot of drills involving the safety, and he has a big job to do."

The Bucks stunned the Cougars at the outset. Slabon picked off Jim Stoneberg's first down pass and returned it nine yards to the 43. On first down, the Bucks once again tried the old "flea flicker" play. This time Rydbom dropped back and rifled a lateral to Pheasant in the right flat, who then turned and saw Kizina wide open behind the Cougar defensive backfield. Pheasant zipped the ball to the former Glendale High receiver for the touchdown with just a minute and a half gone in the game. Ritchie Shoop added the extra point.

Late in the period, the Bucks set up at their own 49 after their defense forced Beaver County to punt for the third straight time. Wayne Rockmore then brought the small crowd to its feet with a brilliant twisting, dodging run through the Cougars for a 51-yard touchdown. Shoop's placement was true again, and the Bucks led 14-0.

Beaver County reached the Bucks' 9-yard line early in the second quarter as Stoneberg connected with Lenny Pushinski for gains of 22 and 35 yards. But Spizzirri stalled that drive by sacking the Cougar quarterback for a nine-yard loss and the Bucks took over on downs at the 19.

One of several poor punts by the Cougars gave the Bucks a chance to score in the last minute of the half. Shoop answered the call and connected on a 43-yard field goal to make it 17-0 at the half. Amazingly, it was the very first three-pointer in the team's two-year history!

Since Ken Rutter was out of action, the injured wide receiver had been acting as the public address announcer for the Bucks' home games. During half-time, Rutter decided to have a little fun with the crowd.

"When Ken got hurt he went up to the press box for the game," recalls his brother Darrel, "He did imitations of [*Steelers' announcer*] Myron Cope."

The imitation was so good that a fan brought his son up to meet him.

"I had to tell him it was just me imitating Cope," remembers Ken, "But he wouldn't believe me, and I had to finally convince him it was just me."

When reminded of the story recently, Wayne Rockmore joked, ""He probably gave that kid an autograph."

In another twist to the story, Darrel Rutter was playing the part of his brother Ken during the game against Beaver County.

"Darrel was on disability from the railroad and wasn't supposed to be playing," says Ken, "so he dressed as me. Wouldn't you know, he fumbled two punts, and I had to announce that I had fumbled two punts! I fumbled twice while sitting in the press box!"

"I guess it was the lights," Ken adds jokingly.

Things like this pointed out the fact that above all else, the Bucks loved to play and have fun. Unencumbered by the strict rules and policies of the NFL, and under no pressure to "protect the shield" as the saying goes, the Bucks were pretty much able to live by their own set of rules. They enjoyed . . . well, they enjoyed being Whitetail Bucks.

"This was semipro ball at its best," recalls Darrel Rutter, "It was the most fun I've ever had in my life. I just wish there was a way to bottle up the kind of enthusiasm we had. Compared to Penn State, it may have seemed like small potatoes, but it was fun. Penn State was not fun. Paterno was a ball-buster.

"In the bus we'd be singing and carrying on. Just a bunch of characters. We had a helluva lot of fun."

"Doug Kritzer." Wayne Rockmore remembers, shaking his head, "He was a funny guy. Went to school together. I took the handoff and got hit just as I did. Had the breath knocked out of me. Guys are asking me, 'Where are you?' So Kritzer comes over and says, 'Rock, you ok? How many fingers am I holding up?' Then he started flashing all kinds of fingers at me . . . first one, then three, then two."

"Up in Sharon, they bulldozed the field right before we played," recounts Ron Roefaro, "Not a blade of grass on that field. There were no locker rooms, so we had to get dressed on the bus. Of course there were no showers, so we had to get on the bus after the game in full uniform. We got to this state park, and the players ran off the bus. Security was running after us trying to get money."

"We all wound up diving in the lake in full uniform," Roefaro adds. "Then we tipped over the lifeguards' platform on the lake, and spilled all these girls into the lake."

Although at times they may have struggled on the field, and they weren't getting paid, above all else, the Bucks had fun and enjoyed their time as semipro ballplayers in Central Pennsylvania. To a man, they say they never had more fun than they did as Whitetail Bucks.

The Bucks lost a golden opportunity against the Cougars early in the third quarter when Rockmore dropped the ball at the Beaver County 12. But the Whitetail Bucks stopped the Cougars cold, and went back on offense at the 14-yard line. Three plays got them nowhere, but on fourth down, the Bucks resorted to some more of their trickeration. Lined up for a field goal, holder Jim Slabon took the snap, jumped up, rolled right and found Pheasant wide open in the end zone for the score. Shoop booted the extra point, making it 24-0.

With Jim Baumbach having replaced Jim Stoneberg at the controls of the offense, the Cougars reached the Central Pennsylvania 19 before running out of downs. The Bucks then responded with a 10-play scoring drive directed by Miller.

Three times the veteran quarterback connected with Pheasant, for gains of 5, 11 and 23 yards. The last one was a great individual effort by the receiver as he made a splendid one-handed grab. Another pass to Doug Kritzer was good for nine yards. Then, at the Beaver County 23, Miller called Rockmore's favorite play, the "15 wham" play, over the left side. The Bucks' offensive line sprung Rock again, and he raced through the hole and was in the end zone before the Cougars knew what had happened. Once again, the Bucks ran the fake on the extra point, with Shoop feigning the kick, and Slabon jumping to his feet and racing around right end for the conversion.

A little over midway through the fourth quarter, Charvi Skillings recovered a Cougar fumble at the Bucks' 42. Just then one of the stadium transformers blew, knocking out one bank of lights. The officials met with safety personnel, and then called a halt to the game.

The Cougars, badly outclassed, didn't object. The Bucks had won 31-0.

Despite the win, head coach Tom Miller was not satisfied.

"I'm still not happy with our offense," Miller stated after the game. "It's not where I'd like it to be. Our power plays aren't getting enough yards and I think our passing can be more effective too."

Starting quarterback Larry Rydbom hit on only two of 14 passes for 27 yards, while Miller spelled him and completed four of six.

The Bucks still had a bit of a quarterback controversy that had started back during the 1975 season. Both quarterbacks had their strengths and weaknesses.

"Rydbom had a helluva temper," states George Walker, "He used to get into fights with Miller all the time on the sidelines."

"I tell you, if you could have put Tom's brain in Rydbom's body, you'd have had something there," Hugh Gibbons recalls.

In any event, the Bucks had won. "I was happy to win that game," said Miller at the time, "We needed a good win."

That they did.

After their big win over Beaver County, the Bucks hit the road again, journeying to Sharon to meet the Old Express at Christian Kennedy Stadium, hoping to continue their winning ways. The Old Express was coming off a tough 19-12 loss to the Ironmen despite quarterback Bob Scrim throwing for one touchdown and running for another.

The Bucks were hoping that the big win over Beaver County would give them some momentum, but personnel problems threatened to eat away at what little depth the Bucks had. Philipsburg's Doug Hrenko, for instance, had replaced Mike McNeish against Beaver County, but after the game he had headed back to Kentucky and would not available against Sharon.

Wayne Rockmore continued to spearhead the Bucks' ground attack. The Rock's fine comeback season was a surprise to some but not to those who knew how hard the Clearfield grad had worked to get himself back into shape. Against Sharon, Rockmore rushed 16 times for 121 yards and a touchdown.

But Central Pennsylvania, which wound up with 264 yards in total offense, fell behind 13-0 after 20 minutes. Sharon's Denny Green stung the Bucks with a 69-yard punt return for a touchdown late in the first quarter, and then Nathan Marshall picked off a Rydbom pass midway through the second quarter and raced 70 yards to paydirt. James Husted added the extra point after the second touchdown.

Not surprisingly, a long run by Rockmore ignited the Bucks' offense on their next possession. The Rock's run set up Rydbom's four-yard scoring pass to Gary Pheasant, and Ritchie Shoop kicked the point-after. Pheasant would wind up with a team-high five receptions for the game.

Moments after Pheasant's score, the Bucks' defense put the clamps to Sharon's offense, and the Old Express punter had to boot out of his own end zone. Unfortunately for him, the punt went straight into the air and came down in Rod Ullein's arms at the two. The big defensive tackle then simply fell across the goal line for the touchdown, and Shoop's placement put the Bucks ahead 14-13 with less than two minutes left in the half.

Central Pennsylvania couldn't hold that edge for long, however, as the Old Express responded by quickly driving into field goal range. Husted then connected from 35 yards away to make it 16-14 at intermission.

The situation did not improve after the half. Sharon took the second-half kickoff and marched 64 yards for a touchdown, with James Campbell driving the last four yards for the touchdown. Husted's conversion upped the spread to 23-14.

But the Bucks wouldn't quit, and once again it was Rockmore who sparked the team to life. Late in the third quarter, The Rock put the Bucks back in business with a 36-yard scoring run, and Shoop's placement sliced the deficit to 23-21.

The game moved into the fourth quarter with neither team doing much on offense. Then the Bucks got a break when the Old Express fumbled and Tom Marlett recovered at the Bucks' 36-yard line. Central Pennsylvania slowly moved the ball downfield, and their drive was helped when a personal foul penalty was called on Sharon. Finally, Joe Good banged into the end zone from the six with a little over six minutes remaining. Shoop's placement failed, but the Bucks were now clinging to a 27-23 edge.

Now it was Sharon's turn to try and beat the clock. They came right back, moving the sticks three times on a long methodical drive that reached the Central Pennsylvania five.

It was there that the Bucks' defense stiffened and halted the march. The Express faced a fourth down and less than a yard to go for the first down.

Sharon tried a running play that didn't go anywhere. The Bucks celebrated when the line judge ruled that the Express had not made the first down and the ball would go over on downs. Suddenly, the referee stepped in and, without even taking a measurement, signaled a first down.

The Bucks were now fuming and held Sharon for two plays. But on third down, with just 57 seconds left on the clock, James Campbell barreled over from the one-yard line and Central Pennsylvania had lost a heart breaker, 29-27.

"Steve Moser, Sharon's general manager, came into our locker room after the game and actually apologized for the officiating," Al Siegel told reporters after the game. "We were playing 11 players and one official, it seemed. The one ref kept overruling the other officials."

The loss still resonates years later with the Bucks.

"We played like hell, but we lost the game on a bad call," remembers George Walker.

"A bad call, a home field call," laments Wayne Rockmore.

The loss was the Bucks' fifth in seven games. The season was slowly slipping away, with Washington and Pittsburgh, both of whom had beaten the team earlier in the campaign, on the horizon.

Maybe Darrel Rutter summed it up best.

"It was the best of times, it was the worst of times," he said recently.

# 6

"When I played, all we got was a party at the Philipsburg American Legion."

—PAUL "BAM-BAM" KANAGY

Life as a semipro football player has never been an easy one. There is no glory involved. No big money contracts, and sometimes no money at all. No endorsement deals. No glitz, no glamour. Long arduous trips to practices and games after working an 8- or 10-hour day, not to mention poor facilities.

But despite facing the hardships involved with the semipro game as well as the possibility of a losing season, the Central Pennsylvania Whitetail Bucks soldiered on in 1976. They played for the sheer love of the game. And although they may seem slight or paltry when compared to the rewards of playing in the NFL, there were some perks involved in being a Whitetail Buck.

"We had some perks," stresses Joe Wales, "They'd hold end of the season parties at this place in Snow Shoe, and we called it the 'Crown Royal Lodge.' Giant lodge. Owned by the mining company that backed the team. They'd cook wild boar, caribou, and elk for us. The coal company owner would haul in sand to make a beach and take us on helicopter rides."

"I went on the Altoona TV station, Channel 10, WTAJ, with Ken Rutter and Dave Belfield to talk football," adds Wales, "On there with Big John Riley."

"Ken Rutter found out that the team had a sponsor that did hair," Wales continues, "He asked if he could get his hair done and they said, 'yes.' So Ken got this huge afro."

"I remember we'd stop on the way back from practices and games at Goody's in Philipsburg to eat," remembers George Walker, "It was owned by Joe Good's

Dad. The surrounding area knew who the Whitetail Bucks were. The towns got behind us. It meant a lot to us. We were the only team that played in an organized semipro league."

Sometimes having people know who you were came in handy for the rough and tumble Bucks.

"Kevin McClincy was an offensive lineman," Hugh Gibbons said in a recent interview, "He was about 350 pounds. Not a big guy like George Walker, just big. We were coming home from a game and stopped in Port Matilda for some food. We ordered and McClincy said, 'I didn't order that.' I guess the owner didn't like it so he called in the town sheriff. He comes in all attitude and loaded for bear, and McClincy just looks at him and says, 'You look like Kojak.'

"Next thing we know the state police are coming in. Thank goodness he was very professional, and he knew the owners of the team. He was able to defuse the situation."

But the perks offered to the Bucks were not always well-remembered.

"When I played," recalls Paul Kanagy, when he learned about the revelries at the 'Crown Royal Lodge,' "all we got was a party at the Philipsburg American Legion."

After the controversial finish in Sharon, the Bucks situation did not look promising. The loss to the Old Express left Central Pennsylvania with a record of 2-5, and they'd have to win all four of their remaining games to fashion a winning record. The odds of that did not look good with Washington and Pittsburgh on the horizon.

Around this time, rumors of an attempt to organize an Altoona-based semipro team began to circulate. The future of the Bucks very much depended on whether these rumors were true, and if so, would this effort turn out to be successful. A majority of the Central Pennsylvania players were from the Altoona area, and might leave the Bucks to join this new franchise that played closer to home.

"There was an attempt to start an Altoona Mountaineers team that was being sponsored by a former player of the older semipro team from the 1940s of the same name," Ron Roefaro recalls, "The sponsor was a pizza shop pioneer in Altoona, Rocco DePiro, who played for the Mountaineers."

"The owners of three pizza shops in Altoona called Pal-Mino's—Joe and Rocco DePiro—had played for a semipro team called the Mountaineers back in the 1940s," remembers Ken Rutter, "They wanted to have a team in Altoona and called a meeting at the Logan Junior High School football field. Some of us attended and they discussed the possible plans for a team.

"We players at that time had little interest in leaving the Bucks because it was a sure bet we're going to have a team. Theirs was only a whim. But it would have been nice to not have traveled for practices."

Sure enough, more and more noise started coming out of the Mountain City about a new semipro team. Sure enough, the owners had approached several Bucks in an attempt to raid the team's roster and recruit players for this new venture. But fortunately for the Whitetail Bucks, the ownership group decided to forget the whole thing soon after, having never really gotten off the ground.

"There was one tryout but nothing happened after that," says Roefaro.

"I think when they saw we weren't going to play in Altoona they scrapped their plans," adds Ken Rutter.

"I vaguely remember something to that affect, but I never paid any attention to rumor," offers Tom Marlett.

With the talk of a possible rival team in Altoona having ended, the Bucks went back to concentrating on their season. Next up on the schedule was Washington. In 1975, the Bucks had easily crushed the Generals twice. But Washington had edged Central Pennsylvania 7-6 earlier in the '76 season, and their new owners, three coal mining companies, spent money and recruited talent from as far as 100 miles away. This helped make the Generals one of the most improved teams in the Mid-Atlantic League. They proved just how much improved they were with another solid performance in Washington, Pa., on Saturday September 18th.

Like their first meeting of the season in Flinton, the game was a bitterly fought defensive battle. Neither team was able to generate much in the way of offense, with the Bucks netting 218 yards and the Generals only 177. There were five punts in the scoreless first quarter alone.

The defensive struggle continued in the second quarter, as Jim Slabon stopped Washington's first real offensive threat with a fumble recovery at his own 17-yard line. Following another punt by the Bucks' Allen Potter, the Generals set up at the Bucks' 38. Four plays later, quarterback John Smith and wide receiver Tom Karpency hooked up for a 25-yard touchdown pass. After the extra point try failed, it was 6-0 Washington.

On the ensuing series, a clipping penalty and a pass that lost yardage had the Bucks deep in Generals' territory. On fourth down, Allen Potter set himself to punt.

But the snap sailed over Potter's head, and the Bucks' punter wisely picked up the ball and retreated into the end zone to surrender a safety rather than give the Generals the ball so close to the goal line. That put the Generals ahead by 8-0.

Washington took the free kick from Potter and marched toward the end zone. From the 32, Smith and Karpency hooked up again for the touchdown. The point after failed again, but Washington now led, 14-0.

The Bucks, desperate to get themselves back into the game, had Ritchie Shoop try a 52-yard field goal on the final play of the half, but it was no good.

Early in the third quarter, the Bucks squandered a couple of scoring chances. Shoop missed another field goal try. Potter then picked off a General pass on the next play, but the Bucks proceeded to fumble the ball right back to the Generals at the 19.

After holding Washington to three-and-out, Central Pennsylvania finally cashed in on a break, as the Generals' punter fumbled the snap at his own two. The Bucks recovered and Shoop crashed into the end zone on the next play. His extra point kick was blocked, keeping the score 14-6, but it gave the Bucks some glimmer of hope.

Early in the fourth quarter Bucks' linebacker Kurt Kessler picked up a General fumble and headed for paydirt. He did a flip as he reached the goal line, losing the ball when he hit the turf in the end zone, and the ball rolled out of play. The Bucks thought they had scored. The officials, however, ruled that Kessler did not carry the ball across the goal line and awarded Washington the ball on a touchback.

The Bucks were so certain they had scored that they sent their kicking team onto the field to try the extra point and then quickly realized they hadn't scored when they saw Washington's offense lining up at the 20. And they were not happy about it.

"We were mad at the refs and stole the 50-yard line marker," says Jay Siegel, "It still hangs in my dad's basement. The '50-yard Line Bar' we called it, which was the site of at least one 'infamous' year-end party."

Central Pennsylvania could not dent the Generals defense the rest of the way, and the Bucks had lost their sixth game in eight tries. Wayne Rockmore had another solid game, rushing for a game-high 94 yards on 16 carries. But coach Miller had to be disappointed in another lackluster performance by Larry Rydbom, who completed only 5 of 15 passes for a mere 76 yards.

Sure enough, after the Washington loss, Miller benched Rydbom and inserted himself into the starting lineup. For the first time all season, Rydbom would not be under center.

The Bucks next faced the Ironmen at Philipsburg's Memorial Stadium. A good crowd of 1,700 people came out to watch, most of them to see the return of hometown hero Alge Jones. The wide receiver had decided to return to the team and would be in uniform for the first time since the '75 season. Working on his farm had not eroded his skills.

Pittsburgh, which had won five straight, came into the game ranked among the Top 15 semipro teams in the country according to a *Pro Football Weekly* poll.

The fans saw a game full of hard hitting, but they had to watch the Bucks blow several scoring chances as well as fumble away other opportunities.

Not surprisingly, the Ironmen threatened first, but Jim Slabon intercepted Gary Shope's first pass at his own 8-yard line. The theft was the ninth of the season for the ball-hawking safety.

Miller then engineered what had to be one of the Bucks' best offensive drives of the season. The veteran signal caller expertly mixed passes to Jones with the running of Wayne Rockmore and Joe Good. The march took 8 minutes and 32 seconds off the clock as the Bucks drove smartly from their own eight to the Pittsburgh 29. The drive stalled, so the Bucks lined up for a field goal. Like they had done so often in the past, Central Pennsylvania went for the fake kick. Slabon took the snap and tried to run, but the Ironmen were waiting and Slabon was hit and fumbled, with Joe Herndon recovering for the Ironmen.

Despite that disappointing end to a great drive, Central Pennsylvania held the Ironmen on downs and then got a big break on fourth down when the snap to punter Howard Lerda was low. This gave defensive end Darrel Rutter enough time to rush in and block the kick. Rutter and another Buck finally corralled the ball at the Pittsburgh 10. The Bucks were knocking on the door.

But the door wouldn't open. Two runs by Rockmore and an incomplete pass left the ball at the six, so Ritchie Shoop lined up for a 24-yard field goal. But Slabon couldn't handle the snap, and Ironman Leo Henne recovered the fumbled ball at the 15.

In the waning moments of the first half, the Ironmen gambled on a fourth-and-one at their own 47. The Bucks were waiting, though, and Ed Farmer lost a yard.

Central Pennsylvania took over on the 46, and then a pass interference call against Pittsburgh gave the Bucks the ball at the Ironmen 7-yard line with time for one more play. Shoop rushed onto the field to attempt a 25-yard field goal, but the ball sailed wide to the left.

The scoreless first half gave the Bucks hope, but after intermission, Central Pennsylvania's troubles began in earnest.

Rich Skillings mishandled a punt and Ironman Chuck Milcic recovered at the Bucks' 29. Shope, who played his high school ball at Huntingdon Area High, hit Dennis Koch with a 27-yard pass and then, after the Bucks' forward wall stopped two plunges, faked a handoff and tossed to tight end Sonny Richardson for an easy six. Pete Ross booted the extra point.

Miller pulled himself from the game and handed the reins to Rydbom. But on the ensuing series, Rydbom was hit from behind and fumbled, with Julius Foy recovering for the Ironmen at the Bucks' 25. Shope immediately went to Koch for 23 yards and then two plays later Melvin McMillan scored from the one. Ross' conversion upped the bulge to 14-0 halfway through the third period.

Pittsburgh was seemingly heading for another score, but Tom Marlett picked off Shope's pass at his own 6-yard line. This only delayed the inevitable. The Bucks gave the ball right back to the Ironmen when Good fumbled and Bob Allen recovered at the Central Pennsylvania 2-yard line. On first down, Farmer skirted right end for the touchdown and Ross tacked on the 21st point.

Despite their lead, Pittsburgh continued to punish the Bucks, proving that semipro ball is not for the faint of heart. Early in the last quarter, Jones caught the ball and went out of bounds. This didn't stop Pittsburgh's Charlie West from laying a hard hit on Jones which sent the receiver up and over the fence surrounding the field. Jones landed hard on the concrete walkway and had to be helped up by the fans who were standing along the fence.

Although the Bucks protested, no unsportsmanlike conduct penalty was called. This didn't come as much of a surprise to some of the Bucks.

"I used to get hit all the time before I caught the punt, which should have been a penalty," recalls Darrel Rutter, "But the refs never called the penalty. I'd say something to them, and they'd say, 'The fans paid to see action.'"

Rydbom finally sparked the Bucks' offense to life midway through the fourth quarter, taking the team 64 yards in 10 plays, all of them through the air. On fourth down at the Pittsburgh 36, Rydbom took the snap, dropped back and was pressured. He then scrambled all over the field like Fran Tarkenton. Rydbom finally spotted Wayne Rockmore down the middle of the field and behind the secondary, and zipped the ball to his halfback. The Rock grabbed the ball and headed for the goal line. Shoop booted the extra point with 2:16 showing on the clock, and the Bucks trailed 21-7.

The Bucks kept up the pressure on the Ironmen. Darrel Rutter chased Shope and then stole the ball from him at the Pittsburgh 29. Rydbom passed to Gary Pheasant for seven yards and Jones for 12 more. From the 10-yard line, he then went to Jones again. The split end made a brilliant catch, snaring the ball just as he fell out of the end zone. Slabon ran around left end for the extra point, and the score was 21-14.

But there were only 49 seconds left in the game, and the Ironmen were able to run the remaining time off the clock. The Bucks had simply run out of time in having to accept their seventh defeat in nine games.

While the team's record was disappointing following their winning season in '75, however, it had been an extremely frustrating campaign as well. The Bucks had lost two games in overtime. They had lost to Sharon when even the Old Express' GM admitted that the Bucks had been robbed. They had lost two close games to Washington, and had just lost to one of the top teams in the country, Pittsburgh, by only a touchdown.

It's also worth mentioning that four of the losses were to teams ranked among the 20 best semipro teams in the country. Mark Azzara Jr. of Danbury Conn, a columnist for *Pro Football Weekly*, had the Brooklyn Mariners tied for eighth, the Brooklyn Golden Knights 10th and the Ironmen 18th. The Bucks had met some of the very best semipro clubs in the United States, and they had proven their mettle on the field by remaining competitive even against the best of teams.

A break here, a field goal there, and the Bucks might have matched the winning record they had in '75.

But close only counts in horseshoes and hand grenades. The Bucks were finding that out the hard way.

Next on the schedule was an away game against the Beaver County Cougars, the Bucks' last road trip of the season. The contest was originally scheduled for the afternoon of Sunday, October 3rd, but was switched at the last minute to Saturday night when the Cougars were able to rent a field in Aliquippa with lights. Although this facility, unlike the team's usual venue, at least offered showers, they were not much more accessible to the Bucks.

"In Aliquippa we had to walk up I don't know how many flights of stairs to shower," laments George Walker.

The Bucks didn't mind making that long climb to the showers after this game.

Central Pennsylvania finally dominated a ball game, running 65 plays to the Cougars' 39 and rolling up 23 first downs and 398 yards total offense, while getting outstanding individual performances from Wayne Rockmore, Tom Miller and Alge Jones.

After Beaver County was forced to punt without a first down on the opening possession, Miller and company went to work. Mixing his running and passing plays to perfection, the veteran quarterback led the Bucks on an 80 yard march in 15 plays. Miller capped the drive with a four-yard pass to Jones. Ritchie Shoop added the extra point to put the Bucks up, 7-0.

With just under three minutes left in the half the host Cougars got on the scoreboard when a quick two-play drive was capped by Jim Baumbach's 49-yard pass to Lenny Pushinski. Darrel Rutter blocked the extra point try to keep Central Pennsylvania in front.

Miller had some time to work with before halftime, and he again got the Bucks rolling. With time running out on the first half, Miller connected with Gary Kizina with a 17-yard scoring pass. Shoop added the extra point and the Bucks had a 14-6 halftime lead.

Central Pennsylvania engineered a 58-yard scoring march to open the third quarter, with 48 of those coming on the running of Wayne Rockmore. The Rock's one-yard plunge and Shoop's extra point gave the Bucks a 21-6 advantage.

The Cougars came right back to score minutes later. An untimely penalty on the Bucks gave the Cougar drive new life, and Beaver County converted on a five-yard run by Dennis Hightower. Leon Tisdale's conversion run made it 21-13.

Beaver County continued its comeback, and managed to pull within a point of the Bucks. Offensive tackle Paul Long hauled in a pass on a tackle-eligible play and barreled 40 yards to the Bucks' one-yard line. On the last play of the third quarter Baumbach scored on a quarterback sneak. Joe Smith added the extra point to make it 21-20. The Bucks' seemingly safe lead had now almost evaporated.

But the fourth quarter was all Central Pennsylvania's, beginning with a crisp, nine-play, 59-yard drive. Miller topped off the march with a nine-yard pass to Jones and Shoop's kick upped the Bucks lead to 28-20.

The Bucks recovered a Beaver County fumble at their own 49, and then marched goal ward. Rockmore's two-yard run capped the drive, and made it 35-20.

Jim Slabon then continued his fine play, picking off his 11th interception of the season. Slabon's last second pick and return to the Cougar 21 came as the final gun sounded.

Rockmore had his—and the Bucks'—greatest rushing game, chalking up 204 yards on the ground in a semipro record 48 carries. The Rock had now pulled within 96 yards of the coveted 1,000 yard mark.

His teammates, the fans and team officials all knew and appreciated that Rockmore's dedication, hard work and sacrifice in the off-season had made Rock one of the top semipro runners around and had helped him rebound from his injury-shortened 1975 season. He was averaging an astounding 5.7 yards per carry, an impressive mark in any league.

Miller, in just his second start of the season, handled the Buck offense with precision and heads-up play calling. He completed 12 of 17 passes for 110 yards and three touchdowns.

Jones, performing like he had played the entire season instead of just the last two games, hauled in 10 of Miller's aerials for 85 yards and two touchdowns.

Defensive coach Gary Baumgardner expressed pride in his charges after the game. Stating that he was most impressed with the fact that his defenders had swiped 23 enemy passes for the season, he singled out the impressive play of Jim Slabon and his 11 interceptions. Baumgardner beamed about his quick, agile linebackers: Dirk Grissinger, Albe Wales, Tom Marlett and Kurt Kessler, all of whom really made Central Pennsylvania's 4-3 defense work. He also raved about his defensive line, anchored by Rod Ullein, Mitch Mancuso, Gary Spizzirri, and a relative newcomer, tackle Jeff Blowers of Clearfield, who had joined the Bucks within the last month and had been the most effective at plugging up the middle.

"We've played good, solid defense." added Baumgardner, "We've held most of the teams down to where we could win. We haven't been out of any game, actually. We have better team quickness this year, and I just think all the guys who played defense have done a rather good job, I think."

The Bucks management continued to do anything they could to appeal to the local community.

On Tuesday, October 5th, Bucks' GM Al Siegel announced that thanks to the generosity of several Clearfield merchants, 23 residents of the Clear Haven Nursing Home would be able to attend the season finale against the Sharon Old Express on Saturday night at the Clearfield Driving Park.

Siegel stated that Kurtz Stationery Store, Sherwin-Williams Paint Store, Nick Prave, Quigley's Drug Store, Rudd's Tobacco Store and Jacobson & Etzweiler's Men's Store purchased the tickets for the game. He added that Fullington Auto Bus Company would provide free transportation to and from the game.

Clearfield, the county seat of Clearfield County and located along the West Branch of the Susquehanna River, was the "unofficial" home of the Whitetail Bucks. In fact, some semipro football sites list the team's name as the Clearfield Whitetail Bucks. With a population of around 6,000, Clearfield was home to four of the county's list of twenty National Registered Historic Places, including the County Courthouse and the Thomas Murray House, the residence of a prominent 19th-century Clearfield attorney.

In 1966, Clearfield, located 22 miles northwest of DuBois, was named as an All-American City, given annually to the top ten cities in the United States.

It's the hometown of *New York Times* reporter and columnist Earl Caldwell, the first African-American to have a regular column in a major national newspaper.

A crowd of more than 2,500 fans was expected for what the local press was calling a revenge match, but rain showers kept the crowd to only 1,500, including the 23 folks from Clear Haven. They saw another exasperating loss that basically served as a microcosm for the Bucks' frustrating season.

The Sharon ballplayers talked some smack before the game.

"We played Sharon the last game in 1976," says George Walker, "and Wayne Rockmore needed only so many yards to get 1,000 for the year. One of their guys came up to me and said, 'He's not going to get 20.' Well, we played like hell and Rockmore wound up with 150 yards or so! We didn't take any stuff from anyone."

The Bucks had been snake-bitten from the opening game, but they dominated most of the season finale. Then the snake bit them once again.

On their first offensive series, they marched from their 20 to the Sharon 30 before running out of downs.

Backed up to their own 22 on their next possession by a clipping penalty on a punt return, the Bucks began a solid 13-play drive. Rockmore capped the march with a 20-yard sprint to paydirt on a draw play.

Ritchie Shoop's first conversion try was blocked, but a penalty gave him a second chance. Shoop never got the second attempt off, however, because of a strong rush.

Central Pennsylvania then had a great opportunity to increase their lead near the end of the half, as they marched to the Sharon 1-yard line. But Tom Miller bobbled a snap from center and the Old Express' Otha Hilton recovered at the seven.

The score remained 6-0 at the half.

The Bucks defense stopped the Old Express at their own 35 midway through the third quarter. The hosts took over and Miller quickly hit Gary Pheasant, who made a great, sliding catch, for 21 yards and then Jones for another 26. That put the Bucks within field goal range, and Shoop drilled a 32-yarder with 4:45 left in the period.

Now ahead by 9-0, the Bucks looked for more to possibly wrap it up and end the season on a high note. Darrel Rutter made his second fumble recovery of the game to turn the ball over to the offense at the Bucks' 39.

Central Pennsylvania then moved swiftly toward a possible clincher, as Rockmore broke off a 33-yard run along the way. At the Sharon 12, Joe Good got the call twice for seven yards. On third and three Rockmore was thrown for a four-yard loss. Miller then attempted to pass to Jones but it fell to the ground incomplete.

That should have been fourth down, but the down marker showed a three, so the Bucks picked up an extra play. It didn't matter. Miller's pass to Gary Kizina was broken up at the goal line.

The Bucks' defense had so far shut out the Old Express, and when Sharon faced a third-and-long at their own nine, the Whitetail Bucks almost sacked quarterback Bob Scrim in the end zone.

But Scrim eluded the rush, rolled left and heaved a desperation pass down the sideline. Two Central Pennsylvania players were there, but halfback Richard Ellebie made a fine leaping grab. To his surprise, he had nobody around him and headed for paydirt. Near the Bucks' 40, safety Jim Slabon cut Ellebie off and tried to wrestle the 6'2", 195-pounder to the ground, but Ellebie shook him off and breezed the rest of the way for a 91-yard touchdown. Steve Moser's placement cut the Bucks' lead to a precarious 9-7.

The situation got a bit more precarious when Miller tossed an interception on first down of the Bucks' next possession, which gave the Old Express excellent field position. But the Central Pennsylvania defense held and stopped Sharon's offense again.

Then, starting at its own 48 following a punt, Sharon pushed to the Bucks' 10-yard line on the running of Ellebie, Scrim and Denny Green before the Bucks defense stiffened. Moser, however, booted a 28-yard field goal to put Sharon up for the first time, 10-9, with 1:44 left.

Al Siegel returned the ensuing kickoff 15 yards to his own 45. Three plays went nowhere, but the Bucks stayed alive when Tom Miller's fourth down pass found Jones for 15 yards to the Sharon 40.

Another Miller to Jones aerial put the ball on the 36. But on third down, Miller's bomb was right into the arms of defender Andrew Woods at the 15. The interception sealed another bitter defeat by the Bucks, and left the team and the 1,500 fans who had braved the inclement weather very disappointed.

On a more positive note, Wayne Rockmore went over 1,000 yards rushing for the season with another great performance, gaining 163 yards on 26 carries. Alge Jones had another fine game with six pass receptions for 74 yards, and the defense was downright fantastic except for two plays. But the 10-9 loss was another bitter defeat and the way it happened essentially typified the way the frustrating season went for the local semipros. They had finished their second season with a record of 3-8 after going 7-5 in their inaugural campaign.

Rockmore wound up with 1,067 yards in 184 carries for a superb 5.8 average. He credited the offensive line for a lot of his success.

"As a running back, our o-line made it easier," the Rock says now, "Everyone did what they were supposed to do. That made it easier.

"That '76 year was not a fluke," Rockmore continues, "We really had something going on offense. It was a pleasure to play with those guys. By that time I had played for a while and I knew what I had to do. I liked to run 40-yard dashes in practice and rode bicycle. I played at around 175 to 185 pounds. Then I got involved with Siegel and was working out with George Walker. I could press 225 pounds 10 times and do that three times in a row.

"I actually preferred to run up the middle," Rock states, "we did great on the inside running game. We had great cohesion with the running game. You never take the guys up front for granted. I can't say enough about our linemen. We just jelled. We got to where we could read each other's minds. I'll tell you, that offensive line, those guys could work together.

"We had trouble with the quick pitch, but it turned out to be a timing thing. I needed to be lined up a half a step wider and should have been a step back. That made all the difference. We could work things out."

Alg Jones, who played only the last three games, finished the season with 22 pass receptions for 213 yards.

Despite their disappointing season, the Bucks were well-represented when it came time to name the All-Star team for the MAFL. Rockmore, of course, made it, but curiously enough as a cornerback, although he hadn't played a game at that position all season! Jim Slabon, Gary Pheasant, Dirk Grissinger and Mike McNeish all made the All-Star roster as well.

But what was in store for the Bucks remained to be seen. Would the team return for another season in '77? The small crowds had been as disappointing as the team's won-loss record and the Bucks, like many semipro teams, were a very financially-troubled franchise.

But the people behind the Bucks—Herman "Hymie" Ziff, Jim Naddeo, and the Johnson Coal Company—soon indicated that, despite the money problems, they wanted to continue fielding a semipro team in the area.

That was definitely a good sign, and after the frustrating season they had just finished, the Bucks certainly needed one.

# CHAPTER

# 7

"It was time for me to move on to a new chapter in my life."

—MIKE McNEISH

So far the Central Pennsylvania Whitetail Bucks had survived two seasons as a semipro franchise. Like most semipro outfits, the Bucks had experienced their share of change and transitioning during their two seasons. The 1977 season would be no exception, and the team would see more than their share of changes both inside and outside their ranks.

First off was the departure of the team's founder, Mike McNeish. The man who had come up with the idea of a semipro team in Central Pennsylvania, helped build it from a dream to a reality and worked hard to make his dream a success, became the epitome of one of the perils of the semipro game.

Unlike professional football, players involved in the semipro game are not tethered as securely to their teams. Since pay, if there is any, is miniscule, players need to hold down daytime jobs, and if that job involves a sudden transfer, or if the player decides to change jobs, the player has to, as the saying goes, "follow the money." So McNeish did what he had to do for himself and his family.

He moved.

"When I left graduate school, I worked for a while as a paralegal assistant for a lawyer in Philipsburg," McNeish says now, "That job was going nowhere so my wife and I decided we'd join the Peace Corps.

"That was a bit of a process but we got everything together, all the paperwork, applications, and documents. We had a prospective assignment but before we left, we went on a whirlwind cross country tour and visited all our relatives and friends.

"When we came back, we found out that the dentist who did the dental work and clearance for that aspect of the application had put the stuff in a drawer and not sent it to Washington, thus ending that avenue.

"We moved briefly to my wife's parents' house on Long Beach Island in New Jersey but found jobs in the Princeton area and moved our stuff to a farmhouse in Bucks County.

"It wasn't really difficult for me to leave the team. It was time for me to move on to a new chapter in my life."

McNeish would be sorely missed.

"Mike McNeish was the guard on my side and we worked well together with traps and cross blocking," recalls Ron Roefaro, "Very good player, blocker and a good football mind."

"He was a great guy, likable guy," recalls Darrel Rutter, "Played semipro up in New York. He was a good player, liked to mix it up."

McNeish would not only be missed because of his on-field ability. He had done a lot of work behind the scenes for the team as well.

"I was involved a whole lot in the background, the administration of the team, though not with the finances," McNeish remembers, "I went to the league meetings, made arrangements for various stadiums, sent out press releases, etc."

"Great business mind, I would say an intellectual," adds Darrel Rutter.

His presence would be greatly missed, but the Bucks had to move on.

So too, did quarterback Larry Rydbom, however.

There was no secret to the fact that Rydbom, who while he struggled at times had performed solidly for the Bucks as their signal caller for 1975 and '76, still entertained serious hopes of realizing his goal of a career in pro football.

In early 1977, Rydbom talked to a scout from the New York Giants. He then attended a clinic in Washington, D.C. run by former NFL player and NFL and WFL coach Ron Waller. These experiences convinced Rydbom that he needed more seasoning at a higher level of football. So he left the Bucks and joined the Chambersburg Cardinals, one the nation's top semipro football teams.

"They told me to get experience, and that this is the best place to get it," he said, "If anybody gets desperate for a quarterback, I want to be ready."

Dave Paganetti, the highly thought-of assistant coach, as well as another assistant, Gary Baumgardner, had also moved on. Both would be sorely missed. Paganetti's offensive innovations had helped Miller, Rydbom and the team tremendously. He had earned the respect of all the players, as had Baumgardner for his quiet, solid leadership. But such was life in the very transitional world of the semipro game.

Another change was uncertainty surrounding the Bucks' affiliation. At a meeting in Gibsonia, Pennsylvania on March 19th, the team voted to join the Southern Division of a new league called the Tri-State Minor Football league.

This was not an uncommon occurrence for minor league and semipro associations. Leagues came and went as did their teams. Many teams were very iffy, fly-by-night propositions, hanging on year-to-year, and sometimes week-to-week, by the proverbial thread.

At the meeting on the 19th, the Bucks decided to forgo their association with the Mid Atlantic League and join their old rivals, the Pittsburgh Ironmen and Washington Generals, in this new setup. Joining the Bucks, Ironmen and Generals were the Allegheny-Kiski Stars from New Kensington, Pa., and the Hardhats from Youngstown, Ohio.

The Hardhats had been one of the premier minor-league franchises in the country in the early 1970s.

Organized in 1972, and owned and run by local construction magnate Ralph Erskine, the Hardhats posted a 38-6 record over three seasons. In its first season, Youngstown pounded its opponents by scores of 47-0, 54-0 and 68-0, only to lose the Midwest League Championship to the Indianapolis Calves. The Hardhats were successful on the field and because thousands of football-starved Youngstown steelworkers were turning out at Struthers High School Stadium to watch the Hardhats, the team gained quite a bit of credibility during their peak years, thanks to ownership under Erskine and his construction/excavation business.

"He was a diehard sportsman," assistant and head coach Al Boggia said of the team owner in the Hardhats' formative years. "Everything came out of his pocket. He was a good owner."

Erskine bought an old house in Struthers, near Struthers Stadium, as a kind of dormitory for his team.

When Boggia, a Semipro Football Hall of Famer, joined the Hardhats as an assistant in 1972, Bill Shunkwiler of Warren was the team's first head coach. When Shunkwiler got a position with a pro scouting organization, Boggia took over the reins as head coach in 1974.

Despite their strong record, the Hardhats' owners announced in March of 1975 that they would not field a team for the upcoming season. This was due to both declining attendance—despite the team's on-field success—and reports that a team from the World Football League was going to locate in nearby Akron, Ohio for the 1975 season.

Boggia said that Erskine made money at first, but then saw it dwindle away as game attendance slipped, while expenses remained constant.

Erskine gave up control of the team a year or so later, but turned the equipment over to the players and permitted the franchise to continue to use of the "Hardhats" name.

But once the players lost Erskine, their financial backbone, they were practically on their own. "We had to bite the bullet after that," Boggia said, "We had to scrape. But it was pure love of the game that kept the guys going."

When the team reorganized in 1977, several community groups and individuals helped out financially.

The Hardhats, like the Bucks, were a mix of former college and high school players who still yearned to play the game they loved. But unlike the Bucks, the Hardhats were able to recruit veteran players, as well as those from big schools like Ohio State and Youngstown State. At first, the Hardhats roster included some players from outside the area, but, eventually, the team's makeup was mostly home-grown talent. To keep talent on their roster, Hardhat players from out of town were offered jobs during the season.

At first, a starter's pay was $50 a game, while reserves got $25.

"That wasn't great money," Boggia said, "but we had some good athletes and our guys managed to hold their own."

Boggia likes to repeat the remark one of his former Hardhats players made to describe the team's collective desire to persist despite financial hardships during their semipro football existence.

While attending a local Curbstone Coaches Association luncheon back in the 1970s, Boggia, as head coach, and some of his players were guests. One player was asked why the men practiced and played for peanuts once the team was no longer properly funded.

"We don't care," Boggia recalled the players' comment. "We'd play on asphalt if we had to."

It was a verbal affirmation of the reason the twenty- and thirty-something Hardhat players, much like the Whitetail Bucks, kept trudging onward during the team's existence.

Representatives from the Clarksburg, West Virginia, Red Devils and the Columbus, Ohio, Stingers, two independent franchises who were on the hunt for opponents to schedule, were also present at this March meeting in Gibsonia.

The new league's Northern Division would include proposed teams from Erie in Pennsylvania, and Tonawanda, Binghamton, Rochester, Syracuse and Batavia in New York.

The division champs would then have a playoff to decide the league champion, who would then advance to meet the winner of the Interstate League, which included teams from Harrisburg, Scranton and Baltimore.

It wasn't long before this new league started experiencing changes and, ultimately, problems.

"We had a league meeting near Pittsburgh last weekend," General Manager Frank Barker of the Salt City Aces out of Syracuse, New York told reporter Mike Holdridge of the *Syracuse Post-Standard* in late March, "and discovered that we were getting inquiries (about franchises) from Connecticut, Michigan, Massachusetts, Maryland, West Virginia and New Jersey. At that rate, we figured our new league name—Tri-State for New York, Pennsylvania and Ohio—wouldn't last too long."

The league itself didn't last too long after that, and vanished without so much as a coin toss or a kickoff.

Instead, the clubs, including the Bucks, slated to join the Tri-State League instead formed two divisions in the—wait for it—Mid-Atlantic Football League. That's right, after all the rigmarole of changing leagues, the Bucks, and most of their old rivals, were right back in the good old MAFL.

Frank Barker went on to tell Holdridge that his Salt City Aces would now play in the Northern Division of the MAFL along with teams from Rochester, Binghamton and Tonawanda. Plans for two other clubs, from LeRoy, New York and Erie, Pa., had already been scrubbed when they couldn't meet the financial or field requirements established by the league and had to drop out.

The Aces had compiled a 6-0 record in 1976 in their first year of New York State Football Conference competition. Overall they were 8-4. Barker insisted at the time that they'd have to do even better to stay with the opposition in the MAFL.

"That Southern Division is loaded with talent," said Barker at the time. "Ed Farmer, a former Pittsburgh Steeler and Philadelphia Eagle, rushed for more than 1,000 yards and scored 16 touchdowns for the Ironmen last year. In one game, he gained 211 yards in 34 carries.

"But that's not all," he continued. "The Whitetail Bucks are loaded with former Penn State players and boast a defensive interior line averaging 278 pounds per man."

Not to be outdone, the new Northern Division had some talent of its own.

The franchise located in Tonawanda, known as the Twin City Geminis, were at one point rated the Number One minor league football team in the nation in 1976. Late cuts from the Buffalo Bills and former Canadian Football League players would make up most of their roster.

Barker pointed out that quarterback Ray Stanton's passing made Binghamton, which went by the name of the Triple-City Jets, one of the toughest semipro outfits around.

"It's the best minor league football in the Eastern part of the country," Bucks head coach and quarterback Tom Miller reported in June, "and we're hoping we can get some of the talent that's around this area to make us competitive."

Due to a rash of defections, the Bucks certainly had a lot of holes to fill, and very big ones to boot. Besides McNeish and Rydbom, top players such as Albe Wales, Jeff Best, Gary Spizzirri, Bill Gordon, Allen Potter, Dale Keith, Jeff McCartney, Phil Flipse, Kurt Kessler, and Glen Brandimarte had moved on to their life's work, as the saying goes. Even though the Bucks had already begun preparations for the '77 season, Miller had to announce that anyone interested in playing for the club was still welcome to attend tryouts, which were being held Tuesdays and Thursdays at 6:30pm and on Sundays at 10 a.m. at the Madera field.

When the Bucks announced their schedule for the '77 season, it was another 11-game slate, with seven of the games listed on home fields. For the third straight year, the Bucks would open the season with a game in State College, this time against the Jersey Oaks. The Mid-Atlantic part of the season would then commence with road games in Washington and Youngstown. On August 13th, the Bucks would host the Allegheny-Kiski Stars in DuBois. After an away game in Pittsburgh, the Bucks would then have three straight home games: against the Brooklyn Knights in State College, the Washington Generals in Curwensville and then Youngstown in Clearfield on September 10th. A week later a trip to New Kensington was booked to face the Stars, and then the Bucks would close out the season with two more home contests, in Philipsburg against Pittsburgh and the season finale against the Twin Cities Geminis from North Tonawanda, New York.

But for awhile that summer, it looked like there wouldn't be any games played in Central Pennsylvania.

Some of the summer practices were held with only 10 or 12 players present, and soon word got around that the Bucks were experiencing financial problems and were on the brink of folding. Due to the extreme manpower shortage, the team did not practice for a time, fueling more talk of the team going under.

In mid-July came more shake-ups within the Bucks' ranks. Tom Miller announced that, because of his duties as a coach and teacher at Tyrone, he was stepping down as head coach of the team to concentrate more on his quarterback duties with Rydbom gone.

Miller's decision left the team in a serious lurch. The season opener was just a couple weeks away and the team was suddenly without a head coach.

To replace Miller as head coach with the season just a few weeks away, the team hurriedly signed Don Turley, who had coached Clearfield High School to a combined record of 5-15 in 1964 and '65, as the new head man on July 11th. As it turned out, Turley was exactly the wrong man for the job.

Gary Passarelli from Curwensville was named the defensive coordinator, but Al Siegel announced that the desperate club was still in need of anyone wishing to help out at the coaching, managerial and training levels.

Siegel told the press that the team had about 30 players committed to play, but added that more players were needed, especially offensive and defensive linemen and linebackers.

The changes continued. Two days after Turley was named head coach, Siegel stepped down as General Manager, and was replaced by investor Herman "Hymie" Ziff.

With the change in the front office, team management announced that all positions on the team were now open and that yet more tryouts were being scheduled. The first of these would be held on Saturday the 16th at 4pm and Sunday the 17th from 10am to 12 noon. Both sessions would be held at the Clearfield Driving Park. Team officials again stressed that the Bucks had a big need for big linemen and linebackers.

In yet another important change, the club announced it would negotiate contracts for 1977 with all candidates who made the squad, meaning players would be assured of at least some pay for the first time. Attorney and team investor Jim Naddeo had been authorized to negotiate expense contracts, which would cover driving and meal expenses. As much as $100 could be paid out to each player. This would be the first reimbursement of any kind in the team's short history.

"There were no contracts at all before '77," says Ron Roefaro.

This was a big announcement for the club. Before the offering of contracts, the outlook of players not receiving any pay kept most of the practice sessions that were held in the late spring and early summer of '77 to only about a dozen or so players.

The Bucks' opener, scheduled for July 23rd against the Jersey Oaks at State College's Memorial Field, was fast approaching. Fortunately for the Bucks, with the announcement that contracts were being negotiated for the first time, the turnouts at the team's practices had swelled to around 35 to 40 players.

"Although many of the players signed contracts," Darrel Rutter explains, "it wasn't enough to quit their proverbial 'day jobs.' Many of the players simply used their playing experience with the Bucks to recover a bit of football glory."

Quite a few of the Bucks returned for the third season. Wayne Rockmore, Ron Roefaro, Al Siegel, Dirk Grissinger, Alex Anto, Mitch Mancuso, Charvi

Skillings, the Rutter brothers Ken and Darrel, George Walker, Gary Pheasant, Jim Slabon, and Ritchie Shoop were some of the veterans who had re-upped for another year. Turley was very impressed with the kicking skills of Shoop, and had him down as both the team's kicker and punter. Like many semipros, a player had to sometimes be quite versatile to keep a job. Shoop was a good example of this, capable of kicking as well as playing several other positions, including running back and tight end.

The Bucks' roster included quite a few newcomers for the '77 season. Among these were the Socoski brothers—"Nick and John, really little guys," recalls Darrel Rutter—from Philipsburg. Both brothers were slated for duty as guards on the offensive line.

"I remember they both had big hair, of course a lot of guys did back then, including my brother Ken" adds Rutter, "They didn't play a lot but helped out, and made a difference that way. They made the other guys work harder."

Greg "Bear" Rowles, who could play both the offensive and defensive lines, joined the Bucks bandwagon. A graduate of Clearfield High School, Rowles was a U.S. Air Force veteran, having served in the intelligence unit in Zweiberken, Germany during the Vietnam era.

"He didn't start much, but he was a helluva player," recalls Darrel Rutter, "Didn't have all the ability in the world, but worked hard and tried hard. He was a no-nonsense kind of guy. Loved to play football, but was not somebody you would have thought played ball."

Another set of brothers, Joe and Lenny Crestani from Bald Eagle, signed up for '77. Joe, the oldest brother, was another Buck who had served with the military. A 1967 graduate of Bald Eagle Area High School, Crestani completed Navy 'A' School (Military Construction Battalion #74) later that year, and then served two tours of duty in the U.S. Navy during the Vietnam War. On his return home he attended Gomaco University in Iowa. Joe was penciled in as a tight end, while Lenny was listed as a safety.

"Lenny and Joey, both solid ball players," remembers Darrel Rutter, "Not real outspoken, just quiet guys. They practiced hard, made a good contribution. Not big partiers. Just good solid people, the kind you liked to know."

The Crestanis were an example of what Rutter likes to call, "brothers separated by a number of years who finally had the chance to play on the same team."

Darrel could have been talking about himself and his brothers, Ken, who was returning for his third year, and John, who had decided to join the Bucks despite some serious health problems.

"Our brother John played for the Bucks," says Ken, "He was playing after seven brain tumor operations. Our family was upset about that. Out playing football after spring surgery. To think he was out there just a couple months after surgery playing football."

Bill Bailey, a native of Hyde who had gone on to become an Eastern Wrestling League champion at the University of Pittsburgh, signed on as an inside linebacker. "Bailey was another good player, he had wrestled at Pitt," recalls George Walker, "Tough kid. He could get good leverage on you."

"He had 'wrestler's feet,'" adds Hugh Gibbons.

"He was good, real good," Darrel Rutter adds when describing Bailey, "Very likeable guy. He played his position well and kept his mouth shut. Very teachable."

Quarterback Kevin Detwiler from Tyrone joined the team to back-up Miller and also play wide receiver and defensive back. He was relatively small at 5'7" and 165 pounds, which put him at a disadvantage in the semipro game.

"He played for Tom Miller at Tyrone," says Darrel Rutter, "He was one of Tommy's boys. He was adequate, but really couldn't play well at the semipro level. He was better as a defensive back. He was just too small. Miller tried to play him in the Veer offense. But he wasn't a good leader. Probably because he was just out of high school, and he was just not that type of player. But give him credit, he showed up and he was a little cocky, which I always liked in a player."

Jerry Shivery, an All-State selection and a local legend from Bellefonte, joined the team as a running back. But his time with the Bucks was unfortunately cut short.

"Shivery played for us," says Hugh Gibbons, "He was the only All-American from Bellefonte. But he got hurt and that was it."

One of the little idiosyncrasies of the semi-pro game was the idea of fluid rosters, where players came and went and sometimes even performed under different names. The Bucks' 1977 roster also included one such person, as one of their players was actually playing under an assumed name. "Ted Castle was actually a kid from Penn State who had some eligibility concerns," says Jay Siegel, "so he and his Dad changed his name on the roster."

Miller retained his role as offensive coordinator. Passarelli was running the defense. Carl Brown, a Clearfield native who had played college football at Millersville State College [*now University*] and had gotten a tryout with the Baltimore Colts, was signed on as a tight end and receivers coach.

Thanks to the National Football League Players Association strike in the summer of 1974, players like Brown got a good long look from coaches who might have otherwise ignored them. The strike was the best thing to happen to the rookies and free agents that season. Brown, a three-sport standout at Clearfield Area High and an All-Pennsylvania Colleges Conference tight end at Millersville, seemed to have a good chance to make the Baltimore Colts' roster as he earned starts in the team's first two preseason games. But then he was sidelined with a hip injury that kept him out of two exhibition games, against Atlanta and Washington.

Because of the injury, the Colts asked waivers on him, but he was claimed by Cleveland. Instead of allowing Brown to go to the Browns, the Colts recalled the waivers. Then they gave him his release. Brown contacted Cleveland, who had become interested in him after he played against them in Tampa. But Carl had received no word as to whether they wanted to take a look at him what with the final cuts already having been made.

"Boy, I just gotta get another chance somewhere, if not this year, then next year," Brown told Fred Kavelak of the *Clearfield Progress*. "It was a long time before I realized how much I want to play football.

"Before the problem was opportunity. I didn't know how good I'd be, coming from Millersville and playing against guys from, say, Nebraska. But when you get a taste, you realize you can play with them.

"It was just unfortunate that I got hurt when I did. I had played all those weeks, twice a day at the beginning when I was the only tight end there with nobody to relieve me, and I got in tremendous shape."

When the Colts cut Brown, he returned to the Clearfield Area High faculty.

"I came back to the area and I taught school and worked for Lezzer Lumber in DuBois," Brown recalls, "One of the Bucks' owners came up and found me, said to me that they'd love to have me play. Offered me $40 a game. He asked me if I wanted to play, and I told him, 'Love to.'"

"He was an excellent ballplayer, big kid, good blocker," Darrel Rutter says of Brown, "He had kind of an attitude, like me. He ran his patterns exact, very precise."

"We pulled in players from all over the area," Brown remembers, "and we had some very good players in that area. We played some good teams— Youngstown, Pittsburgh. We played good, hard football. We also had a lot of parties and a lot of fun."

Turley told the press on July 21st that he didn't expect anything fancy from his team in the opener, mainly due to the lack of practice time.

"We'll stick with the pro set." Turley told the *Clearfield Progress* on the eve of the opener, "We want to keep it at a level where we can execute well."

"I feel we'll be presentable," Turley continued after a practice which saw the largest turnout of candidates for any of the tryouts, "Timing is the problem right now. Also, the players aren't in peak physical shape yet. We are still short a few big linemen, both offensively and defensively, and could use a larger back. The Bucks were on the verge of folding up their young outfit just a few weeks ago, but now players are showing and the third season is indeed a reality.

"At the present time we have 44 active players on the roster with seven or eight players we'd like to keep on the taxi squad," the new Buck mentor stated. "The team was practicing throughout the summer with 10–12 players and we had 46 here tonight."

Turley seemed to be well-liked by some of the players, but he miscalculated when he decided to switch All-Star running back Wayne Rockmore, coming off a 1,000-yard season, to a new position.

"Turley tried to turn Rockmore into a wide receiver from a running back," says Hugh Gibbons, "Rock struggled at this new position. On the field when we went to line up, Rock would say to me, 'What do I do on this play?'"

"I could catch the ball as a running back coming out of the backfield, but I couldn't catch as a wide receiver," says Rockmore, "It was just a mental thing."

Still, hopes were high going into the '77 season. The Bucks were no longer "upstarts" according to Darrel Rutter, but a "seasoned team. We were ready to line it up and play."

The Bucks opened the season against the Jersey Oaks. Based in Plainfield in central New Jersey, the Oaks had been around since World War II. Previously known as the Plainfield Red Oaks, the squad had been a member of the Atlantic Coast Semiprofessional Football League, which was one of the most famous minor league football leagues in the nation during the 1960s.

But the team had been re-organized in 1974. At first they were affiliated with both the New York Jets and the World Football League's New York Stars, meaning they could expect to receive some financial and manpower help. But when these lifelines were cut, the Oaks suffered through some bleak times. One year, the team's survival depended on a sale of raffle tickets in local bars and a pledge by each player to sell $250 worth of ads so they could buy uniforms, insurance and equipment.

Despite their financial woes, the Oaks had managed to finish the '76 season with an impressive 11-2 record and did possess a number of players with good size and speed. In the defensive line was 40-year-old Carl Frank, a 6'3", 260-pound tackle who had ended his playing career in the Canadian Football League 10 years before, and tackle Joe Delouise, a 6'3", 240-pounder from Trenton State College.

Their roster also featured a new recruit, a defensive tackle by the name of "Sir" Gilmore. Nobody seemed to know "Sir's" actual first name. And because he went

6'8" and 300 pounds, no one seemed to be in too much of a hurry to ask him. Gilmore was supposedly being groomed to be a defensive tackle for the New York Giants, and was toiling in the MAFL with the Oaks to acquire more seasoning.

At fullback the Oaks had 6'1", 220-pound Larry Parker from Johnson C. Smith College and at tight end was 6'5", 220-pound Tom Cumpa from the University of Miami.

"All we know about Jersey is what they've sent us," said Turley, "They supposedly have players on the Jets' taxi squad and some major college backs. They have talent and a good establishment."

Because he was hired at basically the last minute, Turley's inexperience as a coach was beginning to show, and manifested itself when he was asked about the league his team was playing in.

"I really don't know much about the league other than what I've read about other players matriculating to these clubs from the pro ranks," Turley said on the eve of the season. "Of course, it's much easier to draw top-notch ballplayers from a metropolitan area than from a rural area."

Of course, like many semipro teams, the Bucks didn't have the luxury of things like game films or highlight reels to study in preparation of their next opponent. Practices were simply exercises in getting the team's timing down. Scouting was virtually nonexistent.

Unlike their games in 1975 and '76, when they more often than not were able to put in a good showing no matter the opposition, the Bucks showed a noticeable lack of organization at times during the 1977 campaign. Some of this could be attributed to the lack of practice time, the poor showing for those practices that were held, and the rumors swirling all summer about the team possibly folding. But some of it could also be placed on the shoulders of the inexperienced of their new, and hastily hired, head coach.

For the third straight season, the Bucks opened their season at Memorial Stadium in State College.

State College, a college town dominated by the presence of Penn State and surrounded by large tracts of farmland, as well as mountains and forests, has become the largest borough in all of Pennsylvania, with a population of around 100,000 people in what is locally referred to as the "Centre Region." The borough itself includes about 40,000 residents.

In 1973 State College adopted a home rule charter, which took effect in 1976. Since that time, it has not been governed by the state's Borough Code, although it retains "Borough of State College" as its official name.

For obvious reasons, the Bucks' roster always included a large number of either State College High or Penn State players.

On July 23rd at Memorial Stadium, the Oaks received the opening kickoff and promptly drove to the Bucks' 10-yard line, where they took the lead on a 27-yard field goal by Otto Ormosi.

The Bucks responded with a march to midfield, mostly on the running of Wayne Rockmore. But an untimely illegal procedure penalty stalled the drive, forcing the Whitetail Bucks to punt. Jamie Winters of the Oaks took the punt on his own 15, and then proceeded to run right through the Bucks for 85 yards and a touchdown. Ormosi added the extra point and the Oaks now led 10-0.

Another big play put Central Pennsylvania even further behind the 8-ball. From his own 24, quarterback Glen Morgan whipped a perfect pass to Joe Henry across the middle and Henry raced the rest of the way to complete the 76-yard play. The extra point made it 17-0.

The outlook got bleaker when Rockmore, the Bucks' only offensive threat, went out near the end of the first quarter with a bad ankle. Joe Good stepped in and did help carry the Bucks to the Jersey 31 late in the half, but Central Pennsylvania failed to convert on a 4th and 13 and lost the ball on downs.

Jersey promptly moved downfield again, thanks to three plays that ate up big yardage. With 13 seconds left in the half, Morgan and Henry hooked up again, this time from the 29, to push Jersey further ahead, 23-0. Dirk Grissinger's block of the extra point was the only positive aspect of the proceedings.

The Bucks were able to put things together a little better offensively in the second half. But the sustained drives they were able to mount ended on turnovers or punts. The third quarter ended with the score still 23-0.

In the fourth quarter, the Bucks' problems continued. A bad snap on a punt sailed over Ritchie Shoop's head, and when Shoop retreated into the end zone to recover the ball he had to bat it over the endline to avoid a possible Jersey touchdown. That made it 25-0.

The Oaks soon had possession again and Larry Parker scored on a 50-yard run to put Jersey up, 32-0. The fans, most of whom lined the sidelines instead of paying for seats in the stands, became restless, hooting and yelling at the home club. The Bucks finally broke onto the scoreboard when they recovered a fumbled pitchout, and then scored on their old razzle-dazzler, as Kevin Detwiler pitched out to Ken Rutter who then hurled a strike to a speedy rookie named Mike Morgan for the touchdown.

Central Pennsylvania attempted an onside kick and it worked as they were able to recover. But after a couple penalties on Jersey, another flea-flicker fell incomplete and the Bucks had lost their 1977 opener, 32-6.

It was the Bucks' worst home loss in their history, and third-worst loss overall. Tom Miller completed just 7 of 20 passes for only 59 yards. Joe Good had a decent game, rushing for 67 yards on 17 carries, but the rest of the team managed only five measly yards on the ground.

The Bucks also had some injury and other personnel woes. Rockmore's bum ankle was going to keep him on the bench, which was a serious blow to the Bucks' offense. Defensive end Ed Ardary, a clean-cut kid with a crew cut from Lumber City, was lost for the season with a knee injury. Gary Pheasant had suffered a concussion in the game and was trying to shake off the effects of that, and Darrel Rutter was sidelined with bruised ribs.

Linebacker Joe Williams left the team, and the Bucks were forced to cut both wide receiver Alge Jones and offensive lineman Doug Hrenko because they were not able to make practice. Both players were veterans who had played for the Bucks since the beginning, and would be sorely missed.

It was not a good sign for the Bucks, or for Don Turley.

To try and bolster their quickly depleting defense, the Bucks re-signed defensive end John Stoneberg from Ashville and added Joe Paddock from Indiana, Pennsylvania. Rod Ullein, who had played so effectively for the Bucks in '76, declared he was ready to return to action.

The Bucks got on their bus and drove to Bethel Park, Pa., to face their next opponents, the Washington Generals. When they got off the bus, they received news that the Generals were having problems securing a field for the game. The Washington team management tried to resolve problems with the Bethel Park School Board right up into early evening in an attempt to use the junior high field. But the Generals could not obtain permission to use the field, and therefore had to forfeit. The Bucks had a win in the books, but it would have been nice if Washington officials had forewarned the team about their issues. But such was life in the minor leagues. Just so the trip wasn't a total loss, the Bucks trucked over to Duquesne to watch the Youngstown Hardhats, their next opponents, crush the Pittsburgh Ironmen.

Their scouting trip did not help the Bucks against the Hardhats. "Youngstown was always tough," remembers Tom Marlett, "They were always big and hit hard all game long. We'd go into those games and we knew we didn't have a chance but we showed up anyhow."

The Bucks showed up in Youngstown.

And they didn't have a chance.

Darrel Rutter and Kurt Kessler try to block a field goal attempt against the Sharon Old Express in 1976. *Courtesy of the collection of Darrel Rutter.*

Don Turley was hired as head coach just a week before the 1977 season. The lack of preparation and organization soon showed. *Courtesy of the collection of Tom Miller.*

For finishing 2nd in 1977, the Bucks won this trophy. Pittsburgh actually finished 2nd but they owed the league money so the trophy went to the Bucks. *Courtesy of the collection of Jay Siegel.*

George Walker (76) and Wayne Rockmore (23) prepare for a game in 1977. *Courtesy of the collection of Tom Miller.*

Quarterback Tom Miller (10) rolls out in the Bucks very first game against Brooklyn in 1975. *The Clearfield Progress.*

Running back Joe Good of Philipsburg on the run against Youngstown. *Courtesy of the collection of Tom Miller.*

Running backs Tom Hipp from Altoona and Charvi Skillings from Tyrone. *The Clearfield Progress.*

Back cover of the 1976 Bucks program.
*Courtesy of the collection of Tom Miller.*

# CENTRAL PENNSYLVANIA WHITETAIL BUCKS

## Semi-Professional Football Team

| | | |
|---|---|---|
| Sat. July 31 | 8:00 | Brooklyn J & A Golden Knights (sc) |
| Sun. Aug 8 | 2:30 | Boonton, New Jersey Bears (p) |
| Sat. Aug 14 | 8:00 | Brooklyn Mariners (al) |
| Sun. Aug 22 | 2:00 | Washington Generals (g) |
| Sat. Aug 28 | 8:00 | Pittsburgh Iron Men (away) |
| Sat. Sept 4 | 8:00 | Beaver County Cougars (cu) |
| Sun. Sept 12 | 1:30 | Sharon Old Express (away) |
| Sat. Sept 18 | 8:00 | Washington Generals (away) |
| Sat. Sept 25 | 8:00 | Pittsburgh Iron Men (p) |
| Sun. Oct 3 | 2:00 | Beaver County Cougars (away) |
| Sat. Oct 9 | 8:00 | Sharon Old Express (c) |

(al) - Altoona High School Field
(c) - Clearfield Driving Park Field
(cu) - Curwensville High School Field
(p) - Philipsburg High School Field
(sc) - State College High School Field
(g) - Glendale High School Field

(*Below*) The Bucks in a practice session at Madera, Pennsylvania. *Courtesy of the collection of Tom Miller.*

# CHAPTER

# 8

"He was a good Christian man who couldn't handle
all the stuff that was going on."
—QUARTERBACK TOM MILLER ON HEAD COACH DON TURLEY

Youngtown was a culturally-diverse city that had been a major producer of coal for much of the 20th century. But when the coal industry fell into decline in the mid- and late-70s, the economy of Youngstown also fell off drastically. Like much of the "Rust Belt," Youngstown's population dwindled, falling from a high of over 170,000 in 1930 to around 125,000 in the mid-70s. Parts of the city fell into disrepair.

"We played in Youngstown, that field was in a bad section of town," remembers Hugh Gibbons.

"There was this nightclub in Youngstown, and it was owned by the Mafia," recalls Darrel Rutter, "We were warned not to ask the women to dance."

But the success of the Hardhats had galvanized the city's sports fans, and brought some sense of pride to a city that like many in the Northeast were going through some very tough times. Lou Piccone had played for Youngstown in the early 1970s and then made it to the NFL with the Jets. According to *Pro Football Weekly* magazine, Youngstown was the Number One ranked semipro football team in the country for the 1977 season. They had opened their season with a 33-28 win over the Pittsburgh Ironmen in Duquesne. The Hardhat players were treated like royalty in Youngstown.

One such player was quarterback Vern Wireman, who was from Warren, Ohio, and had played collegiately at Bowling Green. In the opener against

Pittsburgh, Wireman had tossed four touchdown passes, three of them to Lou Kelson. Wireman would wind up making the Mid-Atlantic All-League team in 1977. On August 6th, he showed why he deserved the honor when the Bucks played the Hardhats in Lowellville High Stadium in Youngstown.

Wireman completed 13 of 18 passes for 180 yards and the Hardhats scored on every one of their first half possessions. For the second game in a row, the Bucks were never in the contest.

Youngstown took the opening kickoff and rolled 70 yards in 10 plays. Running back Sam Fant plowed over from the two and the 'hats led 6-0 after Kirk Andrews' placement sailed wide to the left.

The Bucks, playing without the Rock, Wayne Rockmore, couldn't move the sticks and punted the ball away. Youngstown moved the ball to the Bucks' 32, but Jim Slabon picked off a pass at his own 6-yard line and returned it to the 21. Slabon was hit hard and the ball popped loose, however, and Youngstown had the ball right back. Wireman took advantage of that gift with a 20-yard pass to Rich Morris. Fant then scored his second touchdown on a one-yard burst. Andrews added the extra point and Youngstown led 13-0.

The game quickly went from bad to worse for Central Pennsylvania. Ritchie Shoop was trapped when he went back to punt and was buried for a 13-yard loss at his own 22. Youngstown made it look easy as Wireman hit Morris with an 18-yard scoring toss several plays later to make it 20-0.

"Youngstown especially burned our defensive backs," linebacker Tom Marlett remembers.

The Bucks finally managed to put together a decent drive as Joe Good and Shoop took turns at punching their way through the Youngstown defense, and carried the Whitetail Bucks to the Hardhats' 25. But Tom Miller, who had another ineffective game, picked the absolute worse time to give up an interception. Jim Mayberry stepped in front of Miller's pass at his own 15 and returned it to the 30. Wireman's aerials to Morris and Lou Kelson moved the ball to the 9, from where Jim Smith rolled around left end for the touchdown. The extra point made it 27-0, and the Hardhats weren't done yet.

After another Bucks' possession went nowhere, Youngstown took over on its own 38. Wireman once again marched the 'hats downfield, taking them 62 yards in a drive capped by Lee Stringer's 2-yard run. The placement made it 34-0 at the half.

The Hardhats definitely were making life difficult for the Bucks.

"We played Youngstown in '77, and they were the Number One ranked semipro team in the country," says Hugh Gibbons, "I tackled a guy on the kickoff right near their sideline, and their guys are all flapping their gums at me. Next thing I knew I was lined up and there's this Neanderthal lined up across from me, and he laid into me. That was meant to teach me a lesson."

Just as they had done in the opener against Jersey, Central Pennsylvania showed some improvement in the second half. They did manage to put together solid drives that reached the Youngstown 45, 34 and 12 yard lines, but each march ended with the Bucks turning the ball over on downs. The Bucks finally scored, but it was the defense that did it, as Dirk Grissinger nailed reserve quarterback Rusty Preston in the end zone for a safety.

But the Hardhats piled it on in the last quarter with two more touchdowns, by Preston and Stringer. That set the final at 47-2, the worst loss in team history.

The Bucks' offense had looked helpless against the Youngstown defense. They managed only 22 yards on the ground and a paltry 75 through the air. Miller struggled again, hitting just 9 of 20 passes. Youngstown, meanwhile, rolled up 17 first downs and 324 yards in total offense.

In their two losses, the team had been outscored 79-8. Only the forfeit win over Washington kept the Bucks' record from being worse. This was definitely not the same team that had been competitive in almost every game in their first two years. They had never been embarrassed like they had been in their two losses in 1977.

Something had to be done.

At every level of football—high school, college and the pros—the day after game day is an off-day for the players, with no practice or any other team function scheduled. It's a day used to heal wounds and rest weary bodies.

But not for the Central Pennsylvania Whitetail Bucks. On Sundays after a grueling, hard fought Saturday game and at times a long bus ride home, the Bucks got up on Sundays . . . and played football!

That's right, these men, who played semipro football simply for the love of the game, who traveled great distances for practices and games and got very little, or nothing at all, in the way of a paycheck, loved the game so much that after playing on Saturdays they got out of bed on Sundays and played flag football.

"The Bucks would play on Saturday, then we'd get up on Sunday and play flag football," says Joe Wales, "They hit you just as hard in them as in the Bucks game."

"A lot of the guys who played for the Bucks also played flag football on Sunday," adds Ron Roefaro.

"We all played flag football on Sundays," recalls Darrel Rutter, "We play like hell on Saturday then come back out the next day and play hard again at flag football. Those other teams we played were good. We wound up trying to recruit some of the flag football players to join the Bucks."

The Whitetail Bucks were definitely a unique group of men. Despite having full-time jobs, practicing several evenings a week and then playing on Saturday afternoon or evening, the Bucks loved the game of football and playing the game of football so much that they thought nothing of getting up on their "day off" and playing again.

The Whitetail Bucks were enjoying life, doing what they loved most, playing football. But in the Mid Atlantic Football League, the team was struggling. During their first two campaigns, the Bucks were competitive and played all their opponents, even powerhouses like Pittsburgh and Brooklyn, tough, and the games were hard-fought struggles. Now, however, the Bucks seemed listless. The spark of '75 and '76 seemed to be gone. They had been blown out easily in two games, and had scored a total of eight points. Something just wasn't right. That something was the head coach.

"From what I can remember, Don Turley was a quiet and very neatly organized man who wasn't used to coaching adult players who didn't always follow what you wanted them to do," recalls Ron Roefaro, "He quit after the Youngstown game when we were soundly beaten by them. I think there was some frustration on his part about the team not following most of his suggestions."

"A really great teacher, great guy and good coach and should have stayed with the team longer," offers Darrel Rutter when asked about Turley, "But, it was probably good for the team that he left. He did have problems because he was used to dealing with high school kids, and was not prepared for the hard-nosed guys who played for the Bucks. He tried being a disciplinarian and that didn't work."

"Don Turley," remembers Tom Miller, "He lasted just a couple games. He was a good Christian man who couldn't handle all the stuff that was going on."

To be fair, Turley had been basically thrown to the wolves, named head coach just before the season started and during a period of time when there was real talk of the team folding. What with the management upheaval and front office changes as well as very real rumors of the team going under, the Bucks had very little pre-season practice time, and it hurt the team and its relationship with their coach. Turley also had very little time to instill his own offensive and defensive philosophies, and never was able to get his charges under any sort of control.

This lack of control, however, can be traced in part to the fact that Turley did come in with basically a high school background, and tried to run the Bucks with a disciplinarian attitude. That approach just didn't work with many of the

Bucks. While some of them were just out of high school, many were men who had gone to college or were laboring at full-time jobs in the mills and for the railroad. Quite a few were also veterans who had served with the armed forces and seen action in Vietnam. These were hardened older men who drank, cussed and partied and who didn't take to the methods Turley brought to the table.

"Discipline has to come from within in a situation like that," recalls Carl Brown.

"We lost to Youngstown badly, I mean we had our butts handed to us and all he could say was 'Yeah, yeah, yeah . . .'" says George Walker, "Finally we said to him, 'Why don't you just go home?'"

Shortly after the loss to Youngstown, Turley did just that.

The Bucks named their defensive coordinator, Gary Passarelli of Curwensville, the new head coach. Passarelli had played football and wrestled for the Curwensville High Golden Tide in the late 1960s.

"I didn't have any problems with Gary, I guess maybe because Tom Miller, our quarterback ran the offense," says Ron Roefaro.

At least one Buck, however, didn't see Passarelli as an improvement.

"He was a good guy but I didn't care for him as a coach," says Darrel Rutter when describing Passarelli, "I didn't like how he handled people. My thought is don't be a 'semi-coach' . . . he just didn't step up and was not a good fit."

With their new head coach now at the helm, the Bucks faced the Allegheny-Kiski Stars in Mansell Stadium in DuBois.

For those not from the Central Pennsylvania area, DuBois is pronounced Doo-boys, and not Doo-BWAH. Say it wrong and you'll quickly be corrected. It's located in Clearfield County, approximately 100 miles northeast of Pittsburgh, and has a population of a little over 7,000 people.

Settled in 1812, DuBois was incorporated as a borough in 1881 and as a city in 1914.

The town was founded by a fellow by the name of John Rumbarger, for whom the town was originally named. The Rumbarger Cemetery is all that survives of that original settlement. The town was later renamed for local lumber magnate John DuBois. While the city was founded as a lumber town, the mining of bituminous coal, a huge business in the entire region, quickly became the chief industry in DuBois. But there were other diverse businesses as well, such as paper production, concrete, machinery and equipment.

The city was also home to DuBois Brewing, which opened in the late 1800s. Owner Frank Hahne, who chose DuBois as the site for his brewery due to the excellent local water supply, bought up 2,300 acres of land and by 1906 had four products on the market: DuBois Wurzburger, Hahne's Export Pilsener, DuBois Porter and DuBois Budweiser, which, one could imagine, caused a bit of a controversy what with the presence of Anheuser-Busch on the market. Soon, Hahne was shipping his product to Buffalo, Erie and Pittsburgh.

Hahne did quite well until Prohibition hit, but to battle the new law, Hahne shifted production to items such as "near beer" and soft drinks and also opened an ice company. The brewery won the honor of being one of only two breweries in the entire nation that didn't violate the 18th amendment.

Frank Hahne died in 1932, and the brewery was passed to his only son, Frank Hahne Jr., whose own only son died in infancy, leaving the family without an heir. Hahne Jr. sold the brewery to Pittsburgh Brewing in 1967.

The Allegheny-Kiski Stars were from an area of Western Pennsylvania where the Allegheny and Kiskiminetas—known locally as the Kiski—Rivers form the Allegheny-Kiski Valley where Armstrong, Allegheny, Butler and Westmoreland Counties meet. The area had a rich sports heritage, having produced such figures as basketball coach Buddy Jeannette, football stars Cookie Gilchrist and Dick and Ed Modzelewski, football coach Bud Carson and major-leaguer Mickey Morandini.

The Stars were 1-0 so far in the MAFL, but were experiencing some internal problems. "We had a conflict of personalities on the Stars," recalled safety Henry Lincoln in 1985, "Everyone wanted to be *the* star."

The game was notable for two things—the return of the Rock, Wayne Rockmore, to the Bucks lineup, and as a breakthrough game for wide receiver Mike Morgan from Clearfield.

"Mike Morgan was one of our younger guys," recalls Rockmore, "He was mouthy but quiet. He had a lot of speed and could catch. He was a basketball player which helped him."

Morgan had played little in the first two games of the '77 season, but the Allegheny-Kiski game allowed him to show what he could do and he would wind up as the Bucks' leading receiver in 1977.

"Did a helluva job for us," Darrel Rutter says of Morgan, "Very good wide receiver. If the ball was anywhere near him he'd catch it. Had very good hands and speed. Very smooth moves, and had deceptive speed. He could just outrun guys."

Rockmore, meanwhile, after having rushed for over 1,000 yards for the Bucks during the 1976 campaign, had been counted on to spearhead the Bucks ground game once again in 1977. But the Rock was injured in the first quarter of the season's first game and without him the Bucks' ground game had sputtered to a virtual halt.

But with the Rock's return to the backfield, the Bucks began to show some of their old flash and dash again. They looked like a team reborn.

The opening drive of the game was almost all Rockmore, as he carried the ball five straight times for 31 yards, the last carry going for one yard and six points. The march covered 55 yards on 11 plays, and Ritchie Shoop tacked on the extra point and the Bucks owned a 7-0 edge.

Incredibly, this was the first time the Bucks had led a game all season!

Before the Stars could regroup after the Bucks' first drive, Central Pennsylvania's Al Butler, a 5'10" 165 pound rookie defensive back from Clearfield, pounced on a Stars' fumble on his own 47 yard line. It took just one play for the Bucks to light up the board again. Ken Rutter connected with Morgan on a 53-yard touchdown pass off the team's old staple, the "flea flicker," which had been one of the Bucks' favorite plays since the team's inception in 1975.

Holder Jim Slabon tried to run in the extra point after a mix-up on the snap, but he failed to make it to the end zone, which kept the Buck lead at 13-0.

Early in the second quarter, the Bucks and their newfound weapon, Mike Morgan, struck again. This time Morgan got open in the secondary and grabbed a 14-yard aerial from quarterback Tom Miller to up the Bucks advantage to 19-0. The score capped an 11-play, 57-yard march.

Central Pennsylvania was shortly knocking on the door again. Al Butler registered his second turnover of the game, picking off a Jackie Battles' pass and racing 20 yards to the Allegheny-Kiski 19 yard line. That threat, however, ended on the next play when Miller's throw to Carl Brown was intercepted in the end zone.

The Stars got a break late in the second period when Shoop got a bad snap from center on a punt attempt and was thrown for a 35-yard loss all the way back to his own 12. The Stars failed to cash in, however, when Bucks' linebacker Tom Marlett picked off a pass in the end zone.

The two teams traded punts throughout most of the third quarter before the Stars put together their best offensive drive of the night, using up almost six minutes of the clock to march 77 yards in 17 plays and a penalty. Running back Tom Manley, who wound up as the Stars' biggest offensive threat with 72 yards rushing on 10 carries, got the touchdown for Allegheny-Kiski with a five-yard run. The extra point try was sabotaged by a bad snap.

Allegheny-Kiski refused to quit, and Battles went to the air when the Stars took over on their own 35 late in the game. He quickly completed four passes, the last one a 22-yard touchdown throw to Mike McCloud. The extra point was missed again, but the Bucks' once comfortable lead was now down to 19-12.

The Bucks took over and kept the ball on the ground in an attempt to eat up the remaining time on the clock. The drive was so effective that the Bucks managed to move the ball all the way to the Stars' six-yard line. From there, Miller decided to go to the air one last time, and the veteran quarterback found the speedy Morgan on a third down aerial for the touchdown.

The six-pointer touched off an altercation in the end zone. The field was quickly cleared by the referees but no extra point attempt was made, and the rejuvenated Bucks walked off the field with an impressive 25-12 win.

Morgan finished the game with five catches for 84 yards and three touchdowns. Miller had an efficient evening, completing four of 10 passes. Rockmore rushed for 90 yards on only 10 carries, and Joe Good pounded his way for 53 yards. The Bucks had evened their record at 2-2 and in the process looked like their old selves again. They had played with renewed energy and purpose.

The Bucks would need every ounce of that energy and purpose when they faced off against their old nemeses, the Pittsburgh Ironmen, a week later at Duquesne.

Pittsburgh, the two-time defending league champions, was not having one of their usual stellar years, and had started the season with a record of 0-3. Quarterback Don Folden, who had played so well against the Bucks in 1976 and made the All-League squad, had been switched to defensive back and replaced by Rich DeMao, a 6'3" 205-pounder from the University of Cincinnati. The Ironmen also had Jim Bulger from Notre Dame available to call signals. Bulger was 26 and after 4 years of semipro football had taken a year off. Now he was back.

"I didn't miss it much that one year," Bulger said at the time, "There are a lot of things the fans don't realize. But I'm back, with no aspirations of getting back to pro ball. It's just fun and it's rewarding. It's good just to be playing again."

Another All-Leaguer, running back Ed Farmer, was limping on a bad leg he had injured in a loss to Youngstown. To take his place, the Ironmen had Pitt rookie Ed Brosky.

"I'll run 'til I drop if I can, because I want to make the most of every day," said Brosky, a back-up on the Panthers' 1976 national championship squad, "That's why I play football. I have no dependents. Now's the time if I'm hurt, that's an occupational hazard."

But make no mistake, despite their record, the Ironmen were still a formidable team. Two of their losses had been to undefeated teams, the Columbus Stingers, whose roster featured 14 ex-Ohio State players, and the Clarksburg, West Virginia, Red Raiders.

Their defense, manned once again by All-Leaguers Leo Henne, Julius Foy, Tim Bentley, and Jim "Dr. Sack" Chapas, was still solid. Split end Dennis Koch, another All-League choice, was back catching passes, and kicker Pete Ross was still splitting the uprights. The Ironmen would be no pushovers.

But Rockmore, looking more and more like he was fully recovered from his early-season ankle injury, dented the Ironmen defense for 116 yards rushing and a touchdown. Mike Morgan caught another touchdown pass. The pair, however, could have sued their teammates for non-support. The Bucks reverted to their early season ways as their offense performed inconsistently and made a rash of errors.

The game started out on a positive note as Rockmore raced 63 yards for a touchdown in the first quarter to give the Bucks an early lead. Perhaps there was light at the end of the tunnel for the Bucks after all. But that light turned out to be an oncoming train, and that train was the Pittsburgh Ironmen.

Ritchie Shoop never had a chance to kick the extra point as Pittsburgh poured in to smother the attempt.

A pass interference call on the Bucks got the Ironmen rolling on the ensuing drive and they marched 49 yards on just five plays, with Jerrold Howard running in from the 18 with 3:20 left in the opening quarter. The extra point put the Ironmen ahead 7-6.

Early in the second quarter, Central Pennsylvania found itself in a fourth-and-nine situation at its own 33. Back to punt, Shoop instead took the snap and tried to run around end. The Ironmen were not fooled and buried Ritchie for a 16-yard loss.

The Ironmen took advantage of that break, needing just six plays to take a 14-6 edge. Ed Orendi scored from the two and Pete Ross kicked his second extra point with 9:18 remaining in the half.

The mistakes continued to pile up. Tom Miller fumbled the ball and Pittsburgh returned it to the Bucks' 12-yard line midway through the second stanza. Two plays later Ed Farmer ran in for the touchdown from the 10-yard line. Ross missed the extra point but the Ironmen still led, 20-6.

The Bucks refused to go down without a fight. Albe Wales picked off a pass at his own 49 and returned it 20 yards to the Pittsburgh 31. Back-to-back passes from Miller to Mike Morgan, one for 11 yards and the second for 20 yards and the touchdown, cut the deficit to 20-13 after Shoop tacked on the extra point near the end of the half.

But it was as close as Central Pennsylvania could get. The offense never got inside the Pittsburgh 40 in the second half.

The Bucks were in immediate trouble in the third quarter. The team tried its patented "flea-flicker" play on the first play of the second half. Ken Rutter's pass was intercepted, however, and not long after that Kevin Thompson scooted in from the four to up the Pittsburgh lead to 26-13.

The Ironmen tacked on one last touchdown on a 2-yard run by Brosky, the rookie from Pitt, with 1:43 left in the third quarter. Ross tacked on the extra point, to put the final at 33-13.

The Rock rushed for those 116 yards but got little help in return, as the rest of the team could muster only 78 yards in offense. Joe Good was buried every time he carried the ball and managed only 8 yards in 8 carries. Tom Miller hit on just 5 of 20 passes and had two throws intercepted as well as losing the costly fumble. The offense was so ineffective that Shoop had to punt 7 times.

Still, the Bucks were 2-2 in the Mid-Atlantic League, and 2-3 overall. The season wasn't lost yet.

Next up was a home tilt against the Brooklyn Golden Knights, another old foe, coached by Lou Williams, a former member of the New York Giants organization. The Knights were the seventh-ranked semipro team in the country, and had beaten the Bucks 30-13 in 1975 and 13-7 in overtime in 1976. They had lost just once in 1977.

Twenty-three members were back from that '76 team, including half-back Charlie "Blue" Smith, offensive tackle and George Walker nemesis Earl Belgrave, defensive back and Ohio State grad Alex Hall, Florida A & M defensive back Clark Jones, Kent State linebacker Elijah Stephens and former Penn Stater Glenn Ford, a big, tough defensive end.

The fans at State College's Memorial Field, who numbered somewhere between 350 and 400 people, were hoping for a competitive game, but the Bucks, in the words of Fred Kavelak of the *Clearfield Progress*, "hit rock-bottom."

The game got off to a positive start when John Stoneberg of the Bucks recovered "Blue" Smith's fumble on the very first play from scrimmage. But the Bucks squandered that opportunity and the drive died on the Brooklyn 45.

After a punt, the Golden Knights promptly paraded 74 yards in just five plays, and made it look very easy, too easy in fact, in the process. Halfback Ron West, who opened the drive with a 15-yard run, slashed his way behind the left guard and zipped 16 yards for the TD with just a little over five minutes gone in the game. Louis "Country" Waters, so named because he was from Durham, North Carolina, kicked the extra point.

A 66-yard punt return by Brooklyn's Jerome Wenton on the second play of the second period set up a one-yard touchdown by Smith. Slabon blocked Waters' conversion try, but it was still 13-0.

The Bucks defense performed very well at times and displayed the opportunistic ways that had worked so well in the past. Bill Bailey had a fumble recovery, and Stoneberg and Slabon added interceptions. Offensive lineman Greg "The Bear" Rowles also had a fumble recovery when Brooklyn's Clarence Jones coughed up the ball after making an interception.

But the defense was sabotaged by a pitiful offensive showing, a performance that Kavelak wrote "ranks as the worst in the two and a half years the Bucks have been tangling with generally bigger and quicker clubs."

An attempted "flea flicker" lost 33 yards when the lateral was fumbled and then kicked and slapped backwards. Backup quarterback Kevin Detwiler was sacked several times. Detwiler and Tom Miller could only manage to complete 5 passes in 20 attempts for a scant 19 yards, and each threw an interception. The Bucks muffed two punts and also lost a fumble. Central Pennsylvania ran the ball 33 times in the game. They gained all of eight yards.

The Bucks, who had only three first downs in the first half, missed a golden opportunity when Slabon picked off a Knight aerial on his own 12 and raced all the way to the Brooklyn 36 behind some good blocks by his teammates and a little shifty running of his own. Central Pennsylvania managed to move the ball to the Brooklyn 25, but a Miller pass was intercepted by Jones, the defensive back from Florida A & M, who made a nice return before he fumbled the ball away, with Rowles recovering for the Bucks at the Brooklyn 40.

The Bucks got a break when an offsides penalty against the Knights on fourth-and-four gave the hosts a first down at the Brooklyn 29. But Wayne Rockmore then had the ball stripped away from him on a sweep, and "Bad News" Bonds recovered for the Knights.

Although they played well at times, the Central Pennsylvania defense never could solve the Knights' passing game and were particularly vulnerable to the sweeps Brooklyn ran most of the game.

The visitors marched 53 yards in nine plays for their third score. They got a break on the touchdown when quarterback Tom Green's pass over the middle was deflected by Buck linebacker Dirk Grissinger, but wide receiver Jim Phillips alertly caught the rebound deep in the end zone. Only seven seconds remained in the half when Waters booted the 20th point.

Bailey's fumble recovery at his own 16 halted a Brooklyn drive early in the second half. The Bucks moved into scoring position, but their struggling offense needed lots of help in the way of two 15-yard penalties—for roughing the passer and a personal foul—and a 19-yard penalty—for pass interference—on the Knights. The Bucks' offense contributed just 28 yards to the drive.

Two incomplete passes at the seven prompted Passarelli to opt for a field goal, and Shoop's boot came with 6:07 to go in the quarter. That made it 20-3.

But the Bucks' problems continued. A second muffed punt by Ken Rutter proved disastrous for the Bucks in the fourth quarter. Elijah Stevens picked up the ball and returned it to the Central Pennsylvania 13. On second down from the 11, Wenton circled right end and broke several tackles on a jaunt to paydirt. Waters' conversion put the final at 27-3.

Fortunately for the Bucks, Brooklyn coughed up the ball three times and dropped at least four interceptions which would have been sure touchdowns. Otherwise, the final score would have been catastrophic. The offense managed only 27 total yards. As Fred Kavelak wrote in the *Progress*, "Central Pennsylvania's performance was not one to keep the fans coming back."

The crowd had been disappointing, but the struggling Bucks were not giving the fans a reason to come out and watch. And they needed much bigger crowds to pay the bills. The team was caught in an all-too familiar semipro vicious circle. No wins, no fans, no money.

Hopefully, the Bucks next game, at Curwensville's Riverside Stadium, would draw a better crowd.

That game was originally supposed to be against the Washington Generals. But the Generals, who had been experiencing financial struggles for years, had decided to scrap the season and had folded, while hoping to make a fresh start in 1978. So the Bucks were awarded their second win by way of forfeit of the season.

Replacing the Generals on the schedule were the Pittsburgh Black Knights, a team the Bucks had never played. But they would make an impression on the Whitetail Bucks, and not a very positive one at that. Let's just say they weren't the team's favorite opponent.

"The Pittsburgh Black Knights, now they were a little dirty," recalls George Walker.

"They had a guy who just clubbed me over the head on every play," says Hugh Gibbons.

Fortunately for the Whitetail Bucks, the Black Knights, as Rod Frisco wrote in the *Clearfield Progress*, seemed to be "more concerned with throwing fists than blocks." The game would be marred by a bench-clearing brawl late in the third quarter that brought an early halt to the contest.

"We had a big fight at Curwensville," recalls Carl Brown, "It got a little out of hand."

The Bucks would take advantage of the fairly disorganized Knights and play their best game of the season.

Playing before a respectable crowd of about 600 in Riverside Stadium, the Bucks were consistently in Knight territory. On their first drive of the evening, Central Pennsylvania penetrated to the Pittsburgh 10 before giving up the ball on downs. The Bucks defense held and forced the Knights into a punting situation. The snap, however, sailed through the end zone and the Bucks took a 2-0 lead with exactly seven minutes left in the first quarter.

Just as they had often done in the past, the Bucks decided it was time for a bit of trickeration. Once again, they went to their old reliable "flea-flicker" play, and it worked to perfection. Just 44 seconds after the safety, Kevin Detwiler tossed the ball back to Jim Slabon who whipped a beautiful pass to the speedy Mike Morgan on the run at the 20. Morgan raced away from his pursuers and completed the 50-yard touchdown bomb. Ritchie Shoop's point was straight through for a 9-0 lead.

The teams traded punts and Pittsburgh finally threatened late in the first quarter when quarterback Nate Lee hit Rick Dutrieuille on a 61-yard bomb to give the Knights a first down at the Bucks' 9. The Bucks defense refused to give up any yards to the Knights, and then Al Butler momentarily ended the threat by intercepting a Lee pass at his own 5.

The Bucks proceeded to cough up the ball on a fumble on the next play, however, at their own 12. But once again the defense stepped up, surrendering just one yard on the next four plays to keep the shutout intact.

The Bucks later took possession after a punt at their own 20. From there, they went 80 yards in nine plays with the aid of a 15-yard penalty to score with just 1:57 to play in the first half. Wayne Rockmore raced in from four yards away around left end. But the Rock twisted his ankle on the play and was done for the evening. Shoop drilled the kick to make it 16-0.

Not long after that the Whitetail Bucks missed a chance for three more points. Dirk Grissinger snared an errant Lee pass at the Pittsburgh 42. Central Pennsylvania managed to work their way to the Black Knights' 8-yard line, but Shoop's 26-yard field goal attempt was wide to the right with just three seconds remaining before intermission. Still, the Bucks held a commanding 16-0 edge.

The third quarter was all Central Pennsylvania, as the Bucks pulled away from the visitors with a pair of touchdowns. The first one was set up by Tom Marlett who intercepted a Knight pass at his own 46. The Whitetail Bucks kept the ball on the ground during the drive as Joe Good and Bill "Clicker" Clark from DuBois took turns knifing into the Pittsburgh defense. Clark's 29-yard burst put the ball at the Pittsburgh 12 and the offense worked its way to the 5-yard line. Detwiler then decided to go to the air, throwing toward Carl Brown over the middle. Brown made a terrific one-handed catch for the touchdown, capping a fine night for him. The big rangy tight end hauled in four passes for 55 yards. Shoop's conversion attempt was wide right.

Central Pennsylvania forced yet another turnover on the very next series. Bill Bailey stormed in from his linebacker post to block Jerome Smith's punt. The Bucks recovered at the Pittsburgh 4 and three plays later, Good went over from the one. A bad snap forced Slabon to throw the ball on the extra point try, but he managed to find Joe Crestani open in the end zone for the conversion. For once in 1977, everything was going right for the Bucks.

The frustration of the evening started to show on the Knights. A nifty 18-yard pass from Lee to Sammy Jones ended up being fumbled into the arms of Central Pennsylvania's Bill Mumma at the Pittsburgh 37. That turn of events touched off an altercation that was quickly broken up.

But the extra-curricular fireworks then went off in earnest on the next play. Tom Miller's pass for Brown fell to the ground incomplete. As the ball bounced harmlessly away, a Black Knight defender ran up and proceeded to slam into Brown in a blatant late hit.

"This guy came up and cut my legs out from under me and flipped me over," says Brown.

Tempers then flared and both benches emptied, because, as Brown remembers, "I took his helmet off and belted him in the face."

Nothing else came of it and there were no injuries, ejections—despite Brown's punch—or penalties resulting.

"They started some things, but we finished them," explains George Walker.

The Bucks ran off another play to end the third quarter. Some of the Knights were still fuming and decided to take it out on the officials with a verbal assault. The referee quickly marched off consecutive personal foul penalties and things began to heat up once more. Wisely, the Pittsburgh coaches decided that the game had run its course and both teams retired to the locker room. Some of the Bucks claim that the Pittsburgh players started fighting with their own coaches, and that a locker room door was kicked in. In any event, the Bucks had themselves a solid 29-0 victory, and had played a fine game on both sides of the ball.

Offensively, Central Pennsylvania came alive with 194 yards rushing, 121 yards passing and 20 first downs, a vast improvement over the previous week's fiasco against Brooklyn. "Clicker" Clark and Joe Good paced the Bucks' ground game with 63 and 55 yards, respectively. Meanwhile, Kevin Detwiler was 4-of-4 passing for 61 yards and one touchdown.

On defense, the Bucks were outstanding, displaying the level of play they had shown in '75 and '76 when they had earned themselves a reputation as one of the better defensive units in the MAFL. They picked off four Knight passes, recovered a fumble, blocked a punt and held the Knights' to 150 yards in total offense. Pittsburgh could manage just 39 rushing yards and quarterback Nate Lee connected on just four of 20 passes.

The win was a much-needed one for the struggling Bucks, who were playing better under head coach Gary Passarelli.

"The team jelled," Darrel Rutter says, "We just happened to do better after Turley left."

Despite the team's problems, the players never lost that sense of camaraderie and "family" they had developed over the years. To a man, the Bucks recall that the team grew very close and looked out for each other.

"On the field we were one team," remembers George Walker, "We took care of each other. Give you the shirt off our back."

"We got along although we were from different backgrounds, different parts of the state," offers Joe Wales.

"The team was a very tight-knit group," adds Wayne Rockmore, "I really enjoyed playing with those guys. We joked around a lot, but we were a team. If we were on our game, we were tough to stop."

"We were like a family," recalls Darrel Rutter, "It was unreal. We couldn't be any closer than we were with the Bucks. It didn't matter if you were all-pro, or a sub or whatever, you were a part of it, part of the team. The older guys looked out for the younger guys. Helped them out. We took care of each other. Those guys were closer to me than family . . . you went to war with them. We'd do anything for each other. When it came time to play everyone was serious."

That camaraderie is still evident years later. During interviews for this book in July of 2015, Paul Kanagy excused himself and said he had to go and check on his father, who was battling Alzheimer's. George Walker asked him if he needed anything. "If anybody needs anything, we're still a family," Walker said after Kanagy had left, "We look out for each other."

But like even the best of families, the Bucks had their share of conflict. It's impossible to spend any amount of time together and not have disagreements and clashes of personalities. A lot of these differences came about because even though the players enjoyed playing and had fun, they still cared very much about what they did and took the game they played and loved very seriously.

"We had problems with folks who didn't have the dedication," explains Wayne Rockmore.

"There was not a whole lot of politics involved in semipro ball," says Darrel Rutter, "You either produced or got the hell out. It got to the point where we had fistfights even among our own players. We were serious about the game. If you screwed up you heard about it"

"Alex Anto and I got into a fight during the game," recalls George Walker, "We were pushing and shoving each other."

There was probably nobody on the team that treated the game as seriously as George Walker.

"No one to mess with," Darrel Rutter says of Walker, "Got mad at our punter after a bad punt and chased him around the field."

"We were playing a game at Washington and one of their running backs got into the open field and one of our defensive backs made a half-hearted attempt at a tackle," remembers Hugh Gibbons, "George came after him on the sidelines, and me, genius that I am, tried to get between them. George had that look in his eye but thankfully for me he stopped. But when we got into the locker room, George was still mad, and he picked up the defensive back and threw him across the room. Then a couple guys bigger than me got between them."

But it was the love of the game, and an underlying mutual respect, that made the Bucks a team. And kept them together in tough times, both then and now.

"We all became good friends in the end," states Pat Little, "The respect was always mutual, no matter where you came from. The league was tough and you could see that in the faces of our team in every game. My teammates were one rough group of football players who didn't play for glory, but loved to hit and play the game."

# CHAPTER

# 9

"Teams like Chambersburg could recruit players from all over.
That's what we were competing against."

—BUCKS' WIDE RECEIVER HUGH GIBBONS

So far the Bucks were 3-2 under Gary Passarelli and had shown a marked improvement in their level of play (Okay, so one of the wins was by forfeit, but in semipro football, a win is a win, whether over a live team or a defunct one).

Believe it or not, even after their very auspicious start, and having been outscored 139-24 in their four losses, the Bucks had a real chance to finish the season on a high note, maybe even earn themselves some league hardware.

But the season had taken a toll. First off, recent practices were not drawing the numbers of players needed to keep the Bucks a well-tuned group. The team's performances had been wildly inconsistent, ranging from brilliant to downright awful. And although the team had played better under Passarelli, there still seemed to be a sense of disorganization surrounding the franchise. There was talk of bickering and even some rebelliousness among the players toward their head coach.

One former Buck places a lot of the blame for the team's internal strife on the fact that for the first time the players had contracts with the organization. While the contracts increased the number of players who signed up with the team for 1977, Darrel Rutter feels they hurt the team in the long run.

"The money issues caused problems," says Rutter, "Your contract was dependent on gate receipts and the number of practices you attended. It could be $150 a game or $200 a game or whatever. Some of the players didn't get what they thought they should. It shouldn't have made a difference but it did. It drove a wedge between the players, and the players and the front office. Some of the players didn't like it when some other guy got more money. That certainly hurt us. They say 'money is the root of all evil,' and I believe it. It was that way with the Bucks. Look at these shows about these lottery winners. A lot of them are now broke and unhappy."

The Bucks were certainly not broke, but quite a few of them seemed to be unhappy.

Nobody was happy about the team's offensive performance so far. It was struggling, especially on the ground. Wayne Rockmore was leading the team in rushing but had just 273 yards in 59 carries. Joe Good, with 223 yards, was the only other Buck running back with over 100 yards. The passing game was a little more potent, but had been inconsistent. Tom Miller had completed 28-of-83 passes for 222 yards and three touchdowns, while Kevin Detwiler was 16-of-32 for 131 yards.

Then there were the injuries. Rockmore was still nursing his bad ankle which limited his effectiveness. On top of that, the Rock got a call from former Bucks coach Dave Paganetti, who was on the Chambersburg coaching staff.

"Latter part of the '77 season I went to Chambersburg to try out," says Rockmore, "I drove two and a half hours after work to go, a long drive. [*Former Bucks quarterback Larry*] Rydbom was there, as was Paganetti, who asked me to come down. George Walker went down later. I tried out. Even though I was coming off a sprained ankle, I still ran a 4.36 40-yard dash. Not bad. But I decided to go to work for Xerox instead. It was a tough decision, but I felt like I was really abandoning the team. If I had lived closer it might have been okay. Chambersburg had a good organization, the kind of organization I wish the Bucks had become."

Another Buck who fell to the injury bug was veteran offensive tackle Ron Roefaro, who was felled by a hip injury that ended his playing career.

"I didn't get hurt in a game," Roefaro recounts, "I had pulled my back a little, so my back was feeling weak and I squatted down to pick up a box and popped my hip out. That was at a part-time, under-the-table, job, without any insurance. We were on strike at my teaching job at the time. That ended my playing career.

"I never did get the $100 a game that I signed a contract for because there was a clause in fine print that said you needed to finish the season to get any money from the contract. So, $700 down the drain at a time when I could have used it. This was the first contract that I had in the three years that I was a starter on offense."

So the Bucks went into their next game with some of their most important players either physically or mentally absent. The game was against the league-leading Youngstown Hardhats, who were 5-0 in the MAFL and had easily disposed of the Bucks earlier in the season, 47-2. They were coming off a 20-13 win over the Pittsburgh Ironmen.

The Hardhats still had their potent offense with Vern Wireman under center and throwing to Lou Kelson and Rich Morris, as well as handing the ball to leading rusher Sam Fant. The defense was led by a couple of Youngstown State grads, Mark Kujala and All-Leaguer Ed Craft.

The teams took the field to find that the Driving Park Field was without a scoreboard, clock or numbers for the yard lines since the Clearfield High School Bisons had moved their home games to the new sports complex at the high school. The only positive thing to say about the lack of a scoreboard was that at least Youngstown couldn't light up a blank scoreboard.

And the Hardhats could definitely light up a scoreboard. They were going for their sixth straight win, paced by Fant's 334 yards and six touchdowns rushing on 67 carries, and Wireman's 54 completions for 992 yards and six touchdowns.

The contest drew around 600 fans, another decent crowd that buoyed the Bucks' financial outlook. But they were doomed to disappointment.

Things started out badly for the Bucks. They attempted their long-time favorite play, the "flea flicker," on their first possession but fumbled the lateral. Hardhat Rich Hall scooped up the loose ball and raced 37 yards to the end zone. But the touchdown was nullified when it was ruled the play had been whistled dead after the recovery.

That decision only delayed the inevitable. The Hardhats cashed in on the break anyway five plays later when Wireman hit tight end Rich Morris from 13 yards out. Kirk Andrews then tacked on his first of four extra points to make it a quick 7-0.

Youngstown's next 20 points came even faster, in a span of about three-and-a-half minutes. The Bucks threatened but lost the ball on downs. Quarterback Kevin Detwiler tried to hit a wide-open Carl Brown for what looked like a sure touchdown until Youngstown's Bob Strozier managed to jump at the last-second to tip the ball away to end that threat.

Soon after, thanks to a 33-yard pass from Wireman to Lou Kelson and a 24-yard run by Sam Fant, who wound up with 95 yards on just eight carries, Jim Smith bulled his way in from the one and Andrews added the conversion to up the edge to 14-0.

The Bucks then proceeded to fumble away the ensuing kickoff and defensive back Guido Jannetti, who liked to tell people that he grew a beard to make himself look more intimidating, ran the loose ball back 20 yards to the Buck 26. On the next play Kelson took a 26-yard pass from Wireman for a touchdown and Andrews again converted on the placement.

The Bucks received the ensuing kickoff, and as Yogi Berra said, "It was déjà vu all over again." This time Central Pennsylvania fumbled the ball away on their first play from scrimmage after the kickoff. Youngstown recovered on the Bucks' 41. Four plays later Fant trotted in from the nine to increase the lead for Youngstown to 27-0. Andrews' extra point try was blocked by Joe Paddock, but the Bucks' fans had already started booing.

The boos and catcalls continued as the game approached intermission, especially when the Hardhats increased their lead to 34-0. The score was set up when Youngstown partially blocked Ritchie Shoop's punt and the kick fluttered out of bounds on the Buck 40. Wireman passed to Smith for 11 yards and then Kelson for 29 yards and touchdown number five. Andrews converted again.

The fans decided to stop booing and instead started heading toward the exits as the half drew to a close.

Those fans that left missed the Bucks' lone touchdown and the most exciting play of the game, if not the season. Early in the third quarter Mike Morgan waited for a Hardhat punt and caught it two yards deep in the end zone. Now, in a situation such as that, football wisdom calls for a punt returner to just let the ball bounce through and out of the end zone and then have his team take over at the 20. But Morgan, looking a 34-0 deficit squarely in the face, probably figured he had nothing to lose. He caught the ball and, using plenty of downfield blocking as well as his speed and a couple good moves, outran everyone in sight enroute to a scintillating 102-yard touchdown punt return. Slabon ran in for the conversion. While the play may have been the greatest in Buck history, it only narrowed the deficit to 27 points.

The last touchdown of the night was scored by Youngstown midway through the third period. Backup quarterback Rusty Preston flipped a four-yard pass to Kelson. Andrews added the extra point to make the score 41-7.

Youngstown almost had another score later in the game when Wireman hit William Banks in the end zone from the 11. But an ineligible receiver downfield erased the play and the Hardhats fumbled the ball away a couple plays later, with Slabon recovering.

But the Bucks had been outclassed again. The game was not as close as the final score indicated. Central Pennsylvania's defense had simply been unable to contain either Vern Wireman or Lou Kelson.

Wireman played less than a half but he made the most of his limited playing time by completing eight-of-nine passes for 163 yards and three touchdowns. An interception by Slabon was the only blemish on his otherwise stellar performance.

Kelson, who once had a tryout with the NFL's Atlanta Falcons, outmaneuvered the Buck defense all night, running circles around the Central Pennsylvania secondary. Kelson's slick moves got him in the open often enough to catch seven passes for 160 yards and three touchdowns.

Several of the Bucks claimed after the game that Kelson "was the best athlete we've ever played against." Combined with his earlier game against the Bucks, Kelson managed 14 pass receptions for 244 yards and four touchdowns in the two contests. Not a bad season for most receivers!

The Bucks meanwhile, had resorted to the ineffective offensive efforts they had displayed earlier in the season, managing only 94 yards in total offense. The three quarterbacks—Detwiler, Tom Miller and Shoop—completed just 2 of 14 passes. Central Pennsylvania turned the ball over six times.

It's no wonder that *Progress* reporter Jerry Stewart, in his article entitled "Bucks had Better Regroup," wrote that the Whitetail Bucks were a team that was "beginning to fade fast" and needed to "take a good hard look at itself."

But one has to consider that the Bucks were playing teams that were far better organized and in most cases far better financed than they were. Many were veteran teams that had played together for years and had more depth and were able to recruit big time college players and former professionals.

"Teams like Chambersburg and Youngstown could recruit players from all over," says Hugh Gibbons, "That's what we were competing against."

Since they were often outmanned and had little in the way of depth, the Bucks had to rely on the versatility of their players.

Most of them had to play both offense and defense. Many played multiple positions. The Bucks could not afford the luxury of simple substitutions, much less modern-day football concepts like situational substitutions.

If and when injuries occurred, which was inevitable in any level of football, players had to be ready to step into the breach, sometimes at unfamiliar positions.

"I had to play offensive guard for one play," says Tom Marlett, who usually played linebacker. "Someone got hurt and they sent me in. I didn't even know the offense. I asked Roefaro what we were supposed to do. He said, 'We're crossing.' I asked, 'Who goes first?' and Ron said, 'You do!' Believe it or not, we scored on the play!"

Up next on the schedule was a road trip to New Kensington, Pennsylvania for a return match against the Allegheny-Kiski Stars, who with a record of 1-4 were near the tail end of the Southern Division standings. The Bucks had defeated the Stars earlier, 25-12, and needed a win to stay in the running for a possible second-place finish and a playoff spot. But they would have to face the Stars without their head coach, Gary Passarelli. The young man from Curwensville was, like Turley before him, finding the job to be a little more than he could handle, and decided it was not a one-man job. So Passarelli did not make the trip to New Kensington, and in his place, Tom Miller would be running the offense while Alex Anto was put in charge of the defense. The Bucks were now essentially without a head coach.

The contest was a benefit game for a young man named Scott Doutt, who was injured in a high school game in the fall of 1976, and was paralyzed and confined to a wheelchair. Stars' management reported that the benefit affair was a huge success, as 4,000 tickets were sold.

Central Pennsylvania's first possession went nowhere so the Bucks punted. Allegheny-Kiski then marched smartly downfield and scored first as Fran Graybeagle passed to Mike McCloud. It was one of the game's few passes but was successful from 25 yards out. The Stars were on top 6-0 with 7:34 left in the first period. The run for the extra point fell short.

Late in the first half, an interception by Al Potter set up the Bucks in good shape and then a pass interference call on the Stars moved the Bucks all the way down to the two with a first down and goal.

On first down Bill "Clicker" Clark crashed into the end zone but the point after was blocked and with 2:09 left until the intermission the Bucks had tied things up at 6-6.

Central Pennsylvania got the ball back with 35 seconds to go and Miller went to the air. He found Mike Morgan and the two hooked up for a 64-yard completion that carried the ball all the way to the Stars' one. The Bucks had time for one more play before the half but it failed to find the end zone.

The game settled into a defensive struggle, as neither team could score in the third quarter. The Bucks got a break in the fourth quarter when Les McCoy recovered a Stars' fumble. Ritchie Shoop then completed a 50-yard pass to Carl Brown, but the Bucks squandered the opportunity on the very next play when they fumbled the ball away at the Stars' 28.

As the game progressed, the fog started to roll in as the temperature dropped. It looked more and more like a mistake would win the game. Sure enough, the break came when the Stars got off a poor punt late in the game. Joe Good and "Clicker" Clark took turns running the offense down to the seven. But the Bucks faced a third down with only 18 seconds to go in the contest. Fearful that a play from scrimmage might fail and the clock would run out, the Bucks called on Shoop's foot.

Shoop calmly booted a 24-yard field goal straight through the goal posts and Central Pennsylvania had a 9-6 edge with less than a minute to play.

The kickoff sailed out of the end zone and the Stars' took over on their own 20. On the first play from scrimmage Bill Bailey crashed through the line and chased Graybeagle into the end zone for a safety with three seconds left on the clock. It was 11-6 and the Bucks had their fourth league win of the season.

The Whitetail Bucks now had a chance to finish in a tie for second place in the league standings. Next up on the schedule for the Bucks was a home game with the Pittsburgh Ironmen.

But early in the week Bucks' management learned that the Ironmen had instead agreed to travel to Binghamton, New York to play the Triple-Cities Jets for a guarantee payout instead of fulfilling their league obligations by playing the Bucks.

This sort of thing happened occasionally in the semipro game, as schedules could be fluid affairs that teams had no trouble changing and altering, sometimes at the last minute.

Once they learned of the attempted change by the Ironmen, Al Siegel and "Hymie" Ziff got on the phone and spent the morning and afternoon in an effort to convince Pittsburgh to keep to the schedule and come to Philipsburg to play. As stated earlier, Siegel was a guy who could get things done, and he and Ziff managed to convince the Ironmen management to change their minds. So the game was back on.

Passarelli returned to the team, and would take over as defensive coordinator while Miller ran the offense. But there's an old adage that says too many cooks spoil the broth, and the idea of using co-coaches instead of having one head coach had never worked very well in the history of football, and didn't succeed with the Bucks either.

If the Bucks could somehow beat Pittsburgh, something they had never done before, then both teams would have three losses in the league, which would set up a playoff to determine the winner of the second place trophy.

The game was held in Philipsburg, and despite the importance of the game, a smaller-than-expected crowd of around 500 fans was on hand.

Ownership had to be disappointed in the crowd, especially since management had organized a promotion called "Prize Night" for the season finale. Ten area residents won a wide array of prizes donated by local merchants which included everything from a bucket of Kentucky Fried Chicken to dinner for two at several local restaurants to a carton of cigarettes.

The fans saw another in a long line of fine defensive performances by the Bucks. Although their offense had traditionally performed erratically and inconsistently, mainly due to a woeful lack of practice time, the defense had always been the team's strong suit. In those simpler times of the 1970s, the defense didn't need as much practice time, as playing the position took a more reactive mindset than the offense did. Defenses could still perform well despite a lack of time on the practice field.

And on September 24th, the Bucks defense, despite a lack of practice time and a notable lack of participants in those practices, once again displayed a tremendous effort.

They held the Ironmen to just 2.2 yards per rushing attempt and only 152 yards in total offense. The Bucks allowed the Ironmen to cross midfield only once in the first half, and held Pittsburgh without a touchdown until there were only 23 seconds left in the game. Every member of the defense was to be congratulated—linemen Bill Bailey, Jeff Blowers, John Stoneberg and Joe Paddock, linebackers Albe Wales, Alex Anto, Dirk Grissinger and Tom Marlett, and defensive backs Mark Stewart, Al Potter and Jim Slabon.

But their efforts went for naught, and were sabotaged by another anemic performance by the offense. The Bucks managed just 98 yards in total offense, with Wayne Rockmore accounting for a third of that total with 37 yards. Central Pennsylvania passers completed just three passes all night, and Ritchie Shoop had to punt nine times.

The Bucks managed to reach the Pittsburgh 27 midway through the first quarter when Mike Morgan grabbed a Kevin Detwiler aerial and raced for a 31 yard gain, but a procedure penalty and an eight-yard loss by Detwiler on a pass attempt forced a punt. It would be Morgan's only catch of the game, as either his quarterbacks couldn't find him or the Ironmen defenders kept the speedster under wraps.

Late in the half, Grissinger played a Pittsburgh pass play in the flat beautifully. He dropped back in coverage then stepped up in front of the receiver and proceeded to rumble 39 yards down the right sideline. Ironmen quarterback Rich DeMaio finally pulled Grissinger down at the Pittsburgh 9-yard line. But Central Pennsylvania's offense couldn't capitalize on this gift. The Bucks had time for one play from scrimmage, but Detwiler was sacked for a three-yard loss. Head coach Passarelli quickly sent in the field goal unit. Shoop's kick definitely had enough leg, but tailed off to the right, keeping the game scoreless at the half.

A strong wind kicked up at halftime, which turned out to be an ill wind for the Bucks. Early in the third quarter, Shoop's punt was high and short thanks to the wind, then took a bad bounce for the Whitetail Bucks and wound up at their own 34.

The Ironmen ran five plays but got very little yardage as the Bucks' defense once again played superlatively. The Ironmen had to settle for a 36-yard field goal by Tom Dolfi from the University of Florida and went in front, 3-0.

Another poor punt by Shoop gave the Ironmen great field position at the Bucks' 30, but the rugged Buck defense wouldn't budge once again. Dolfi was sent in to try another field goal. However, the snap sailed high over his head, and he was tackled at his own 49.

The Bucks offense continued to flounder, and soon became a chorus line—one, two, three, kick. Meanwhile, Pittsburgh finally put the game away in the final minutes. The Ironmen drive was set up when they picked off an attempted "flea-flicker" by Slabon. DeMaio, a former University of Cincinnati signal-caller, had an off-night passing but hit two big ones when he had to during the 54-yard drive. Ed Brosky from Pitt finally capped the march with a two-yard plunge. Pete Ross' attempt on the conversion sailed off to the right.

The 9-0 edge with 23 seconds left was certainly enough, but Gerald Barroffio, a defensive end from Boston College, tacked on two points for good measure when he tackled back-up quarterback Jim Stoneberg in the end zone for a safety.

Stoneberg, who had quarterbacked the Beaver County Cougars in 1976, had been signed by the Whitetail Bucks and was the fourth quarterback used by the team in 1977. None of the quartet, however, had been able to move the Bucks with any kind of consistency.

The 11-0 loss was the first time the Bucks had been shutout in their three year history, but was also the third time in 1977 that their offense had failed to find the end zone. But while the losses were to some very good semipro clubs, the Bucks had not been competitive in most of those games.

The loss to Pittsburgh in the last game of the season dashed any hopes the Bucks' had of finishing in second place. Their 4-4 league record placed them third in the Southern Division. But in the wacky world of semipro football, the Bucks still came away with some hardware.

"We actually got third in the league that year but the second-place Pittsburgh Ironmen owed the league money," states Jay Siegel, "so we got their trophy."

The Whitetail Bucks obviously needed a major overhaul to their offensive unit before they would return to the field in the summer of 1978. Tom Miller had indicated he might break ties with the team due to his commitments at

Tyrone High School. While he didn't have a great season, the signal caller added a veteran presence and had shown he was more than a capable offensive coach on the sidelines. Miller's possible departure would leave the Bucks with Kevin Detwiler as the de facto starter, but while the Tyrone grad had performed well in spots, he had been inconsistent and there were questions as to whether his 5'7" 170 pound frame could take the game-by-game pounding.

Wayne Rockmore had been slowed by his ankle injury and was questionable for '78, but if anybody could fight back from an injury it was the Rock.

The offensive line already missed Ron Roefaro, and couldn't afford any more defections or injuries.

Despite a lackluster season, the Whitetail Bucks had nine players named to the 1977 Mid-Atlantic Semipro Football League Southern Division All-Star Team in mid-December. Interestingly, they had more offensive players named to the team than defensive ones.

The only players who made the first team defense were linebacker Bill Bailey and cornerback Jim Slabon. Alex Anto was a second team defensive selection at linebacker.

Meanwhile, first team offense selections included Big Al Siegel at guard, Carl Brown at tight end and Wayne Rockmore at running back. Making the second team on offense was running back Joe Good.

Despite the number of All-League selections, however, the Bucks needed some serious help and also needed to show some definite improvement if they expected to attract a more avid following. But some folks weren't going to wait. The rather poor attendance figures, coupled with rising costs, had given some of the owners a case of cold feet. Late in 1977, most of the owners bailed on the team.

"The owners were unhappy, since they were not getting great gate receipts," says Darrel Rutter, "Certain owners just didn't want to dump more money into the team because they lost money on the gate receipts. Plus all the expenses like uniforms, insurance, rent on stadiums."

"The lawyers who owned the team got out of it," states Hugh Gibbons, "The coal mining industry started to go downhill as well."

"Coal industry went bust," adds Ron Roefaro when asked why the team experienced such deep financial difficulties late in 1977.

Finally, late in December of 1977, Al Siegel, who had helped save the Bucks when they were on the brink of extinction back in the spring and summer of 1975, did it again, buying up all the shares of the Bucks franchise and becoming sole owner of the club.

"Apparently by 1977, Dad became sole owner of the corporation," recalls Jay Siegel, "as evidenced by a sole stockholder certificate I found after his passing in June of 2011."

This stockholder certificate, filed under the name White-Tailed Bucks, Inc., showed that Allan Siegel purchased all 10,000 shares in the corporation for a dollar a share on December 30th, 1977.

"Siegel took over ownership of the team after the '77 season," remembers Darrel Rutter, "I believe he had been paying a lot of bills out of his own pocket."

Siegel was once again putting his neck out for the Bucks. He believed in the team and he believed that the area fans would support the team.

As the calendar flipped its inevitable pages over into 1978, Siegel's row became a lot harder to hoe. Big Al must have begun to wonder what kind of team, if any, he'd have in 1978. For various reasons, players began to leave the Bucks.

"The time I played for the Bucks was one of the best times of my life," says linebacker Tom Marlett, who'd had a very solid '77 campaign, "so the reason for my departure from the team was not for any reason other than time to get my career together and finish my education. Accordingly, I moved to Pittsburgh for a short time, and in 1979, I entered active duty in the Army."

Marlett was only the first of the men who played linebacker for the Bucks in 1977 to decide to leave the team. When all was said and done, all five linebackers, all of them smart savvy veterans and good hitters, had cut ties with the team—Marlett, Alex Anto, Bill Mumma, Dirk Grissinger and All-Leaguer Bill Bailey, who went back to Pitt to concentrate on his wrestling career with the Panthers.

The defections literally tore the guts out of the defense. But that was life in the world of semipro football. Players didn't sign long-term contracts or stay with a team for great lengths of time. These men were playing the game simply for the fun and the joy of it, to revel in the experience for another year or two before moving on with their lives. Unfortunately for the Bucks, quite a few of their players decided to do this after the '77 season.

Many left because the threat of injury was too great and far outweighed the joy of playing. An injury could mean some serious time off work from their "day" jobs, and that didn't stop the bills from coming due.

"You were not being paid if you got hurt," explains Darrel Rutter, "You got paid for an injury but not for the lost work. There was no worker's comp. The chance of injury was always present."

Pass receiver Gary Pheasant and running back Joe Good, both solid long-time veterans who had contributed much to the Bucks' cause over the years, had packed their bags and called it a career. Carl Brown, like Good an All-League selection, was another veteran who left the team after the season.

"Even playing semipro ball there's a risk of injury," Brown remembers, "I already had had five knee injuries. I got out of it what I wanted to, and wanted to move on."

Al Butler, who had done so well as a rookie defensive back in '77, was gone.

Tom Miller announced that he was indeed leaving the team to concentrate on his teaching duties at Tyrone High School.

"I didn't play the last season," Miller says now, "It got to be too much of a hassle what with my obligations at Tyrone High."

Something positive did occur when ex-Buck quarterback Larry Rydbom announced he was seriously considering a return to the Whitetail Bucks after a year with the Chambersburg Cardinals to be closer to home in Coalport. That was good news for Siegel, since the departure of Tom Miller left the Bucks with limited options at the signal caller position. Siegel stated at the time that Rydbom would also be the offensive coordinator for the team.

So the Bucks faced a lot of question marks, both on the field and off, as they headed into the 1978 season. Siegel and the Whitetail Bucks hoped to put the disappointing 1977 season behind them. But as the team headed into the 1978 campaign, they were unaware that in a very short time, that mediocre 1977 season would seem like the salad days.

# CHAPTER

# 10

"That last year we were really just scraping by;
it was just not fun anymore."

—GEORGE WALKER

D espite the uncertainty facing the team following the 1977 season, the Bucks geared up for their fourth campaign early in 1978.

Al Siegel was now the Whitetail Bucks' sole owner, as well as serving as general manager, an assistant coach and a player. He wore so many hats he looked like the guy in the old children's book "Caps for Sale" by Esphyr Slobodkina.

"My Dad did it all for that team," Jay Siegel says now.

Big Al approached his duties with all the sense of purpose and resourcefulness he had displayed all his life. He was bound and determined to make the Whitetail Bucks a success.

In April, Siegel announced that he hoped to fill the two open dates in the team's schedule and also add a pre-season game to give the Bucks an 11 game slate.

"We have four home games for sure, and we'll definitely play them in Clearfield, Curwensville, DuBois and State College," Al told the press, "I've got approval from all those school boards. We'd like to play two maybe three games at Clearfield. We want to open our league on July 22nd at Clearfield for sure.

"One of our additional games will be with the Brooklyn Golden Knights, who have agreed to come without a guarantee just for the good of our team."

But he had quite a mountain to climb. So many players had cut ties with the organization that only nine men on the prospective roster had been with the team since 1975. Many of the players who said they'd sign up with the Bucks were woefully inexperienced, and on top of that there just weren't a whole of them either. But the Bucks had persevered before when the number of candidates at tryouts were not tremendous.

The Whitetail Bucks were not the only team facing some big question marks for 1978. The Washington Generals were hanging on by a thread. But this was not a new situation for the Generals. After folding up their tents early in '77, Washington finished 0-9. They were back to give it another try thanks mainly to Tom Averell.

"I've played minor league football for 22 years, and I'd guess for 20 to 30 different teams," said Averell, who worked leasing new cars for a dealer in Etna, Pa. "All those teams are gone now—all of them folded up. The Generals may be minor league football's last stand in Western Pennsylvania. But I happen to think it can survive. Maybe it'll never make money, but at least it'll survive."

With someone determined enough like Averell to push them, the Generals had at least a longshot's chance to make it. Sort of like Al Siegel and the Bucks.

"There are four of us who are trying to keep this thing together," said Averell, a short chunky offensive lineman, "George Robinson, the coach; Blaine Popp, special teams; Jim Lacko, former quarterback now a darn good linebacker, and myself. I played last year, and I guess if I could lose about 15 pounds I might still suit up and run down under some kickoffs."

The Generals had existed since the early 1960s, first as the Washington Mustangs and then known as the Washington Merchants. But in recent years the club had struggled financially and had moved around the area like homeless waifs—playing for a time in Charleroi and other Mon River towns before landing at Bethel Park for the past few seasons.

"What we need more than anything—except money, of course—is to find a place to play that we can afford in Washington County to re-establish our identity and to promote minor league football as an attraction," Averell went on to say in an interview in March of 1978, "It's a good game. We know it's not the NFL, but it is the next best thing."

"We have had some terrible teams for at least the past three years," Averell continued, "But if everybody who ever had a bad team quit, where would the Pittsburgh Steelers have been for the first 42 years? Or the New York Jets or the Tampa Bay Buccaneers."

But while the Generals had compiled the league's worst record over the past several seasons, they were without question minor league football's most resilient franchise. The 20-to-30 teams that Averell had played for were testimony to the Generals' staying power.

"We will do everything in our power to get back into Washington County, "said Averell, "As a matter of fact, I'll be sending out letters to all the high schools seeking quotations for use of their stadiums. And then we need people of all kinds—some who can help coach, others to take tickets or repair equipment, plenty of fans and guys who can play the game, not just talk about it.

"We have 18 or 19 really good football players on the team right now, but if they get injured we have nobody to take over. Washington County has got to be loaded with fellas who were pretty good football players in high school and college and who want to continue in the game a little while longer."

But Washington was not an isolated situation. There were problems elsewhere. The Pittsburgh Ironmen reportedly ran out of money in 1977 right around the 14 thousand dollar level. While the team had another decent year on the field, they had struggled financially.

In fact, the Ironmen wound up so deep in debt that finally, in a desperate bid to survive in some form, the team was purchased by a new owner and merged with the Allegheny-Kiski Stars, forming a new team that was at first going to be named the Pittsburgh Stars and then changed their name to the Pittsburgh Wolf Pak (PAK standing for Pittsburgh-Allegheny-Kiski), which then moved to the Atlantic Football Conference. But even this new team got off to a rocky start. After sinking some money into the project, new Wolf Pak owner Rob Baker decided he didn't have that kind of dough to throw away. He finally gave up on the idea. But then Atlantic Football Conference Commissioner Warren Unholz talked to him. It took a nine-hour marathon session, but Baker was convinced.

Baker, who had turned a fledgling fencing business into a $2 million-a-year operation, was counting on some of those same techniques and concepts to make a success of his latest venture. Matched with a little good fortune, Baker's hard work and determination was responsible for a quick turnaround in the club's fortunes.

"I didn't know if we would be a success, but I knew we would try to be very good," said Baker, "Then lo and behold, Joe came on the scene. I hope we'll have him for a whole season. If not, fine. One thing's for sure, it's been quite an experience."

The "Joe" Baker was referring to was former Pittsburgh Steeler quarterback Joe Gilliam, who had signed on with the Wolf Pak.

"He's a very fine young man. I think he's got it back together," Baker said.

But signing Gilliam was a gamble. When he was cut by the Steelers just before the 1976 season, he was already hooked on drugs. Gilliam shook his drug habit at a rehabilitation clinic in Richmond, Virginia, but when he went back to Nashville he couldn't find work. He tried out for the Saints but was released.

By 1978, he was free of drugs, but was on probation—on weapons and marijuana possession charges—and at the age of 27 was fast approaching middle age for a pro athlete. Baker seemed to be putting a lot of his eggs in a very flimsy basket.

Baker said Gilliam viewed the Wolf Pak as a step back to the big time and that he would be free at any time to sign with an NFL team. "We will not hold him back," said Baker. "Our prime purpose is to give experience and exposure to players who have potential."

Despite the struggles teams seemed to be facing, Baker felt the time was ripe for minor league football. The National Football League had cut its preseason by two games and, at the insistence of the courts, trimmed its annual college draft from 17 to 12 rounds. Colleges were also giving out fewer scholarships, and that combination meant that a lot of talented ballplayers were bound to be overlooked, and therefore, prime candidates for spots with semipro squads.

The merger of the Ironmen and the Stars and their subsequent move to the Atlantic Conference left the Mid-Atlantic League without two of its franchises from 1977. The New York franchises which had made up the MAFL's Northern Division in 1977 decided to join the new Wolf Pak in the Atlantic Conference. With all the defections, the Mid-Atlantic League would consist of the Bucks and only four other teams—the Youngstown Hardhats, Washington Generals, Cleveland Academes, and Erie Express.

The Bucks announced they would be holding a team meeting on Sunday April 30th at 11am, with Siegel saying he encouraged all interested players to report to the Community Building in the Driving Park at Clearfield. The GM said he wanted "to set up tryouts and the start of practice. We want to have a 35-man team that wants to come to practice as well as play football."

So the Bucks, skating on thin ice as it was, were one of several unstable franchises in a now somewhat unstable league. It all didn't bode well for a successful season. Unfortunately, the uncertainty surrounding the team continued into the spring and summer months.

In mid-April, Siegel was still in the hunt for a head coach, a chore which he stated was high on his very long priority list. "Several players have volunteered to help coach, but I'm still looking for a take-charge guy to be the boss on the sidelines," Siegel said.

A month later, the Bucks announced the team would open their fourth season on July 15th with a non-league game against the Connecticut Sea Raiders at 8pm at State College's Memorial Field. Siegel also announced that the team had filled out its 11-game schedule, and would open league play on July 22nd against a new addition to the MAFL, the Erie Express, in DuBois. The team's schedule included seven home contests, at least one of which was still being finalized. A week after hosting Erie, the Bucks were scheduled to tangle with the Brooklyn Golden Knights at Philipsburg, and then battle the Cleveland Academes, another newcomer to the league, on August 5th in State College. The Bucks would face Washington in Curwensville and a week later Youngstown in Clearfield on September 23rd. Another as yet to be named opponent would provide the opposition in the Driving Park on September 2nd.

But those home contests were not selling many season ticket plans the team was offering to provide the club with some "upfront" money to cover expenses. Siegel described the team's financial situation as "shaky, definitely shaky. I'm just disappointed in ticket sales."

Another problem continued to be the search for a head coach. "At this point, there is no head coach," Siegel told the press, "and I'm just about resigned to the fact we may be going with player-coaches, although we still have a couple guys in mind."

If no one stepped forward to be the head man, Siegel said he would serve in that capacity and finally hang up his cleats, but added, "I'd prefer to play."

The team was still counting on Larry Rydbom to return and play quarterback and serve as offensive coordinator. Veteran defensive back Jim Slabon would coach the linebackers and defensive secondary. Siegel said he would be in charge of the linemen.

"We're still looking for more players, especially linemen and linebackers," Big Al said, adding that practices would begin June 4th, a Sunday, and that the Bucks would work out three times a week in preparation for their opener.

"We won't have any formal tryouts, but anybody who shows up June 4th will get a look," Siegel said.

The team took a serious hit, however, when Rydbom, who had said he was going to return to quarterback the Whitetail Bucks, and was being counted on to be the offensive coordinator as well, decided to stay in Chambersburg and play another year with the Cardinals. That meant that neither Rydbom nor Tom Miller, both seasoned veterans, would be under center for the Bucks in '78, and that left a big hole at quarterback.

"It really crushed the team when Rydbom decided not to play," says running back Ron Rehmeyer.

Finally, as the season drew closer, the Bucks were able to find that "take-charge" guy Siegel said he was looking for to man the sidelines and coach the team. His name—none other than Allan J. Siegel.

"Siegel was a human encyclopedia of football," states Rehmeyer, "He knew all the nuances of the game. He liked to be innovative, using things like trap plays."

In late June, however, more uncertainty dogged the team. The Bucks were originally scheduled to open the 1978 season with a non-league game on July 15th against a new team from the Atlantic Football Conference, the Connecticut Sea Raiders. The Sea Raiders had been formed in March of 1978 and would quickly become one of the strongest semipro squads in the Eastern United States.

But money issues forced the Bucks to scrub the opening game against Connecticut.

"We can't afford to play that game right now, because the league commitment has to be met first," explained Siegel, who by now had assumed the offensive coordinator duties along with being head coach, general manager and owner. "Our first commitment is to the Mid- Atlantic League. We can't afford to bring in a team like the Connecticut Sea Raiders, so we have to go right into our league schedule.

"Monetarily, we're not as shaky as we were earlier because we have a fund-raiser going with a rifle, a gift certificate for $50 at the Grice Gun Shop and an official NFL football as prizes. However, that's our only source of income right now. Nobody has bought a season ticket in the past few weeks, and very few businessmen or individuals have sent checks."

Siegel noted that he had sent out 200 letters appealing for financial support for the Bucks, stating, "Most of those letters went out to those who gave us money last year, but I've heard from only seven or eight so far. Others have said they'll send something but haven't done so yet.

"I'm at the point right now of cancelling that July 15th game, which could kill us. That's a game we need monetarily as well as a tune-up for our league. I don't have insurance for the ball players, which was told to them point blank at practice Sunday. I know we're gonna lose a couple of key players over that.

"We'll start hitting in pads next Sunday. If we can't get insurance on the players because of lack of money, it will be a potential problem."

In an effort to work around not having to come up with the guarantee for the Connecticut team on July 15th, Siegel was trying to arrange a home-and-home series with a non-league opponent, getting the home draw July 15th at State College and returning the visit on Sept. 30th, which was an open date for the team.

Some of the possible opponents Siegel mentioned were the Chambersburg Cardinals, the Baltimore Warriors, the Oneonta, New York, Indians, and a team from Spring Valley, New York.

When asked to discuss the 1978 Bucks squad, Siegel's tone changed to a more positive one.

"We have 29 sure, 100 percent ball players, with 11 shaky as far as I'm concerned as far as making a commitment," he remarked. "Those 11 haven't been coming to practice on a regular basis.

"Right now, we have more players coming on a regular basis, but most of them are on the offensive unit."

With Larry Rydbom having decided to go back to Chambersburg, another ex-Glendale Area High grad had been signed and had quickly moved up the depth chart and was now considered the team's Number 1 quarterback. He was Brian Lightner, who had played some varsity ball at Lock Haven State College [*now University*]. At 6'2" and 205 pounds, he had the size and the arm strength to make a good impression on Siegel. Lightner added another dimension to the offense in that he could also run the option play, especially out of the Veer.

"We had a good quarterback in Lightner," says Ron Rehmeyer.

When asked who would be backing up Lightner, Siegel said, "Ritchie Shoop of Hollidaysburg is No. 2, and we also have Kevin Detwiler of Tyrone back."

Siegel stated that he liked the group of running backs the team had put together, which included returnees Wayne Rockmore, Doug Kritzer and Bill "Clicker" Clark, as well as newcomers Tom Primerano of Johnsonburg, Ron Rehmeyer from Boalsburg and Kevin Mickey of Altoona.

"I had boxed and played intramural football at the University of Miami," recalls Rehmeyer, "I then transferred to Penn State, and also got a job selling sports cars. I met Wayne Rockmore, one of the best athletes on the team. Rock said I should try out for the Bucks. I tried out for the team in 1977 and actually made the squad, but the 60 mile one way commute to Madera was just too far to travel. Well, Rock stayed in touch, and in 1978, the team switched practice sites to Philipsburg, and that wasn't such a haul. Rockmore said I should come and try out again and I did."

Rehmeyer quickly earned a new nickname with the Bucks.

"My style of playing running back was to hit the hole instantly," Rehmeyer says, "then make cuts. I always tried to make the first person miss, and kept doing that. My teammates would tell me, 'If you'd have run straight you'd have scored!' They said I always cut toward the tackler and hit him head on, like a 'Baby Bull.' So the name stuck. People have shortened it to just 'Bull' now. Even my son calls me that."

The Bucks' new head coach said he planned to install a multiple offense with Straight-T, Power, and Winged-T sets, adding, "Basically, we want to stress execution."

But there were still a lot of question marks on defense, since Siegel had no idea what to expect due to the lack of personnel at practices, especially at linebacker, where five of the men from 1977 had cut ties with the team.

"John Stoneberg of Ashville and Joe Paddock of Hastings came out for the first time Sunday, which was good news," Siegel said, sounding almost relieved.

But the money woes were hanging over the Bucks like the sword of Damocles. The team needed money fast to keep its head above water. Any individuals or businesses thinking about offering a donation to the team were encouraged to contact Siegel immediately.

If not sooner.

"That 1978 season was kind of a blur. I had begun to feel the inevitability of it being over," recalls Wayne Rockmore, "It was sad, but we tried to hang on. We just didn't have the tools we had before."

In early July, the Erie Express was named as the opponent for the Whitetail Bucks' July 15th 1978 opening game at State College's Memorial Field. Siegel told the press that a lack of financial support was the reason for the schedule change.

The Express was originally listed as the July 22nd opening game opponent for the Bucks, with Mansell Stadium in DuBois the site for that contest. With the schedule change, however, Siegel said he was hopeful of lining up another opponent for that date.

Just when the team managed to get that problem sorted out, yet another one cropped up. The Bucks' July 29th home game against the Brooklyn Golden Knights, scheduled for Philipsburg's Memorial Stadium, was now in jeopardy. Siegel stressed that the status of that non-league game depended a lot on how the attendance was for the opener in State College.

"Our only source of income the last month is from the fund-raiser our players have going," said Siegel. "I've had a couple of calls from people saying they're going to help, but that's all."

"There was a lot of uncertainty about the team," recalls Ron Rehmeyer.

Just when it looked like the news couldn't get any worse for the Bucks, it did. Wayne Rockmore had to go under the knife for a knee operation. He would be out a few weeks at least, and there was the possibility that his whole season was in question. The Rock had sparked the Buck offense for three years. He would be sorely missed.

"I had had knee surgery and not sure if I could play," says Rock now, "Plus I had started working for Xerox."

Since Rockmore couldn't play, Siegel asked if he would serve as an assistant coach for the team. It didn't take Rock long to decide.

"I filled in as an assistant coach," recalls Rockmore, "I was the offensive coordinator for Siegel. It wasn't my preference but I knew the guys and I knew the plays."

John Appleton of Curwensville, yet another newcomer who could play both offensive guard and linebacker, had been named the defensive coordinator with veteran Buck safetyman Jim Slabon tutoring the defensive backs.

Despite the changes and uncertainty, Siegel told reporters that the team was adjusting to the new set-up quite well.

"We've got enough player-coaches that two of us will be on the sidelines at all times," said Siegel, "Like this week, Rockmore won't be in uniform and Appleton is not starting."

Because of the incredible turnover in personnel since the end of the '77 campaign, the squad, which numbered around 36 players, depending on injuries and the day of the week, was somewhat different than in the past with no less than 15 new faces in camp.

Siegel remained upbeat, however, and tried to put a positive spin on things as the Bucks embarked on an 11-game regular season schedule.

"The attitude is great, and I think we've got what we have to have at this point," said Siegel, "We hit hard in practice tonight. I feel this group has the attitude that approaches that of the 1975 team, when we started. We're peaking right now. All we need is a game. I'm very optimistic about this weekend."

The fact that injuries or any other of a number of factors could have quickly and easily trimmed the roster to less than three dozen players in a hurry didn't seem to concern Siegel.

"Several players can play more than one position, so I feel we're deep enough in what we need," said Siegel, "I don't think you'll see any 60-minute players, but some of the guys on offense will play some defense. Everybody is gonna play Saturday night."

The Bucks planned to utilize a Multiple-T offense, showing full house, wing and pro sets in the backfield. "We'll mix up our ground and air game," said Siegel, "From what I've seen so far, I think we have quite an impressive ground game."

This was despite the loss of Rockmore. With the Rock sidelined, the majority of the ball-carrying duties would fall on the shoulders of two veterans, "Clicker"

Clark and Doug Kritzer, and the newcomer Primerano when the Bucks lined up in a Straight-T. Siegel said he was impressed with Kritzer's improvement and Primerano's potential. Clark had always been a hard-nosed runner who was good for the tough, inside yards.

"Tough kid, more of a plow," Darrel Rutter says when asked about Clark, "Not shifty or fast, he'd just as soon bull you over. He was not big, but he was strong and ran with a low center of gravity."

"Clark was the prototypical team leader—loud, Big 33 choice, slated to be the star," adds Rehmeyer.

When the Bucks went into a two-back alignment, veteran flanker Hugh Gibbons, one of the nine players who had been with the club since the beginning, would enter the lineup.

Siegel had been counting on Kevin Mickey, a first-year running back from Altoona, but he injured his knee high jumping in mid-July.

Brian Lightner was set to direct the attack. He would be backed up by Ritchie Shoop, a Bucks' veteran, who could also be used as a running back and would handle all the teams' kicking chores. In a pinch, the diminutive but exciting Kevin Detwiler could step in as the signal caller, but Siegel projected him as more of a wide receiver and possibly a defensive back.

The speedy Mike Morgan, the leading receiver for the Bucks as a rookie in 1977, was set at split end. Big Joe Crestani, another returnee from the '77 squad, was slated as the starting tight end but could also move in to play offensive tackle. Phil Crotzer, a rookie from Clearfield who had impressed Siegel, was the back-up receiver.

His other duties were not going to stop Siegel from strapping on the pads for another campaign, and Big Al was all set to play another season at center at the age of 40. The rest of the o-line had rookie Mark Rusnak, a 1978 Mo Valley grad, and veteran Joe Wales at guards, with two other veterans, George Walker and Kevin McClincy, at tackles.

"George Walker was just a rock," says Ron Rehmeyer, "indestructible. A boulder. The guy across from him just wasn't going to get around him."

George Walker also made an impression of a different sort on Rehmeyer. As the reader may recall, one of George's idiosyncrasies was his pre-game ritual of throwing up before each game.

"Whenever we'd start the game in the huddle, I would be listening to the quarterback," says Rehmeyer, "Then I hear George was making all kinds of grunts and groans. I nudged him and said, 'What's wrong?' and he threw up all over my shoes! He'd do this every game and it was always MY shoes!"

Other possibilities for the offensive line were putting Crestani at tackle, Appleton at guard and Rusnak at center. Greg Walker was also available to play tackle.

What with the loss of many of the veterans who had played in 1977, the defensive unit wasn't settled yet, but Siegel was able to at least name some probable starters. The unit was a little green, however, with Mitch Mancuso, Darrel Rutter, John Stoneberg, Jim Slabon and Denny Kurtz being the only players who had logged a lot of playing time.

Tackle Terry Graham, a 270-pounder who had recently moved back to the Clearfield area and had played for the Bucks in 1975, was being counted on to help anchor the front wall.

The linebacking crew was all-new and full of question marks, with George "Peachy" Williams flanked by Joe Williams and Ron Davison.

"Joe Williams was my best friend on the team," Rehmeyer says, "We used to go 1-on-1 in practice all the time."

Another one of the new linebackers was a young man named Larry Lane from State College.

"He was a tall, thin guy," Rehmeyer recalled recently, "He played on the kick coverage team. In almost every game, he would invariably get his bell rung on the opening kickoff. It got so that we nicknamed him 'Liberty Bell' Lane."

Rookie John Challingsworth from St. Mary's and Rusty Noel of Altoona were penciled in to possibly join Slabon and Kurtz in the secondary, where Howie Wilcox of State College was also a candidate to start. This was another area full of inexperienced players.

Siegel announced that the Bucks would carry a roster of 35 men.

"We're totally self-supporting," said Siegel of his ballclub, "and nobody is out here to make money. We're made up of good high school players who never went to college for some reason or another, and some college players who just never made the pros.

"I think we'll be an exciting team with a balanced offense. We'll show a lot of formations and even run options because our quarterbacks are that type of player."

As they had always done in order to save money, players carpooled—and in some cases "truckpooled"—to practices and games.

"I had a Toyota pickup truck," recalls Rehmeyer, "and several of the guys would ride in the back to practice. Usually George Walker and a couple others. Of course, they'd fight over who would ride up front with me."

As they had done every year since 1975, the Bucks opened their fourth season with a game in State College. Tickets for the game were priced at $3 for adults and $1.50 for school-age students at the gate. However, tickets were made available from team members in advance. Those tickets were all $2 but could admit one adult or two youths.

Erie came into town off the heels of an embarrassing 77-0 loss to the Pittsburgh Wolf Pak. Joe Gilliam, with scouts from at least two NFL teams watching from the stands, threw for four touchdowns and ran for another and completed 10 of 12 passes—including eight in a row—for 180 yards in the two quarters he played.

"The Erie coach told me they just got overpowered by an awesome football team," said Siegel, "The Wolf Pak is big and fast, and those second- and third-stringers kept pouring it on because they want to be first-stringers too."

When asked to describe the Express, Siegel said, "They aren't very big, if the figures are correct. They only have two guys on defense who are over 210 pounds. According to the positions on offense, they use either a pro-set or a Power-I with two wide receivers."

The team featured offensive tackle Jim Chambers, a 6'3" 280 pounder, tackle Novell McMathis and guard Mark Dylewski, both who weighed around 230 pounds. David Green, a star running back for Edinboro State College [*now University*], was a highly-touted 200-pound tailback.

On defense, the Express featured a pair of 230-pound ends in Eric Dinicola and Jeff Miller, and a fellow by the name of Jimmy "Notorious" Jones in the backfield.

After the embarrassing loss to Pittsburgh, the Express went through a complete reorganization. They certainly looked reorganized on July 15th in State College.

Siegel was hoping for a solid win, but the game got off to an auspicious start for Central Pennsylvania when veteran Darrel Rutter was hurt early in the game.

"I got hurt second play of the game," Rutter says now, "Hurt my Achilles tendon. Heard it snap and I knew I was done."

"That was a big loss to the team," Rehmeyer says, "Rutter was a great player."

Shortly after Rutter went down, another Bucks' vet, Mitch Mancuso, suffered a bruised leg and retired to the bench. The Bucks had lost both their defensive ends in the first quarter of the season! These injuries were, unfortunately, a sign of things to come.

The Bucks' offense also got off to a difficult start. Lightner bobbled the snap on the team's first play, and Miller recovered for the Express. Erie could not convert that turnover into points when placekicker Pat Comer missed a field goal try from 44 yards away.

Lightner and the Bucks continued to struggle, as the rookie quarterback misfired on three straight passes on the next series. Then on their next possession the Bucks gambled on fourth-and-two at the Erie 40 and lost six yards. The Express took over and marched 54 yards in nine plays. Green scored the season's first touchdown with a one-yard plunge. Comer's extra point try was wide right.

Central Pennsylvania's problems continued. Shoop fumbled the ball on the Bucks' very next play from scrimmage, and Jimmy Clark recovered for the Express at the Bucks 48. Ten plays later, Sam Scott passed 11 yards into the end zone to Dave Overton for an easy score. A mix-up in defenses created confusion in the Bucks defense, with the team not aligned properly at the snap and then left without a defender to cover Overton. Comer's conversion made it 13-0 with 13:07 left in the first half.

Finally, the Whitetail Bucks were able to get their first game jitters out of the way. The team drove from their own 26 to the Erie 47. Lightner then called the "Mo-Fly" to the speedy Morgan, who broke free and streaked down the middle. The rookie quarterback put the ball right on the money for a picture-perfect touchdown bomb. Shoop added the seventh point to draw the Bucks within six at 13-7.

Near the end of the half, Erie tried to cross up the Bucks on a fourth down-and-three play. The Express showed punt, then called time. On the sidelines, the Express opted to try a pass.

It looked for all the world like Erie had pulled off that bit of "trickeration" because the Bucks had their punt return unit on the field and didn't have time to switch when the Express came out of the huddle in a pro set.

But what looked like misfortune quickly turned to fortune when Morgan, doing double duty as a defensive back, stepped in front of Scott's pass over the middle and with clear sailing in front of him, raced downfield for a 68-yard touchdown. Shoop's conversion shoved the Bucks ahead for the first time 14-13 with a little over two minutes remaining in the half.

At halftime, the Bucks organization gave out the prizes from their fund raiser. The prize winners were Luella Lines of Clearfield, who won a rifle, Boyd Houck of Philipsburg, who took away a Grice Gun Shop gift certificate, and Bill Flanagan of Clearfield, who was now the proud owner of an official NFL football.

When the second half began, the Bucks suffered yet another injury.

"On the first play of the second half, Bill Clark hurts his leg," remembers Ron Rehmeyer, "There were no other fullbacks on the roster, and so they put me in. But there was no pressure on me. I loved to practice, treated them like a game, and went full out. I wound up losing about 30 pounds that season from playing all the time."

The game then settled into a defensive struggle as neither offense was able to do much. The clock wound down until there were only about two minutes left in the game, with the Whitetail Bucks still clinging to their slim one-point lead.

Then disaster struck.

Shoop boomed one of his typical punts, a very high kick, that Erie return specialist Herb Ford fielded at his own 47. Ford veered quickly toward the left sideline, cut back sharply near the Bucks' 25 and then sped across the field against the grain to send the Express bench into a frenzy.

Only 1:04 remained on the clock when Ford, who was a teammate of Pittsburgh Steeler running back Jack Deloplaine at Salem College in West Virginia, reached the end zone, with no Buck having put so much as a hand on him.

"David Green gave me the key block just after I caught the ball," said Ford, a 5'9", 160-pounder who had aspirations of getting a tryout as a kick returner and defensive back with some NFL club. "It seemed like they over pursued when I cut back. There was nobody over there."

"I was playing in punt coverage for the first time," recalls Ron Rehmeyer, "When the guy caught it near the sideline I ran straight for him. Now you're supposed to use the sidelines as another player, and I should have just pushed him out of bounds. But I wanted to really light him up and I missed him completely. He ran it all the way back."

The Bucks didn't go down without giving it one last shot. Morgan provided his team with great field position by returning the ensuing kickoff 40-yards. Shoop was now playing quarterback because Lightner had sustained a cut on his head that required stitches when a hard tackle had knocked his helmet off. Ritchie connected with Kevin Detwiler, who made a brilliant fingertip grab, on a clutch, fourth down pass for 19 yards to the Erie 26.

In the huddle, Rehmeyer tried to tell Shoop that if he went out on a flare pass he'd be open. The play had worked earlier in the game for a nice completion.

"Shoop was a good athlete," says Rehmeyer, "He had a tryout with the Cowboys. But sometimes it seemed like some of the established guys wanted nothing to do with a new guy like me. He wouldn't listen to me about the flare pass, just wanted me to block. Even the guys on the sidelines are telling Shoop to call the flare pass. But he wouldn't."

After two incompletions, the Bucks tried to cross up the Express defense with a draw play, and it worked as Rehmeyer barreled to the 18.

The Bucks had one last shot with just 11 ticks left on the Memorial Field clock. Finally Shoop went to Rehmeyer. "But I'm covered and it's incomplete," says Rehmeyer now. Game over.

"I don't think we were outplayed," shrugged Al Siegel after his debut as head coach. "We lost two defensive ends, Rutter and Mitch Mancuso, in the first quarter.

"Then, without Lightner, we couldn't use the flea flicker we have, and I think it would have worked.

"We made a tactical mistake on their last touchdown. We had two tackles sent in to protect the punter, but they weren't going for the block. They had the runback set up all the way."

It was one of the toughest defeats of the team's four-year history, as the Bucks were only seconds away from victory after overcoming the early 13-0 deficit in their Middle Atlantic Conference opener.

Green, who lasted two months with the Cleveland Browns in 1977 and was anticipating a call from the Montreal Alouettes of the Canadian Football League for a tryout that week, slashed through the Central Pennsylvania defense for 157 yards in 25 carries.

"Baby Bull" Rehmeyer's 22 yards in four carries topped the Bucks, who netted only 79 yards on the ground.

Lightner settled down after his jittery start and showed real potential, winding up with five completions in 13 tries and 100 yards passing before he was injured.

"Rehmeyer and Phil Crotzer really impressed me, and Lightner was as cool as a cucumber back there just before he got hurt," said Siegel, "They were all untested before this game.

"We just have to get it back together for next week," Siegel continued. That's when the Bucks were scheduled to host the Chambersburg Cardinals, who were the defending 1977 Interstate Semipro League champs.

"I'm concerned about Chambersburg, because they're a big, fast team," the head coach concluded.

The coach was especially concerned since the Bucks had suffered a rash of injuries in the game. Lightner, Mancuso, and Rutter were joined on the injury list by "Clicker" Clark, who had sustained the lower leg bruise early in the second half. Their status for the next game would be determined later.

In the other Middle Atlantic Conference opener on July 15th, the defending champion Youngstown Hardhats buried the Washington Generals 71-0. The victory was a portent of things to come in the MAFL. Washington was living on borrowed time, and Youngstown's domination of their opponents would hurt their attendance figures.

With Lightner and several others on the injured list, the Bucks needed warm bodies. During the week, the team added Kerry Snow, a former Bucknell University quarterback, to the roster. Snow had his name plastered all over the Bucknell record books, and had helped lead the Bison to a 24-16 upset win over Colgate in 1975. Later that season he was Division II Player of the Week by throwing for three touchdowns as he helped engineer a 32-25 upset of Lehigh. In 1976 alone he set nine school passing records, completing 138 of 256 passes for 1,451 yards and averaging 177.1 yards per game in total offense. He was expected just to see spot duty as a kick returner and receiver until he could get more practice time under his belt.

"Great quarterback for us," says Rehmeyer, "He was a good find for the team. But he was rich, a bit of an elitist. He'd come to games in a motor home."

Les McCoy, who had played for the Bucks on-and-off since 1975, had rejoined the team during the week and was slated to replace the injured Darrel Rutter. Another Bucks' vet, Dave Gregg, had decided to give the semipro game another shot and was penciled in at linebacker.

But a shortage of offensive linemen was giving Siegel headaches as he tried to figure out how to arrange his personnel. He was considering several options—move Joe Wales from guard to tackle and insert defensive coordinator John Appleton at guard, or shift himself from center to tackle, switch Mark Rusnak from guard to center and start Appleton at guard.

Chambersburg came into DuBois ranked Number 8 among the nation's semipro teams by *Pro Football Weekly* magazine. They were indeed a big, fast team and they had not lost a game since the 1976 season.

Chambersburg's roster was packed with top-notch talent. Three of the Cardinals—kicker Dave Schminke, wide receiver Averill Harris, and cornerback John Duncan—had all been chosen for the 1977 national semipro all-star team by *Pro Football Weekly*. Harris had been signed by the Los Angeles Rams in 1977 but was cut. He returned to Chambersburg in time to catch 76 passes for the Cardinals for 1,362 yards in 10 games. Those three and quarterback Greg Hare, offensive guard Jesse Johnson, center Steve Oldt, and linebacker J.C. Hyder made the All-Interstate League team.

The Cardinals not only had some impressive talent on their roster, but also some impressive size.

"That team had huge players," recalls George Walker, "Even at 270 I was smaller than all their linemen!"

The Cards huge defensive front, featuring 6'3" 267 pound Leroy Broaders from Albany State, 6'5" 253 pound Joe Mason, and 6'8" 299 pound Johnny Walker from Merican Junior College completely shut down the Bucks running game as the makeshift offensive line struggled to gain a foothold against the massive Cards' line. Plus, a former teammate was coming back to haunt the Bucks again.

Larry Rydbom returned to the area to stick it to his old mates.

Rydbom had shown some big improvement since leaving the Bucks and joining the Cards. His attitude and work ethic had both improved, and he had benefited by being around new teammate Greg Hare from Ohio State.

Still determined to make it to the NFL, Rydbom traveled about 200 miles from his home in Coalport to Chambersburg and back for practices or games.

"He's the first guy to practice and the last to leave," lauded Card head coach Don Heiges. "He's my kind of player. I love the kid."

"Greg has really been a big help to me," said Rydbom of Hare, "I've learned more than just fundamentals down there. Coach has the practices so organized that he just blows a whistle and everybody knows where to go."

He added, "It feels good to have 270-pound linemen blocking for you, too," a not too subtle reference to his days playing for the mostly undersized Bucks.

Heiges, a former Cumberland Valley High School and Cumberland semipro team coach, analyzed Rydbom's two-season progress with the Cards.

"At first, I didn't think Larry could fill in and do a good job against a good team, but we're very confident with him now," said Heiges, ""Like I said before, he's my kind of player, very coachable. He's shown a lot of progression. He's gained a lot of poise, both from being around Hare and the coaches.

"Larry is a very important part of our team. He's become a leader, and he leads by example.

"Although he's playing in the shadow of Hare, he's not really a benchwarmer. He played the equivalent of about seven games last year. He'll play a lot for us this year, too."

Another former member of the Bucks, assistant coach Dave Paganetti, was serving as the Cards' special teams coach.

"Chambersburg basically is a passing team, and that's the way we're going to play them," said Al Siegel before the game. "We're going to do quite a few unconventional things."

Lightner, despite the head injury suffered in the opener against Erie, was given the okay to play. The possibility of a duel between the two former Glendale High quarterbacks led to speculation that the game would draw a big crowd.

"I hear half of Coalport is coming," said Siegel.

The Bucks fully expected to have a difficult time against the Cards.

"We knew we were outmanned and outgunned going into that game but as always we tried to meet the challenge with everything we had," says Wayne Rockmore. But what the Bucks had was simply not enough, and they certainly weren't prepared for what happened on July 22nd.

A 50-yard punt runback by Jerome Kater, the Cards' kick return specialist, set up Rene Posey's 14-yard sprint around left end for the first score of the game. Schminke's extra point gave the visitors an early 7-0 lead.

The Bucks fought back gamely. From his own 26, Lightner called for the "Mo-Fly." At the snap, wide out Mike Morgan streaked downfield, and Lightner, from the shot-gun formation, let it fly. Morgan sprinted under Lightner's bomb to put the hosts back in the game, 7-6, with 4:46 left in the first period.

The rest of the game, however, was an absolute nightmare for the Bucks.

"I was on the kick coverage team after our touchdown," says Ron Rehmeyer, "I was running downfield and saw this dark shadow out of the corner of my eye. I glanced in time to see this guy 6'7" or 6'8" try to clothesline me. If I hadn't seen him he'd have broken my neck."

Posey, a former Mount Union High and Shippensburg State College [*now University*] standout, who was in his rookie season with the Cards, scored from four yards out on the first play of the second quarter.

The Bucks had a couple chances after Posey's score, when an interception by safety Jim Slabon and a fumbled punt gave the hosts the ball in good field position. But the Bucks simply could not budge the massive Chambersburg defensive line. They were practically impenetrable.

Posey added his third touchdown, barreling in from a yard out with 3:15 left in the half to move the score to 21-6.

Chambersburg used their three timeouts to stop the clock late in the second quarter and then made that bit of strategy pay off when, after a 27-yard pass interference penalty against Slabon, Hare found Charles Williams all alone down the middle and hit him with a 33-yard scoring strike. Schminke booted the 28th Card point with 39 seconds left in the half.

Rydbom, who started the game because Hare was hobbling with an ankle injury suffered in a softball game, returned to quarterback for the second half and really put on a show for the Coalport area fans who had made the trip to DuBois to see him go against Lightner.

Chambersburg's superior offensive and defensive lines made the anticipated duel between the two ex-Viking signal callers a mismatch, however.

A diving interception by Johnny Duncan of a Lightner throw set up an 11-yard touchdown run by Posey's backfield mate, halfback Tom Brown from Harrisburg.

Then Rydbom went to work. He threw deep to Keith Boykin, and the former Tulane wide receiver skipped away from Howie Wilcox for a 62-yard touchdown play.

Chambersburg's lead was 44-6 moments later when a bad snap on a punt by the Bucks sailed out of the end zone for a safety.

On the second play of the fourth quarter, Brown scored from the two, and Schminke's conversion made it 51-6. When the Bucks got the ball back, Shoop was in at quarterback. His deflected pass was picked off by Bernard Anderson at the Bucks' 26. Instead of sitting on their huge lead, the Cardinals went for more. Rydbom immediately went for the payoff strike, zipping the ball to Tom Forman sprinting down the right side.

But the Cardinals still weren't finished yet. A pass reception by tight end Joe Crestani was fumbled away and recovered by Kater at the Bucks' 43. Rydbom, still going for the end zone, fired two more completions, one of them to Williams wide open deep down the middle. The Cards' wide out stepped away from Slabon's try at a tackle inside the five and completed the 35-yard scoring play.

The final touchdown came with 7:45 to go when Doug Fesler picked off Lightner's pass in the flat in full stride and breezed into the end zone. Two long runs by Posey had the Cards perched at the goal line in the final minutes, but Rydbom was intercepted by Denny Kurtz of Clearfield to avoid even more damage.

The relatively small crowd had watched Chambersburg amass 505 yards in total offense while limiting the Bucks to 126. Central Pennsylvania wound up with just 27 yards in 29 rushing attempts, and managed just one measly first down.

Rene Posey had 19 carries for 176 yards and scored three touchdowns from his fullback position. The Coalport fans were happy to see Rydbom, the former hometown boy, connect on six of 10 passes for 161 yards and three touchdowns, but the 71-6 loss was the worst the Bucks had experienced in their three-plus seasons of attempting to make a semipro football team a success in the area. And they weren't happy about it.

"I mean they wiped us off the map," remembers Darrel Rutter, who was working the press box for the team since being injured, "They'd have never done that to the '75 or '76 team."

"We lost big to Chambersburg," Wayne Rockmore says quietly, his voice revealing the emotion still present to this day.

Later he added, "I don't hold grudges but to be honest it did piss me off, for lack of a more appropriate phrase, I think to this day it showed a lack of class. If there was any animosity on Larry's part, I surely, to this day don't understand why. But in retrospect I recall thinking it was more the coach of the Chambersburg Cardinals than the players. Because the players reflect the wishes of the coach."

"I got to play a lot and was just enjoying it, and didn't take it personally," recalls Ron Rehmeyer, "but a lot of the guys were pissed off at Rydbom for leaving the team."

Rydbom still throwing late in the game with a huge lead didn't sit too well with the Bucks, either.

"Chambersburg ran up the score on us," George Walker says today, his voice still tinged with disgust. In fact, it was one of the first things he mentioned to the author when he met to interview the former Buck. "The Chambersburg coach liked to run up the score."

Despite the score and the hard feelings associated with the game, the Bucks really had nothing to be ashamed of. In 1978, the Cardinals would wind up with a 14-0 record and would average over 48 points per game. They also won the semipro national championship. In fact, between 1977 and 1984, the Cardinals won 72 straight regular season games, including five perfect seasons, a record for non-collegiate football.

As Al Siegel said in summing up the loss, "We got beat by a big, experienced team. We're just not deep enough in people to stay with them, but we're not demoralized."

But, the loss was enough to demoralize Siegel into giving up his coaching duties. A day after the loss, Big Al announced he had relinquished his job as head coach to concentrate on playing and handling his ever-challenging front office duties.

"Siegel asked me if I'd like to take over as head coach," recalls Wayne Rockmore, "I thought about it a little bit, but like I said before, I knew the guys. You didn't have to push me into things like that, it was a natural thing. I couldn't play so I wanted to do something to contribute. I'm glad I had the experience to coach."

So Rockmore was now head coach of the Central Pennsylvania Whitetail Bucks.

"Rocky is not gonna play at all this season," Siegel explained as the reason he was giving up his role as head coach for the team. "He wants to make sure his knee is 100 percent before he plays again."

The Rock would continue in his capacity as offensive coordinator and Siegel would still help out with tutoring the linemen.

"Rock was a good coach," remembers Ron Rehmeyer, "He taught me a lot about being a running back. I remember he always told me that on my first step my knee should hit my chest."

In another coaching move, Jim Averill of DuBois was hired to help John Appleton coach the defense. This move came about when Appleton was forced into action on the offensive line.

Siegel also announced that the game booked for the following Saturday at Philipsburg against the Brooklyn Golden Knights had been canceled because of "monetary reasons." He didn't elaborate, but the team's faltering financial situation was not a secret.

"I never got paid, although some guys did," recalls Rehmeyer with a shrug of his shoulders, "but I did get free hamburgers and free bus rides."

Also, the Aug. 5th Mid-Atlantic Football League game with the Cleveland Academes set for State College's Memorial Field had been switched to DuBois' Mansell Stadium.

"The extra week should help us regroup," added Siegel. "We've got quite a few minor injuries that should heal, and we're expecting more players to try out."

But the mood surrounding the team was bleak. Money and personnel woes were dogging the team at every turn.

"We just had a ton of injuries that ate up the team," remembers Rehmeyer, "and a lot of the 15-to-20 guys we had left were too small to take the pounding."

"That last year we were really just scraping by," says George Walker, "it was just not fun anymore."

# CHAPTER

# 11

"The fourth year was not that good;
a lot of the better players had left by then."

—WIDE RECEIVER KEN RUTTER

The Bucks were reeling. They had lost their first two games of the season and had now put their faith in a popular but inexperienced head coach. A spate of injuries had depleted the Bucks' already thin roster.

Jim Slabon joined the injured list when it was discovered that he had bruised his instep and would be unavailable for the next game against Cleveland. It would be the first game he ever missed as a member of the Bucks. That left only Big Al Siegel as the one player who had played every Bucks game in their history. Mike Morgan, who had scored all three Buck touchdowns so far, had missed the second half of the Chambersburg debacle because of a muscle spasm. But thankfully Mike was back at practice. "Clicker" Clark's leg bruise had also healed and he was deemed fit to return to action.

The Bucks had a week off due to the cancellation of the Brooklyn game that had originally been scheduled for July 29th. Next up on the schedule were the Cleveland Academes, a new club in the MAFL. In a world full of strange nicknames for semipro football teams, this had to be one of the oddest. When researching the word Academes, one finds a definition that states it's a poetic name for the garden or grove near ancient Athens where Plato taught, supposedly named for its former owner, the hero Akademos. Okay, then.

Both teams entered the game with 0-and-2 records, and both were 0-and-1 in the MAFL. The Academes had been outscored 74-9 in two losses to Clarksburg,

West Virginia and Youngstown. The two clubs faced off at Mansell Stadium in DuBois in a rain storm before a very small crowd.

For the third straight game, the Bucks struggled. The week off had not helped. Whether it was the conditions, the injuries, adjusting to their new head coach, or an overall lack of motivation, the Bucks put on another poor performance for the home fans.

The rain was falling when the game began and continued throughout. The Bucks won the toss and things went downhill from there. Joe Crestani returned the short opening kickoff to his own 49. "Clicker" Clark picked up a yard, then so did Tom Primerano. Brian Lightner then took to the air on third-and-eight but the pass was incomplete. A defensive pass interference call on the play gave the Bucks a first down at the Cleveland 44. On the very next play, however, the Bucks fumbled the ball away with Cleveland's Lonnie Kelly recovering.

An 11-play drive by the Academes produced the first score of the game. James Carter's rushing helped Cleveland pick up three first downs on the drive and quarterback Dwight Patrick passed to Victor Bailey for another. Ernie Brewer then bounced in from the one and although Cleveland missed the extra point, they led 6-0 with 9:02 still left in the first quarter.

The Bucks offense then did something that was becoming all-too familiar: it ran three plays and Ritchie Shoop had to punt. Cleveland took over on its own 31 and proceeded to drive 69 yards in twelve plays. Brewer capped the march by running the ball in from the 8. The kick was missed again but Cleveland still had a 12-0 lead with a little over three minutes left to go in the opening quarter.

When they took over after the ensuing kickoff, the Bucks offense once again gained little yardage, running only four plays before being forced to punt. This time at least the Whitetail Buck defense managed to stop the Academes at their own 36 after they had picked up a pair of first downs.

The running of Shoop and Lightner gave the Bucks one first down on their next possession, but once again the drive stalled, this time at the Cleveland 42.

When Cleveland got the ball back, they were able to move the sticks again. Patrick went to the air, hitting Blake Chamberlin for 16 yards and Steve McCoy for 22 more. Tommie Davis then sprinted 20 yards for the score halfway through the second quarter. It was now 18-0, and the Bucks were in a very deep hole.

The hole kept getting deeper. The next time they had the ball, the Bucks ran only four plays and punted again. Ritchie Shoop got off a beautiful kick that traveled 45 yards. But Ernie Brewer's 26-yard return to midfield set up the Academes in good field position. From there it took just six plays for Cleveland to score once again. A 42-yard pass from Patrick to Bailey was the big play in the drive. Davis went over from the 1 to make it 24-0 at the half.

The Academes took the second half kickoff and proceeded to march 67 yards, all of it on the ground, for yet another score. They picked up four first downs along the way and used up almost six minutes on the clock before Brewer scored from the 5 yard line. It was now 30-0.

The Buck offense, anemic up to then, finally showed some signs of life. Kerry Snow replaced Lightner at quarterback after the ex-Glendale signal caller had missed every one of his 10 passing attempts. Snow rambled for 9 yards to start the next Buck possession and then passed to Ron Rehmeyer for 19 yards and a first down. It was the only pass the Bucks managed to complete in the game. Rehmeyer then ran 11 yards to move the sticks again, but that was as far as the Bucks could get. The drive died and Shoop then punted to the Academes' 15.

Cleveland stuck to the ground to run time off the clock and moved to the Buck 47 before giving up the ball on downs. But the Bucks then fumbled it back two plays later with Harry Edwards recovering for the visitors. Two plays later Patrick passed to Chamberlin, who wound up with six catches for 105 yards, for 21 yards and the final score of the game. The Bucks had lost again, 36-0.

Central Pennsylvania was completely outplayed. Cleveland had 23 first downs to 5 for the Bucks, and outgained the home team, 398 yards to 60. The Academes didn't have to punt once all game. Lightner was 0-for-10 passing, and the best the team could manage on the ground was 18 yards each from Rehmeyer and Shoop. The Bucks offense turned the ball over three times and never really threatened to score.

With the team in what appeared to be an irreversible downward spiral, players soon became discouraged and disenchanted. Unlike past seasons, the Bucks were getting beaten badly every time they played. The games were not competitive and were usually over by halftime.

"I got sick of the losing," Ron Rehmeyer recalls, "I wanted to win. But one single mistake would usually beat us. It was amazing."

"Things got bad the last year," says Hugh Gibbons, "It got to the point where I told myself, 'I didn't want to do this anymore.'"

"The fourth year was not that good, a lot of the better players had left by then," adds Ken Rutter, one of those better players who had left before the season started and was working full-time as a carpenter and mason with the railroad and would soon become a locomotive engineer.

"That last season, we either weren't getting paid, or the checks were very miniscule. It just took something off of the experience," says Wayne Rockmore.

"I think that we all knew that the Central Pennsylvania Whitetail Bucks were coming to an end," Rockmore goes on, "There were rumors and stories concerning the dissolving of the organization and with that it just wasn't the same. Not the best of times for our team. But we hung on as long as we could, and fought the best we could, that always stands for something positive."

"There didn't seem to be the same camaraderie there had been in previous years," Rehmeyer adds, "I think the older teams had more—the '78 team not as much. There were 4 or 5 guys on the team that I thought would be my friends for life and I haven't seen them since. What's odd is that Ritchie Shoop, who I felt never liked me, has kept in contact with me and visits my office all the time."

But Rehmeyer goes on to say that no one on that '78 team, despite being severely undermanned due to all the injuries, ever quit.

"Nobody gave up," he says, "We played hard and kept at it. The guys on that team were brave, absolutely fearless. Just a fearless bunch of people. But if you don't have the size, you're gonna get destroyed."

"That last year so many guys had jumped ship," offers Darrel Rutter, "Guys had had enough. They had families and decided it was time to move on. I worked the press box for a while but things with the team were coming unraveled."

Unraveled indeed, mainly due to the continuing rash of injuries. The versatile Kevin Detwiler broke his hand in the Cleveland game and joined the ever-growing injury list.

"If we hadn't been so decimated by all the injuries, we might have done much better that year," says Rehmeyer.

Next up for the Bucks was a road game scheduled for August 12th against the Washington Generals, another struggling franchise. The Generals season had gotten off to a bad start, as they had lost to Youngstown, 71-0 and the Clarksburg, W. Va., Red Raiders, 31-6. They managed to edge Erie 10-9 but the game revealed a lot of internal strife. On one play, a General cornerback and linebacker got into a fight on the field, as the defensive back obviously felt he should be getting more help on defense from the middle.

Then on the 10th, Al Siegel got a call from Washington team officials.

"They just don't have enough money to pay for the field and the officials," explained Siegel, who sounded a little numb as he announced that the Generals had to forfeit the game.

But while the Bucks would get another weekend off, Siegel was anything but happy about the circumstances.

"I'm just so fed up its unbelievable," said the Bucks' general manager, "We needed a game this week. The forfeit means nothing. Our guys were hopped up at practice tonight, too."

For the Bucks, the forfeit was their third from the Generals during the past two seasons. In 1977, the Bucks traveled all the way to Washington, Pa., a 150-mile journey, only to learn the game couldn't be played because the field had not been prepared. The organization wound up folding, resulting in a home field forfeit win for the Bucks later that season.

Finally, on August 15th, 1978, just five days after telling the Bucks they had to forfeit their game, the Generals had to announce that after 18 seasons, the team was finally giving up the ghost and folding for good.

The team had started playing back in 1960 as the Washington Mustangs. They later changed their name to the Merchants and then finally, to the Generals. For years they had struggled, hanging on by the proverbial thread. They finally died as a result of semipro football's natural cause of death . . . lack of money.

"We just ran out of money," Tom Averell, the team's general manager and publicist said when he announced the news, "We didn't have the money to continue so we just shut it down tonight."

Averell, who worked days as a lease manager for a suburban Pittsburgh car dealership, played for the Generals for eight seasons as an offensive guard until he retired after the 1977 season.

Dedicated to his team and to saving it, Averell had assumed the duties as general manager and, in his words, "we had it going pretty good there for a while. What hurt us most, and probably what ultimately killed us off, was the fact that we couldn't find a home field to play on anywhere near Washington County."

The Generals soon resorted to wandering around the county looking for a field to play on and fans to root them on. They never really found either. For two seasons they played in Monongahela and in 1977 at Bethel Park High School before they had to fold up their tents.

"We tried everything we could to play again in Washington County," Averell said, "but nobody had a field for us. We wouldn't have started the season at all if I hadn't made arrangements to use Stone Field at North Park."

But the long 50-mile drive from Washington to North Park was just too much to ask of the few surviving local fans. At their only home game at North Park, the team lost $600 due to rent and other expenses.

The death of the Generals left the Mid-Atlantic League with just four teams. The question around the league was, 'Who would be next?' Almost everybody's answer was the Whitetail Bucks.

The team indeed had a steep hill to climb if they wanted to survive, especially with Youngstown next on the schedule. The Hardhats were ranked Number 11 in the country among semipro teams. Among their wins was a 71-0 shellacking of Washington, and a 40-13 smashing of a team from Tonawanda, New York, a game in which the Hardhats displayed line play that "was the best I've seen all year," according to head coach Al Boggia. Youngstown was seeking its 14th straight win in MAFL play since joining the league in '77.

The Bucks meanwhile, traveled to Youngstown with only 26 players eligible to dress for the game. At least one of those wasn't at 100% health wise.

"I had gotten hurt at a particularly intense practice," Ron Rehmeyer says, "Got hit in the back between my shoulder pads and hip pads. Later that night I couldn't stand up, and couldn't sleep. I went to the doctor the next day and told him my back was killing me. He told me he was not going to give me pain pills to practice.

"My teammates talked me into going to a chiropractor. He was a physical therapist and I liked him. He told me, 'When I'm done, you'll feel so good you'll feel like you can play right now . . . but don't do that.'

"So I missed practice and then the doctor called and I told him I still needed some kind of meds, so he prescribed a muscle relaxant for me.

"On the bus to Youngstown, I took 1 or 2 of the pills and drank a six-pack of beer, my own prescription you might say. Now realize, this is a four-hour bus ride so it wasn't like I was drinking right before the game. Due to the pills and the beer, I was feeling okay. But when we were warming up I couldn't catch a thing, my hands wouldn't coordinate to catch the ball. So anyway, the game starts. Kerry Snow is the quarterback, and on the first play of the game calls a draw play to me. He hands me the ball and immediately two big Youngstown linebackers who had both played at Ohio State and were on a level with All-American Tom Cousineau, just plowed me under. Just buried me. I walked back to the huddle, looked at Snow and said, 'Don't ever call that play again as long as you live!'"

The outmanned Central Pennsylvania team did their best, but the powerful Hardhats were just too much for them.

Despite some fine play by the Bucks defense, Youngstown had no trouble scoring in the game.

The first Hardhat score came on the hosts' first series when standout quarterback Vern Wireman, who had just been sacked for an 11-yard loss moments before, fired a 52-yard scoring strike to his favorite receiver, Lou Kelson. It was one of 26 touchdown receptions Kelson would score in 1978, a semipro record. Kirk Andrews' conversion made the score 7-0 in Youngstown's favor.

Youngstown scored its second touchdown on its next play from scrimmage. Central Pennsylvania made one first down on its possession, but was soon forced to punt. Youngstown returned the kick to its own 43, and on the very first play, running back Jim Smith was sprung loose on a trap play and raced 57-yards to score. Andrews missed the extra point but the Hardhats still led 13-0.

And they were far from finished. In the second quarter, Youngstown scored three touchdowns to blow the game wide open. The first was a two yard run by Smith and the second a four yard burst by Rick Ellebie. Both touchdowns came on the 'hats' first play from scrimmage. That was the kind of great field position the Bucks were giving the Hardhats.

The final score of the half came when Wireman hit Kelson with a 35 yard scoring strike, making the score 33-0 at intermission.

At halftime, the Youngstown fans were treated to an exhibition game between two midget football teams.

The rout continued, although Youngstown, unlike Chambersburg a few weeks before, eased up in the second half. The Hardhats scored a touchdown in each of the two remaining quarters. The first came when Luke Tabor recovered a poor Central Pennsylvania punt in the end zone for a touchdown. In the last quarter, Youngstown's third string quarterback got into the act by tossing a long scoring pass to make it 46-0.

It looked like the Bucks were heading for their second straight shut out until Phil Crotzer ran under Kerry Snow's 35 yard touchdown pass with 16 seconds to play in the game. Siegel's placement attempt was wide.

After the game, Siegel, while admitting that the loss was hardly unexpected, praised his defensive unit for a deceptively good job.

"Don't let that score fool you." said Siegel "The defense looked pretty good, but they spent a lot of time playing with their backs against the wall. We had poor field position most of the game and due to inexperience with our punter and center, it didn't improve much."

"I didn't remember a thing after that first play," recalls Rehmeyer, "Nothing of the game and not the ride home."

The rest of the Bucks probably wished they could have forgotten the experience as easily. Offensively, the Bucks had little to show for their efforts, as they rushed for less than 50 yards. But for the first time all season they showed they were capable of putting together a decent passing game.

"Our quarterback, Kerry Snow, did well considering he was pressured every time he went back to pass," Siegel commented, "He completed 11 of 33 passes and had three intercepted."

"We actually played a decent game despite the fact that we were missing key players," said Siegel, "We're looking forward to playing a team of our own caliber next week. We have some new players from Bellefonte and Cresson that should help stabilize our offensive line."

Above all else, despite the score, the team hadn't quit. They were just out-manned by a superior opponent. But unlike previous seasons, that was hap-pening much too often. The Bucks had scored only four touchdowns all year, and had been outscored 172 points to just 26. The forfeit over Washington was the only thing that kept the team from being winless.

It had been a rough week for the Bucks. "We had a real shakeup because of what happened last week," said Al Siegel, who due to the manpower shortage was playing both offense and defense, "We added six or seven guys to the roster and should have about 34 ball players on the bus."

The outcome of the Youngstown game had driven Siegel to desperate measures.

"We actually went around and picked up equipment from several guys who weren't coming to practice and gave it to players who couldn't work out because they didn't have any gear," said Siegel, "I don't know how many of the new players will start, but they'll all play a lot."

Because of the rash of injuries or other reasons, such as being unavailable to play, the Bucks roster no longer included Jim Slabon, Brian Lightner, Kevin McClincy, George Walker, Greg Walker, Joe Williams, Ritchie Shoop, Randy Arthur, John Challingsworth, and Keith Graham. Kevin Detwiler was still on the injured list due to the broken hand he had suffered against Cleveland, and Larry Lane had suffered a bruised sternum in the Youngstown game. Bill "Clicker" Clark's leg had not responded to treatment and he was through for the season.

New additions to the team included linebackers Tom Monahan and Fred DeHaas, and defensive back Jack Volpe. Siegel stressed that several Bucks, in-cluding himself, would have to go both ways against the Express.

"Erie hasn't won since they beat us, but they don't have their good running back, Dave Green," Siegel noted, "He's with Montreal in the Canadian Football League now.

"We're prepared and confident to start the second half of our season."

Despite Siegel's optimism, the team bused to Erie with only 27 players, five of whom had never worn a Bucks' uniform before. "It's a losing season, so the guys don't want to travel," Big Al lamented.

The undersized, outmanned Bucks had not quit against Youngstown.

The same could not be said in Erie.

"The guys got frustrated in this one," Siegel said afterward.

The Bucks were down by only 17-0 at the half, but then proceeded to mail in the last two quarters. It turned into yet another ugly loss.

Due to a lack of numbers, many players had to go both ways, playing both offense and defense. Fatigue set in, and apathy followed. The Bucks found themselves deep in their own end of the field for much of the game. Erie scored two safeties thanks mainly to the constant bad field position that the Bucks found themselves in.

When the final gun sounded, the Express had rolled over the Bucks, 53-0.

"It was similar to what we did last week at Youngstown," Siegel said it trying to explain the rout. "But we didn't quit at Youngstown."

The Bucks had scored just one touchdown in their last three games. Their record now stood at 1-and-5 and they had been outscored 225 to 26 for the season. The campaign was quickly becoming an embarrassment. While the Bucks had struggled financially their first three seasons—what semipro team doesn't?—they had at least been competitive and at times even superlative. Their defense, loaded with hard hitters and smart ballplayers, had always been strong. The offense ran hot and cold but when it was hot it could score from anywhere and everywhere on the field.

But now the team was just a shadow of its former self. Bam-Bam Kanagy was serving with the military in Germany. Ken Rutter was working on the railroad. His brother Darrel was out of action with a snapped Achilles tendon. Tom Marlett was living in Pittsburgh and preparing to start a career in the Army. Larry Rydbom was in Chambersburg heaving passes for the Cardinals. Wayne Rockmore was coaching on the sidelines instead of running for big yardage with the "15 wham" play. Ron Roefaro was teaching and coaching football at Altoona High. Alge Jones was throwing hay bales on his farm instead of catching passes with the Bucks. All these players had performed solidly for the Bucks and had helped make them a very good football team, one opponents knew was a squad to reckon with. Now the team had a lot of younger and inexperienced players who were missing that veteran presence and guidance that pros like Rydbom, Marlett, Rockmore, Jones and the Rutters had been able to provide. As Ron Rehmeyer says, the kind of camaraderie that had turned the upstart Bucks into a tough squad and that had been so prevalent in 1975, '76 and '77 was not as strong in '78. That absence was beginning to show.

Another problem was that although the team had never carried a lot of players on its roster that number was now in the mid-20s, which meant many players had to play both offense and defense, which increased the risk of injuries, a situation that really doomed the Bucks in 1978.

When he was asked about the state of team affairs, Siegel said of his players, "They're gonna have to make a decision. I told Rocky that if we don't have two

decent practices this week, I'm gonna fold the team to try to salvage something
for next year.

"We have two league games to go, one in Cleveland and one at Clearfield
against Youngstown, and I'd like to honor our league commitments."

The non-conference game with the Pittsburgh Black Knights originally
scheduled for September 2nd had been cancelled, because, according to Siegel,
the Knights had joined a league and had adjusted their schedule accordingly. So
the Bucks had two weeks to regroup before their next game, in Cleveland.

Then on Thursday the 7th, it was announced that the Whitetail Bucks would
indeed return to action on Saturday the 9th. But not at Cleveland as scheduled
but at Braddock against—you guessed it—none other than the Pittsburgh Black
Knights. Yep, the exact same team who's game with the Bucks that had been
originally scheduled for September 2nd, but then had been canceled. At this
point the author will let Al Siegel explain the bizarre circumstances that led to
this case of a "scheduled/canceled/scheduled again" nonconference game.

"Youngstown is just too strong for the rest of the league, and it's affecting
their draw," stated Big Al, "They were scheduled to play Erie at home Saturday,
we were supposed to go up to Cleveland and the Black Knights scheduled a
game at Toronto because they had the bye in their league.

"There was no way Youngstown wanted to play Erie because they had
beat them bad earlier so this is the deal that was made through a lot of phone
calls. Youngstown is going to Toronto, Erie is going to Cleveland to play in our
place. They were scheduled for next week anyhow. We're forfeiting our game to
Cleveland because it means nothing in the standings. In turn, we're going to play
the Black Knights, one of the teams we feel we can compete against."

Everybody get all that? There was nothing quite like semipro football. Fluid
scheduling situations such as this required team GMs and front office personnel
to think on their feet, at times think outside the box, and become very flexible
in terms of schedules and opponents. Then Siegel continued.

"It looks like our league is definitely going to fold," the big veteran said, "or at
least we're going to back up and regroup. We're trying to save our program, too."

So it looked like the rumors that had circulated for weeks were true. Not
only were the Whitetail Bucks on thin ice financially, but the whole Mid-Atlantic
League was hanging on by its collective fingertips. The clock was ticking, and the
writing was on the wall.

As they prepared to face the Black Knights, the Bucks announced that since
the Washington Generals had folded, Siegel had managed to scrounge up another opponent to take their place for the Bucks' next game on September 16th.

The Franklin County Minutemen, from Chambersburg, Pa., and the Mason-Dixon League, were proclaimed as the team's opponent for a game on the 16th in Curwensville. The Minutemen were a new but solid franchise, and would go on to win the Mason-Dixon title in 1978. The team featured Semipro Football Hall of Famer Chazz "The Hammer" Brown, a Vietnam veteran who had been bouncing around the minor leagues since 1969. They also had two Mount Union High School grads on their roster—Eddie Rogers, a flanker and Nat Fortson, a defensive tackle.

On the 9th, the Bucks took their Penn State Fullington bus to Braddock, Pa., another decaying Eastern town feeling the brunt of the decline of the steel and coal industries. The city had seen its population decrease alarmingly from its peak of almost 21,000 residents in 1920 to around 6,000 in the late '70s. Around this time crack cocaine was introduced to the community, which would ultimately lead to an epidemic of the drug in the early 1980s. The combination of the two problems nearly destroyed the community. By 1988, Braddock would be designated a financially distressed community. It may just have been the buckle in the Rust Belt.

By September 9th, the Bucks themselves were pretty financially distressed as well. They got off the bus in Braddock with only 20 players ready to suit up, not enough manpower to field complete offensive and defensive units. Almost everyone would need to play both ways.

"We played in Braddock and the stadium was underground," Ron Rehmeyer says, "below ground level. There was a baseball diamond right in the middle of it."

The Bucks, outmanned as usual, put up a pretty good fight for a while against the Black Knights. For most of the first half, the defenses dominated. Then came the moment that may just have sounded the death knell for the Central Pennsylvania Whitetail Bucks.

Fred DeHaas was a linebacker who had graduated from Bellefonte High School in 1972. He had joined the team during the season, recruited to help stock the roster when the players began getting hurt at an ever more alarming rate. Late in the first half, DeHaas made a tackle against the Knights—and didn't get up.

An ambulance arrived on the field and EMTs placed DeHaas on a stretcher and rushed him to Braddock Hospital. He had a cracked vertebrae.

The injury was a crushing blow to the Bucks. Watching their teammate fall and then get carted off the field was more than the already dispirited Bucks could take. It took away what little fight the team had left. The Black Knights scored four times in the second half and walked off the field 28-0 winners.

Siegel told reporters about DeHaas' injury after the game, stating that he would "probably be in Braddock Hospital all week."

"We only had 20 players but it was 0-0 when Fred got hurt," Siegel went on, "The team wasn't the same after that."

Soon after, there was no team at all. Siegel, citing both player and fan apathy, finally gave up the ghost after fighting a losing battle all season. He told reporters he was folding the team.

"Interest is just waning at this point," Big Al finally admitted. "There's a lack of interest by ball players, supporters and fans."

"Siegel just didn't have the money to keep it going," says Hugh Gibbons.

At least one player, however, contends that the reasons the Bucks folded were not solely financial.

"I remember that player breaking his back," says Joe Wales, referring to the DeHaas injury, "They disbanded the team to avoid a law suit."

Whatever the reasons might have been, the Bucks were now history, consigned to the graveyard of defunct sports franchises, now just pedestrians on the boulevard of broken dreams. For four years these men had tried to keep the dream of Mike McNeish and Al Siegel alive. They had fought the good fight, both on and off the field, fighting their opponents as well as the apathetic attitudes of teammates and fans alike, the perceived stigma of semipro football, and the constant uphill struggle to try and make a team from a rural area successful.

The Bucks drew good crowds their first couple years as they played competitive, exciting and at times top-notch football. But as the team started to struggle on the field, they felt the effects of this at the gate. The Central Pennsylvania sports fan can be a finicky creature, given to quickly jumping on and off the bandwagon of their favorite team. Even Penn State and Joe Paterno, despite their success, felt the wrath of local fans, when even a single a loss by the Nittany Lions would have fans cursing under their breath and calling for Paterno's head.

For four years, the dream had been a reality. But now the dream was gone.

"When it ended, and the team had folded, we came back from the last game, and went to the bar and had one last drink together," recalls Wayne Rockmore, "It was a sad thing, there was so much potential there. It was sad to see it go. But it was an enterprise, and success comes from the balance sheet. But it was still tough to see it go."

"It was sad to see it end," says Darrel Rutter.

With the Bucks having folded, there was talk that some of the players had been offered an invitation from the management of the Pittsburgh Black Knights to play with that team for the remainder of the 1978 season.

"I don't recall anyone going," says Ron Rehmeyer, "When it was over, it was over."

Quite a few former Bucks did go on to play for the Chambersburg Cardinals, thanks to an assist from a former Cardinal and minor-league legend.

"King Corcoran made it possible for a lot of us to play for Chambersburg," says George Walker.

"Some of us later went down to Chambersburg and played for them," adds Rod Ullein.

"A few of our guys moved up to play for the Chambersburg Cardinals, which was one of the top teams in the country," says Joe Wales, "My brother, Albe, played there and so did Jeff 'Mother' McCartney."

"I got into power training while I was hurt," recalls Darrel Rutter, "The Cardinals called me about playing but I didn't go."

In the years since the team passed into the mists of sports history in 1978, some former Bucks feel that they and the team did not get the respect they deserved.

"It upsets me that the Bucks were and are perceived as a joke," says Hugh Gibbons, "We didn't get the respect we should have. We had some great athletes on our team."

"We'd play everybody tough, it was no joke to us," states George Walker, "We took it seriously. Put our heart and soul into it."

Others, however, think the problem was that the local area did not support the team, and that the local media didn't properly promote the team.

"I think a lot of this perception stems from the fact that the local media in State College virtually ignored us" offers Pat Little.

"I do not think we were treated as a joke," declares Tom Marlett, "But I also do not believe any of us gave a rat's ass what the people in the community thought, especially the 'arm-chair quarterbacks' in the area. We treated the people in the area to a very good game, so let the minions be the minions. We were like the Steelers of the 50s and 60s; you knew we may not win, but you will get your ass beat with a lot of hard hitting."

"Most people did not know about the team or really cared for that matter," states Bill Luther, "Semipro football was new to the area and we played during the summer. I would agree that most did not take it very seriously, but I don't recall hearing it referred to as a 'joke.'"

"The talent on that team was unbelievable," says Darrel Rutter, "I just wish the area would have supported us like they do the [*Altoona*] Curve. They built them a nice stadium and everything."

At least one player believes the local community didn't realize the effort put forth both on and off the field by the Bucks to try and make the team successful.

"I don't think some people realized the commitments that everyone had to make just to have an organized team," says Ron Roefaro, "The players had to have most of their own equipment, except for team jerseys. You had to make family and job sacrifices to practice and play in the games. And, if you got hurt, you were on your own. You even had to have your own supplies to prepare your body with tape, pads and devices for protecting small injuries.

"It wasn't like today's soccer moms that carry the drinks and kiss the wounds for their children. Those of us that were married, our wives were usually pissed at us for playing, getting injured and taking time away from the family. So there was always that ubiquitous dichotomy at play.

"Also, the team players that doubled as the organizers, managers, planners, personnel seekers, schedulers, trainers and finders of financial backers for the team, those guys did a lot of work for the dream of having a team. Guys like Al Siegel were sometimes also player/coaches. They deserve a lot of respect as they spent thankless hours for the time they put towards the team."

As to the perceived lack of respect, Roefaro goes on to say, "I know that for me, and I believe for many of our teammates, we didn't care what anyone thought! I think the State College area suffers from that elite attitude that comes from the Penn State program."

While the *Clearfield Progress* offered solid coverage of the Bucks during their existence, a lot of other local newspapers and media outlets did not. This could have been caused in a large part to the fact that the Bucks just got lost in the shuffle when it came to coverage by the local media outlets.

"I was the sports editor at *The DuBois Courier-Express* during the time of the Whitetail Bucks," says Tom Schott, now a member of the DuBois Historical Society, "They were not a prominent part of our coverage. I had a staff of one at that time and a part-time game to game assistant. We covered all the sports for four high schools, Little League, Legion baseball, local recreation baseball and softball, etc. We did try to provide reports of the games because of the players from DuBois on the team. These were obtained when available from sports desks in other towns or given to us by the team."

"At the paper we didn't do a lot of coverage of them," states Ron Bracken, who was a sportswriter for the *Centre Daily Times*. "They were kind of an extra thing we had to deal with outside of P.S.U. and the high schools, which kept us busy enough."

The Whitetail Bucks did have some identity problems when it came to coverage in out-of-town newspapers, being referred to quite often as simply the "Bucks," which is understandable. But at other times—and for some unknown reason—the team was called the "Vikings" and the "Stars." Sometimes they were listed in game accounts as simply "Central." Then there's George Walker's story of the team being mistaken for a hunting club at a local luncheon, more associated with the NRA than the NCAA. But many still remember the Bucks fondly.

"I bought one the purple jackets that Al had made up with a picture of the tail end of a Whitetail Buck on the back" states Mike Leone, "I had that jacket for many years and I finally gave it to my son."

In 2000, John Hartsock wrote an article in the *Altoona Mirror* marking the 25th anniversary of the team. Neil Rudel, another *Mirror* sportswriter, penned a "Where Are They Now?" article about Darrel Rutter.

Whatever the attitudes of the area's football fans and media might have been regarding the team, all the former Whitetail Bucks have one thought in common—they all cherish their memories of playing semipro football for the Bucks, and they relish the idea of passing their stories along. Most significant of all, they have absolutely no regrets.

"We all knew that we would never play in the NFL," remembers Ron Roefaro, "We didn't have all the natural talents, size, speed and athletic abilities that those unique individuals who make it to the NFL are so blessed with by God. Not all of us had the God given size, speed, and athletic ability that a Division 1 program and pro teams demand. But, there are many good football players out there that have 'bigger hearts' than ability and size would dictate. They 'play big.' Division 2 and 3 schools are filled with them. Semipro football provides a venue for many football players to compete at the next level, and even though it is a long shot, they may get the notice of someone at the next higher level. Those things got them there and dedication, training and luck keeps them in the battle.

"For most of us, what we did have was heart and a burning desire to compete in a sport that we loved. We couldn't quench our thirst for that impact that you get when you hit someone. I know that you can get that in other sports, but ours was football.

"Also, the team concept was addicting to us. You actually do your role as an individual but all the parts come together to form a team. And those teams that are successful gel together both physically and mentally. You become a band of brothers that bleed and sweat together. For most of us, we played for nothing but our pride and dedication and love for the game. The semipro leagues and teams gave a chance to live this desire once again.

"Our bodies have the same physical wear and tear that the pros suffer. Personally, I have had three hip replacements and an operation on my right shoulder. Other joints, back and hands suffer from arthritis, especially when overused or when rain is coming. But, when asked if I would do it again, my answer without hesitation is YES!!! I would go back in a minute! My name will never show up in the record books or on the stat sheets. I was a lineman and we got our rewards on every play in the trenches. I miss that feeling!

"We were getting a chance to play again the game that we loved at the next level. I played each week because I had a passion for the game and had a family connection to my fellow warhorses.

"When we played teams that were located close to areas where pro teams were located or larger Division 1 schools, we played against many of the guys that were on pro practice squads and players that graduated from big school programs. So we played against some very good individuals and teams.

"Perception is in the eye of the beholder! Even after all these years, once-in-a-while someone will say, 'Hey, didn't you play for the Whitetail Bucks?'

"To hear that is even better that eating a Banana Split!"

"Love of the game was what drove most of us," says Pat Little, "I think we played for each other. Initially, the mixture of rival schools was a little tense. We had played each other in some very important games and there were mixed feelings. However, shortly after joining the team we became friends and teammates. We bonded in a common purpose. We were a little disorganized at first, but we kept at it and somewhere in the first season it began to click. I am not sure when that happened, but it was pretty cool when it did. Soon we were playing for each other."

"We won some pretty good games, and were close in all the games we lost, except the Pittsburgh Ironmen and Youngstown Hardhats games," states Tom Marlett, "Those Youngstown boys were both BIG and good; they were mainly the guys from Youngstown State and a few former pros."

"We had some great football players on that team," Darrel Rutter states without hesitation, "I saw some great ones at Penn State, but the Bucks had some that were just as good. That's not bravado, that's truth. We had guys who were railroaders, miners, steelworkers; we had kids out of high school, laborers, professors, lawyers, state cops, even a writer, me.

"I've had my shoulders separated, ribs hurt, knees hurt, I don't know how many concussions I've had. I do have trouble remembering things sometimes. Despite playing under the constant threat of injury, most of the players felt like they were the luckiest people on the face of the earth. We weren't making any money, but it was the most fun I've ever had in my life."

"We were serious about it," offers Ron Rehmeyer, "but we had a lot of fun too."

"Football was always a big part of my life. I had dreams of playing in the NFL, but I didn't make it," Carl Brown says now, "But the Bucks were a good time in my life. I had the most fun doing that."

"We played for the purity of the game," remembers Wayne Rockmore, "I had fun playing, I was very proud of us and what we did. None of us liked to lose. We practiced and played hard."

"They are good guys," Bill Luther says of his teammates, "Haven't seen most of them in many years. I still can't believe that was all those years ago. We all have one thing in common—great stories, great memories of the old days as Whitetail Bucks."

Then Luther adds, "Our pension must be worth about five bucks now!"

"Some good years to remember with good friends," offers Joe Wales.

"It was a good time," says Tom Marlett.

"Something I will always remember and tell my grandkids," states Pat Little.

# EPILOGUE

Before we close the book for good on the story of the Central Pennsylvania Whitetail Bucks, both literally and figuratively, there's one more thing that should be mentioned.

That is despite having been around for only four years, never winning a championship and struggling both on the field and off, the Bucks managed to make history. They were the first semipro football team to play a prison team outside the prison walls.

Okay, so it wasn't actually the Whitetail Bucks team, just some members of the team recruited to play in the game, and it was only an exhibition, but it was a game nonetheless. The exhibition occurred in State College, and was played at Memorial Field. The Bucks have quite a lot of vivid memories about the game.

"There had been softball games played against a prison team, but never a football game," says Ron Rehmeyer.

"We played a team from Rockview Prison, the only team to ever do that outside the prison walls," recalls Hugh Gibbons, "We played them at State College. But talk about pressure. Trying to play and all those guns pointed at us!"

While the game made history, it wasn't quite Pennsylvania's answer to "The Longest Yard."

"We beat 'em up pretty good," remembers George Walker, "They were actually pretty wimpy."

"I remember scrimmaging the prison team and if I recall it didn't last any longer than a half," says Ron Roefaro, "It wasn't very well organized and if I remember correctly there weren't any officials there. It wasn't like the movie "The Longest Yard" with Burt Reynolds. They weren't very good and when they saw that they weren't going to run over us, they kind of gave up. I think I remember them walking off the field in disgust and ending the scrimmage. The anticipation was greater than the actual event!"

"The prison team game was a scrimmage game," offers Wayne Rockmore, "it was a big deal because it was to raise money for Muscular Dystrophy. I had a fun time, but we were out of shape. I couldn't even scratch the back of my head the next day I hurt so much."

"It was what you might say pretty casual," adds Rehmeyer, "The refs weren't calling anything, and while we had the equipment on, not much was happening. It was not really the Bucks playing as a team, and there was really just a lot of general standing around."

There were no newspaper articles that reported on the game, and nothing but the memories of the players to verify it. One former Buck has a theory on why the press didn't cover the game.

"That game against the Rockview team, the newspapers didn't cover it, because the newspaper guys didn't show up," explains Darrel Rutter, "They didn't want to get killed."

Since 1978, when the Whitetail Bucks joined all the other teams in the semipro football graveyard, there have been other attempts to place semipro teams in the area. The North East PA Miners, Altoona Bouncers, Williamsport Wildcats, Central Pennsylvania Piranha, Western PA Wildcatz, Butler County Bears, and DuBois Mountain Lions have all tried to gain a foothold in the area. The latest addition to this list is a team called the Moshannon Valley Vikings, who have announced plans to enter the Great Eastern Football Association, which includes 20 teams from around Pennsylvania, including the DuBois Mountain Lions, State College Flash, and the Mifflin County Tomahawks.

Whether or not these teams and leagues make it, they will never replace the Central Pennsylvania Whitetail Bucks. It was a special time, and a special team, manned by special players who played for simply the love of the game. No pretensions, no glitz, no glamour, no feelings of self-importance, it was just men playing and enjoying the game they loved. There will never be another Whitetail Bucks no matter how many times they try to recreate that feeling. There will never be another George Walker, standing on Atherton Street in his full uniform, ready to play before his teammates picked him up; never another Wayne Rockmore, The Rock, racing up the middle on the 15 Wham play and then simply handing the ball to the referee after he scored; never another Darrel Rutter, defensive end, kick returner and self-employed philosopher; never another "Bam-Bam" Kanagy, playing an entire game with three broken bones in his hand; never another Mike McNeish, who took a dream and turned it into reality; and certainly never another Big Al Siegel, who did it all for the Bucks, acting as owner, general manager, assistant coach, head coach, and player, just in an effort to keep his and McNeish's dream alive against the longest of odds.

People like this and so many others who played and worked for the Bucks should never be forgotten, never resigned to the foggy mists of forgotten history. They deserve respect and their well-earned place in the annals of Central Pennsylvania, even if sometimes it seemed as if they were playing for just a hoagie and a beer.

# 1975

## 1975 BUCKS' GAME BY GAME

| | | | |
|---|---|---|---|
| **8/9 Brooklyn Golden Knights (H)** | L | 13-30 | at State College (500) |
| 8/17 Beaver County Cougars (A) | W | 19-6 | |
| **8/23 Washington Generals (H)** | W | 40-6 | at Philipsburg (1,100) |
| **8/30 New York Tigers (H)** | W | 47-6 | at Curwensville (400) |
| **9/14 Pittsburgh Ironmen (H)** | L | 18-27 | at Philipsburg (1,300) |
| 9/20 Johnstown Miners (A) | L | 8-45 | |
| **9/28 East Palestine (H)** | L | 8-9 | at Curwensville |
| **10/4 East Ohio (H)** | W | 13-0 | at Altoona (600) |
| 10/11 Washington Generals (A) | W | 27-0 | |
| **10/18 Johnstown Miners (H)** | W | 40-2 | at Clearfield (300) |
| 10/26 Pittsburgh Ironmen (A) | L | 12-36 | |
| Latrobe Laurel Leopards (A) | W | (Forfeit) | |

## GAME ONE—8/9/75 BROOKLYN GOLDEN KNIGHTS 30, WHITETAIL BUCKS 13

**SCORE BY QUARTERS**

| | | | | |
|---|---|---|---|---|
| Knights | 7 | 3 | 13 | 7 - 30 |
| Bucks | 0 | 0 | 0 | 13 - 13 |

Brk—Bonham 1 run (Jamison kick)
Brk—Jamison 27 FG
Brk—Meyers 55 fumble return (Kick failed)
Brk—Bonham 1 run (Jamison kick)
Brk—Phillips 11 pass from Green (Jamison kick)
CP—Hipp 5 run (kick blocked)
CP—Kyler 14 pass from Miller (Rutter pass from Slabon)

| STATISTICS | KNIGHTS | BUCKS |
|---|---|---|
| First Downs Rushing | 4 | 1 |
| First Downs Passing | 7 | 1 |
| First Downs Penalties | 0 | 2 |
| Net Rushing Yardage | 92 | -72 |
| Passes Att.—Com. | 22-8 | 31-13 |
| Passing Yardage | 104 | 170 |
| Penalties—Yards | 6-55 | 6-30 |
| Punts—Average | 2-24.0 | 2-29.5 |
| Fumbles—Lost | 3-2 | 5-2 |

## GAME TWO—8/17/75 WHITETAIL BUCKS 19, BEAVER COUNTY COUGARS 6

### SCORE BY QUARTERS

| | | | | |
|---|---|---|---|---|
| Bucks | 6 | 0 | 7 | 6 - 19 |
| Cougars | 0 | 0 | 0 | 6 - 6 |

CP—Miller 29 run (Kick Failed)
CP—Hipp 16 run (Skillings kick)
BC—Tisdale 26 pass from Palkowoski (Kick Blocked)
CP—Rydbom 4 run (Kick Blocked)

| TEAM STATISTICS | BUCKS | COUGARS |
|---|---|---|
| First Downs Rushing | 4 | 5 |
| First Downs Passing | 10 | 6 |
| First Downs Penalties | 0 | 2 |
| Net Rushing Yardage | 126 | 73 |
| Passes Att.—Com. | 25-14 | 23-10 |
| Passing Yardage | 218 | 164 |
| Penalties—Yards | 6-51 | 3-15 |
| Punts—Average | 2-37.0 | 4-35.5 |
| Fumbles—Lost | 3-2 | 2-1 |

## GAME THREE—8/23/75 WHITETAIL BUCKS 40, WASHINGTON GENERALS 6

### SCORE BY QUARTERS

| | | | | |
|---|---|---|---|---|
| Generals | 6 | 0 | 0 | 0 - 6 |
| Bucks | 7 | 6 | 20 | 7 - 40 |

CP—Rydbom 4 run (Skillings Kick)
W—Bucci 69 Interception Return (Kick Blocked)

CP—Kyler 4 run (Kick Blocked)
CP—K. Rutter 3 pass from Rydbom (Jones pass from Slabon)
CP—Rydbom 8 run (Kick failed)
CP—D. Rutter 76 Punt Return (Skillings Kick)
CP—Sommer Recovered Blocked Punt in end zone (Hipp pass from Slabon)

## GAME FOUR–8/30/75 WHITETAIL BUCKS 47, NEW YORK TIGERS 6

### SCORE BY QUARTERS

| | | | | |
|---|---|---|---|---|
| Tigers | 6 | 0 | 0 | 0 - 6 |
| Bucks | 0 | 20 | 14 | 13 - 47 |

NY—Newkirk, 57 pass from T. Jackson (kick blocked)
CP—Rydbom, 1 run (Jones pass from Slabon)
CP—Jones, 79 pass from K. Rutter (Skillings kick)
CP—Skillings, 28 pass from Rydbom (Kick failed)
CP—Skillings, 13 pass from Rydbom (Skillings kick)
CP—Rydbom, 5 run (Skillings kick)
CP—White, 8 run (Kick failed)
CP—White, 21 run (Skillings kick)

| TEAM STATISTICS | TIGERS | BUCKS |
|---|---|---|
| First Downs Rushing | 0 | 12 |
| First Downs Passing | 4 | 8 |
| First Downs Penalties | 2 | 4 |
| Net Rushing Yardage | -4 | 212 |
| Passes Att.—Com. | 23-5 | 26-13 |
| Passing Yardage | 123 | 253 |
| Penalties—Yards | 8-64 | 10-87 |
| Punts—Average | 4-33.5 | 1-32.0 |
| Fumbles—Lost | 7-4 | 8-2 |

### INDIVIDUAL STATISTICS

**RUSHING—Bucks:** Kyler 14-83, Rydbom 21-56, White 7-66, Rockmore 14, Slabon 1-10, Kritzer 2-2, Hipp 5-2, K. Rutter 1- minus 6, Potter 1- minus 15. **Tigers:** Marlon 4-7, Smith 3-7, Winton 2-5, Justice 4-2, T. Jackson 6- minus 2, Newkirk 3- minus 23.

**PASSING—Bucks:** Rydbom 23-11, 148 yards, K. Rutter 3-2, 105. **Tigers:** T. Jackson 20-4, 120, Winton 1-0, 0, Newkirk 2-1, 3.

**RECEIVING—Bucks:** C. Skillings 5-71, Jones 1-25, Rutter 2-23, Kyler 1-8, Gibbons 1-26, White 1-0. **Tigers:** K. Jackson 2-39, Newkirk 2-81, Jones 1-3.

## GAME FIVE—9/14/75 PITTSBURGH IRONMEN 27, WHITETAIL BUCKS 18

**SCORE BY QUARTERS**

| | | | | |
|---|---|---|---|---|
| Pittsburgh | 0 | 14 | 13 | 0 - 27 |
| Bucks | 6 | 0 | 0 | 12 - 18 |

CP—Jones to pass from K. Rutter (Kick failed)
P—Richardson 1 run (Ross kick)
P—Fullum 43 pass from Folden (Ross Kick)
P—Fullum 30 pass from Folden (Kick failed)
P—Smith 10 run (Ross kick)
CP—Jones 7 pass from Miller (Kick failed)
CP—Jones 11 pass from Miller (Pass failed)

## GAME SIX—9/20/75 JOHNSTOWN MINERS 45, WHITETAIL BUCKS 8

**SCORE BY QUARTERS**

| | | | | |
|---|---|---|---|---|
| Bucks | 2 | 6 | 0 | 0 - 8 |
| Johnstown | 6 | 13 | 6 | 20 - 45 |

J—C. Gunby 17 run (Kick failed)
CP—Safety, White, Arnelle and McCoy sacked McCabe in end zone
J—N. Gunby 4 run (Layo kick)
J—Wyatt 63 tumble return (Kick failed)
CP—Rydbom 1 run (kick failed)
J—C. Gunby 13 pass from McCabe (kick failed)
J—Hall 26 pass from McCabe
J—C. Gunby 6 run
J—N. Gunby 21 run

## GAME SEVEN—9/28/75 EAST PALESTINE RED DEVILS 9, WHITETAIL BUCKS 8

**SCORE BY QUARTERS**

| | | | | |
|---|---|---|---|---|
| East Palestine | 3 | 0 | 6 | 0 - 9 |
| Bucks | 0 | 0 | 6 | 2 - 8 |

EP—FG Andrews 43
CP—Skillings 6 pass from Rydbom (Kick blocked)
EP—Jordan 2 run (Kick blocked)
CP—Safety, Dugan ran into own end zone

| TEAM STATISTICS | EP | CP |
|---|---|---|
| First Downs Rushing | 8 | 6 |
| First Downs Passing | 2 | 8 |
| First Downs Penalties | 0 | 2 |
| Net Yards Rushing | 136 | 94 |
| Passes Att.—Comp.—Int. | 7-3-2 | 24-9-1 |
| Passing Yards | 59 | 136 |
| Penalties—Yards | 9-80 | 6-43 |
| Punts—Average | 2-42.5 | 4-32.5 |
| Fumbles—Lost | 3-3 | 6-1 |

### INDIVIDUAL STATISTICS

**RUSHING—East Palestine:** Pancake 14-73, Schmidt 19-55, Jordan 8-16, Dugan 2- minus 3, Smith 1- minus 5. **Bucks:** L. Rydbom 19-57, White 17-50, Skillings 1- minus 13.

**PASSING—East Palestine:** Jordan 7-3-2, 59 yards. **Bucks:** L. Rydbom 22-8-1, 121, Potter 1-1-0, 45, White 1-0-0, 0.

**RECEIVING—East Palestine:** Bruno 2-28, Preston 1-21. **Bucks:** Jones 4-49, Little 2-55, Skillings 2-21, Miles 1-11.

## GAME EIGHT—10/4/75 BUCKS 13, EASTERN OHIO DUKES 0

### SCORE BY QUARTERS

| | | | | |
|---|---|---|---|---|
| Dukes | 0 | 0 | 0 | 0 - 0 |
| Bucks | 7 | 0 | 0 | 6 - 13 |

CP—Jones 57 pass from K. Rutter (Luther kick)
CP—Skillings 34 pass from Rydbom (Kick failed)

| TEAM STATISTICS | EO | CP |
|---|---|---|
| First Downs Rushing | 1 | 2 |
| First Downs Passing | 5 | 1 |
| First Downs Penalties | 3 | |
| Net Rushing Yardage | 56 | 45 |
| Passes Att.—Com | 27-10 | 27-12 |
| Passing Yardage | 82 | 235 |
| Penalties—Yards | 3-15 | 5-40 |
| Punts—Average | 7-25.9 | 5-34.2 |
| Fumbles—Lost | 2-1 | 4- |

**INDIVIDUAL STATISTICS**

**RUSHING—E. Ohio:** Myers 9-57, Holland 8-9, Grafton 1-3, Jones 1-1, Bowman 1-0, Thorton 5- minus 5, Hubler 12- minus 11. **Bucks:** Robinson 12-42, Kritzer 4-9, Rockmore 1-t, Slabon 1-2, K-Rutter 2- minus 3, Skillings 1- minus 1, Rydbom 16- minus 7.

**PASSING—E. Ohio:** Hubler 23-9-4-79, Grafton 2-1-1-3. **Bucks:** Rydbom 25-11-2, 178, K. Rutter 1-1-0-57, Potter 1-0-0.

**RECEIVING—E. Ohio:** Myers 3-19, Lemal 3-15, Sprowle 2-20, Hutton 1-21, Holland 1-7. **Bucks:** Jones 4-153, Skillings 2-38, K. Rutter 1-22, Little 1-10, Miles 1-2.

**GAME NINE—10/11/75 WHITETAIL BUCKS 27, WASHINGTON GENERALS 0**

**SCORE BY QUARTERS**

| | | | | |
|---|---|---|---|---|
| Bucks | 7 | 13 | 7 | 0 - 27 |
| Washington | 0 | 0 | 0 | 0 - 0 |

CP—Pheasant 45 interception return (Luther kick)
CP—S. Robinson 1 run (Kick blocked)
CP—Kritzer 12 pass from Slabon (Luther kick)
CP—24 pass from Rutter (Luther kick)

| TEAM STATISTICS | CP | W |
|---|---|---|
| First Downs Rushing | 5 | 2 |
| First Downs Passing | 7 | 3 |
| First Downs Penalties | 2 | 3 |
| Net Rushing Yardage | 80 | -52 |
| Passes Att.—Comp.—Int. | 28-7-5 | 18-7-4 |
| Passing Yardage | 111 | 84 |
| Penalties—Yards | 14-126 | 13-120 |
| Punts—Average | 1-41.0 | 4-30.3 |
| Fumbles—Lost | 6-2 | 5-2 |

**INDIVIDUAL STATISTICS**

**RUSHING—Bucks:** Robinson 11-42, Rydbom 10-23, Rockmore 5-11, Kritzer 1-2, Slabon 1-2. **Washington:** R. Scharbrough 9-3, A. Scharbrough 1-3, Karpinski 3-2, Miller 3-0, Ioli 1- minus 10, Newhouse 2- minus 13, Peller 9-minus 37.

PASSING—Bucks: Rydbom 22-5-5, 75, Slabon 3-1-0, 12, Rutter 3-1-0, 24.
Washington: Newhouse 8-2-3, 27, Peller 10-5-1 57.
RECEIVING—Bucks: Jones 3-44, Rutter 2-39, Miles 1-16, Kritzer 1-12.
Washington: Karpinski 4-41, Smith 1-16, R. Scharbrough 1-15, Hughes 1-12.

## GAME TEN–10/18/75 WHITETAIL BUCKS 40, JOHNSTOWN MINERS 2

## GAME ELEVEN–10/26/75 PITTSBURGH IRONMEN 36, WHITETAIL BUCKS 12

SCORE BY QUARTERS

| | | | | |
|---|---|---|---|---|
| Bucks | 6 | 0 | 0 | 6 - 12 |
| Pitts. | 3 | 10 | 10 | 13 - 36 |

CP—Kizina 6 pass from Rydbom (Kick blocked)
Pitt—Ross 33 field goal
Pitt—Jancosko 5 run (Ross kick)
Pitt—Ross 24 field goal
Pitt—Brumbaugh 41 pass from Shope (Ross Kick)
Pitt—Ross 31 field goal
CP—Shoop 2 run (Pass failed)
Pitt—Jenkins 22 run (Kick failed)
Pitt—Sanders 25 Interception Return (Ross kick)

# 1976

## 1976 GAME BY GAME

**7/31 Brooklyn Golden Knights (H)** L 7-13 (OT) at State College (350)
**8/8 Boonton Bears (H)** W 12-0 at Philipsburg (779)
**8/14 Brooklyn Mariners (H)** L 14-20 (OT) at Altoona (2,250)
**8/22 Washington Generals (H)** L 6-7 at Flinton (500)
8/28 Pittsburgh Ironmen (A) L 13-40
**9/4 Beaver County Cougars (H)** W 31-0 at Curwensville
9/12 Sharon Old Express (A) L 27-29
9/18 Washington Generals (A) L 6-14
**9/25 Pittsburgh Ironmen (H)** L 14-21 at Philipsburg (1,700)
10/3 Beaver County Cougars (A) W 35-20
**10/9 Sharon Old Express (H)** L 9-10 at Clearfield (1,500)

### GAME ONE—7/31/76 BROOKLYN GOLDEN KNIGHTS 13, WHITETAIL BUCKS 6 (OVERTIME)

**SCORE BY QUARTERS**

| | | | | | |
|---|---|---|---|---|---|
| Brooklyn | 0 | 7 | 0 | 0 | 6 - 13 |
| Bucks | 7 | 0 | 0 | 0 | 0 - 7 |

CP—Rockmore 27 run (Skillings kick)
B—S Green 7 run (Walker kick)
B—Smith 1 plunge (no PAT attempt)

### GAME TWO—8/8/76 WHITETAIL BUCKS 12, BOONTON BEARS 0

**BUCKS—Ends:** K. Rutter, Kizina. **Tackles:** G. Walker, Roefaro. **Guards:** Anto, McNeish. **Center:** Keith. **Backs:** Miller, Belfield, Rockmore, Flipse.

**Subs:** Rydbom, Slabon, Griffith, Kurtz, E. Futrell, Gibbons, Best, Kritzer, Dick, Skillings, Camuso, Good, Gordon, Houghtaling, Potter, D. Rutter, Marlett, Wales, Grissinger, Morrison, Jeffries, Siegel, Pheasant, Noel, McCartney, Mancuso, Kessler, Morgan, Brandimarte, Shoop, Spizzirri, Kline, Ullein, Pletcher.

## SCORE BY QUARTERS

| | | | | | |
|---|---|---|---|---|---|
| Boonton | 0 | 0 | 0 | 0 - 0 | |
| Bucks | 0 | 6 | 6 | 0 - 12 | |

CP—Skillings 44 pass from Rydbom (kick failed)
CP—Rockmore 16 run (kick failed)

| TEAM STATISTICS | B | CP |
|---|---|---|
| First Downs Rushing | 2 | 10 |
| First Downs Passing | 3 | 3 |
| First Downs Penalties | 0 | 1 |
| Net Rushing Yardage | 47 | 186 |
| Passes Att.—Comp. | 22-6 | 22-9 |
| Passing Yardage | 67 | 130 |
| Penalties—Yards | 2-30 | 5-35 |
| Punts—Average | 8-34.3 | 5-35.8 |
| Fumbles—Lost | 2-1 | 4-3 |

## INDIVIDUAL STATISTICS

**RUSHING—Bucks:** Rockmore 15-66, Shoop 9-51, Rydbom 5-26, Belfield 8-19, Kritzer 3-10, Camuso 1-9. **Boonton:** Bouroult 9-33, Reiley 10-6, Pirrello 2-3, Walker 2-3, Cunningham 2-2.
**PASSING—Bucks:** Rydbom 15-5-3-90; Miller 6-3-1-28; Slabon 1-1-0, 12. **Boonton:** Cunningham 22-6-3, 67.
**RECEIVING—Bucks:** Flipse 3-35, Kizina 2-23, Belfield 2-10, Skillings 1-44, Rockmore 1-18. **Boonton:** Hagen 3-38, Wilfong, 2-12, Reiley 1-17.

## GAME THREE—8/14/76 BROOKLYN MARINERS 20, WHITETAIL BUCKS 14 (OVERTIME)

**BUCKS—Ends:** Pheasant, Kizina. **Tackles:** Roefaro, Walker. **Guards:** McNeish, Anto. **Center:** Siegel. **Backs:** Rydbom, Rockmore, Belfield, Flipse. **Subs:** Slabon, Gordon, Shoop, Houghtaling, Grissinger, A. Wales, Kessler, McCartney,

D. Rutter, Spizzirri, K. Rutter, Ullein, Brandimarte, Mancusso, J. Wales, Keith, Jeffries, Wayland, Pletcher, Marlett, Potter, Good, Camuso, Skillings, Dick, Kritzer, Best, E. Futrell, Griffith, Miller.

## SCORE BY QUARTERS

| | | | | | |
|---|---|---|---|---|---|
| Brooklyn | 0 | 14 | 0 | 0 | 6 - 20 |
| Bucks | 0 | 0 | 14 | 0 | 0 - 14 |

B—Sommers 6 run (Tarpey kick)
B—Curtin 6 run (Tarpey kick)
CP—Shoop 1 run (Shoop kick)
CP—Houghtaling 3 run (Slabon run)
B—Lucan 1 run (no kick)

| TEAM STATISTICS | B | CP |
|---|---|---|
| First Downs Rushing | 7 | 7 |
| First Downs Passing | 9 | 1 |
| First Downs Penalties | 2 | 7 |
| Net Yards Rushing | 127 | 54 |
| Passes Att.—Comp.—Int. | 32-14-3 | 16-7-1 |
| Yards Passing | 161 | 48 |
| Penalties—Yards | 11-67 | 6-47 |
| Punts—Average | 5-40.4 | 6-37.0 |
| Fumbles—Lost | 2-0 | 3-1 |

## INDIVIDUAL STATISTICS

RUSHING—**Bucks:** Rockmore 14-43, Shoop 5-18, Belfield 7-18, Houghtaling 3-1, Miller 1- minus 13, Rydbom 9- minus 13. **Brooklyn:** Curtin 17-64, Sommers 13-46, King 7-21, Lucan 3-13, Gagliardi 4- minus 17.
PASSING—**Bucks:** Rydbom 15-7-1-48, Miller 1-0-0,0. **Brooklyn:** Gagliardi 32-14-3-161.
RECEIVING—**Bucks:** Pheasant 3-28, Flipse 1-9, K. Rutter 1-8, Skillings 1-5, Belfield 1- minus 2. **Brooklyn:** Rupp 7-89, Curtin 6-65, King 1-7.

## GAME FOUR—8/22/76 WASHINGTON GENERALS 7, WHITETAIL BUCKS 6

BUCKS—**Ends:** Kizina, Pheasant. **Tackles:** Roefaro, Walker. **Guards:** McNeish, Anto. **Center:** Keith. **Backs:** Rydbom, Rockmore, Shoop. **Subs:**

Kline, D. Rutter, J.Wales, McCartney, Kessler, A. Wales, Grissinger. Marlett, Ullein. **Backs**: Brandimarte, Gordon, Slabon, Griffith, Pletcher, Futrell, Belfield, Camuso, Potter, Siegel, Good, Jeffries, Gregg, Spizzirri, Mancuso.

## SCORE BY QUARTERS

| | | | | |
|---|---|---|---|---|
| Generals | 0 | 0 | 7 | 0 - 7 |
| Bucks | 6 | 0 | 0 | 0 - 6 |

CP—Kizina pass run from Rydbom (kick blocked)
W—G. Smith 1 run (Hughes Kick)

## GAME FIVE—8/28/76 PITTSBURGH IRONMEN 40, WHITETAIL BUCKS 13
## SCORE BY QUARTERS

| | | | | |
|---|---|---|---|---|
| Bucks | 0 | 6 | 7 | 0 - 13 |
| Ironmen | 0 | 20 | 0 | 20 - 40 |

## GAME SIX—9/4/76 WHITETAIL BUCKS 31, BEAVER COUNTY COUGARS 0

WHITE TAIL BUCKS—**Ends:** Siegel Kizina. **Tackles:** Roefaro, Walker. **Guards:** Hrenko, Anto. **Center:** Keith. **Backs:** Rydbom, Rockmore, Good, Pheasant. **Subs:** Kline, D Rutter, Spizzirri, Ullein, Grissinger, Houghtaling, Marlett, Kessler, Gordon, Potter, Slabon, Shoop, Kurtz, Kritzer, Futrell, C. Skillings, R. Skillings, Pletcher, Mancuso, Morgan, Garito, Miller, Gibbons, Martz, Gregg.

## SCORE BY QUARTERS

| | | | | |
|---|---|---|---|---|
| Cougars | 0 | 0 | 0 | 0 - 0 |
| Bucks | 14 | 3 | 7 | 7 - 31 |

Bucks—Kizina 43 pass-run from Pheasant (Shoop kick)
Bucks—Rockmore 51 run (Shoop kick)
Bucks—Shoop 43 FG
Bucks—Pheasant 7 pass from Slabon (Shoop kick)
Bucks—Rockmore 33 run (Slabon run)

## INDIVIDUAL STATISTICS

**RUSHING—Bucks:** Rockmore 16-123, Good 6-21, Rydbom 2-17, Shoop 4-11, Kritzer 1-4, Skillings 1-1. **Beaver County:** Hightower 10-33, Tisdale 4-28. Greenham 1- minus 1, Stoneberg 3- minus 26.

**PASSING—Bucks:** Miller 6-4-0-51 yards, Pheasant 1-1-0-43, Rydbom 14-2-1-22, Slabon 1-1-0-7. **Beaver County:** Stoneberg 18-4-2-66, Baumbach 7-5-0-37, Hightower 1-1-0-12.

**RECEIVING—Bucks:** Pheasant 5-67, Kizina 1-43, Kritzer 1-9, Good 1-4. **Beaver County:** Pushinski 5-108, Tisdale 1-4, Greenham 1-3, Hightower 2-0, Smith 1-0.

## GAME SEVEN–9/12/76 SHARON OLD EXPRESS 29, WHITETAIL BUCKS 27

### SCORE BY QUARTERS

| | | | | |
|---|---|---|---|---|
| Bucks | 0 | 14 | 7 | 6 - 27 |
| Sharon Old Express | 6 | 10 | 7 | 6 - 29 |

S—Green 69 punt return (Husted kick failed)
S—Marshall 70 interception return (Husted kick)
CP—Pheasant 4 pass from Rydbom (Shoop kick)
CP—Ullein 2 punt return (Shoop kick)
S—Husted 35 FG
S—Campbell 4 run (Husted kick)
CP—Rockmore 36 run (Shoop kick)
CP—Good 6 run (Shoop kick failed)
S—Campbell 1 run (Husted kick failed)

## GAME EIGHT–9/18/76 WASHINGTON GENERALS 14, WHITETAIL BUCKS 6

### SCORE BY QUARTERS

| | | | | |
|---|---|---|---|---|
| Bucks | 0 | 0 | 6 | 0 - 6 |
| Generals | 0 | 14 | 0 | 0 - 14 |

G—Karpency 25 pass from Smith (Kick failed)
G—Safety, Potter touched ball down in end zone
G—Karpency 32 pass from Smith (Kick failed)
B—Shoop 2 run (Kick blocked)

| TEAM STATISTICS | CP | W |
|---|---|---|
| First Downs Rushing | 6 | 4 |
| First Downs Passing | 1 | 4 |
| First Downs Penalties | 1 | 1 |
| Net Rushing Yardage | 90 | 82 |
| Passes Att.—Comp. | 15-5 | 15-6 |
| Passing Yardage | 76 | 123 |
| Penalties—Yards | 5-55 | 6.60 |
| Punts—Average | 4-49.3 | 5-35 |
| Fumbles—Lost | 1-1 | 3-3 |

## GAME NINE—9/25/76 PITTSBURGH IRONMEN 21, WHITETAIL BUCKS 14

### SCORE BY QUARTERS

| | | | | |
|---|---|---|---|---|
| Ironmen | 0 | 0 | 21 | 0 - 21 |
| Bucks | 0 | 0 | 0 | 14 - 14 |

P—Richardson 1 pass from Shope (Ross kick)
P—McMillan 1 run (Ross kick)
P—Farmer 2 run (Ross kick)
CP—Rockmore 36 pass from Rydbom (Shoop kick)
CP—Jones 10 pass from Rydbom (Slabon run)

| TEAM STATISTICS | P | CP |
|---|---|---|
| First Downs Rushing | 11 | 4 |
| First Downs Passing | 4 | 6 |
| First Downs Penalties | 1 | 1 |
| Net Rushing Yardage | 138 | 86 |
| Passes Att.—Comp. | 21-9 | 24-12 |
| Passing Yardage | 114 | 129 |
| Penalties—Yards | 3-35 | 4-16 |
| Punts—Average | 5-23 | 3-43 |
| Fumbles Lost | 1-1 | 5-4 |

### INDIVIDUAL STATISTICS

RUSHING—**Pittsburgh:** Farmer 17-91, Smith 9-31, McMillan 5-24, Ellison 2-7, Shope 2- minus 15. **Bucks:** Rockmore 18-63, Good 8-14, Rydbom 5-12, Futrell 1-3, Shoop 1-2, Slabon 2- minus 8.

PASSING—Pittsburgh: Shope 21-9-2, 114 yards. Bucks: Rydbom 13-6-1, 80, Miller 13-6-1, 49.

RECEIVING—Pittsburgh: Cook 3-72, Farmer 3-12, Richardson 2-22, Lerda 1-8. Bucks: Jones 6-54, Pheasant 3-38, Rockmore 2-35, Good 1-2.

## GAME TEN—10/3/76 WHITETAIL BUCKS 35, BEAVER COUNTY COUGARS 20

### SCORE BY QUARTERS

| | | | | |
|---|---|---|---|---|
| Bucks | 7 | 7 | 7 | 14 - 35 |
| Beaver County | 0 | 6 | 14 | 0 - 20 |

CP—Jones 4, pass from Miller (Shoop kick)
BC—Pushinski 49, pass from Baumbach (kick blocked)
CP—Kizina 17, pass from Miller (Shoop kick)
CP—Rockmore 1 run (Shoop kick)
BC—Hightower 5 run (Tisdale run)
BC—Baumbach 2 run (Smith kick)
CP—Jones 9 pass from Miller (Shoop kick)
CP—Rockmore 2 run (Shoop kick)

| TEAM STATISTICS | CP | BC |
|---|---|---|
| First Downs Rushing | 18 | 6 |
| First Downs Passing | 5 | 4 |
| First Downs Penalties | 0 | 1 |
| Net Rushing Yardage | 288 | 99 |
| Passes Att.—Comp. | 17-12 | 16-8 |
| Passing Yardage | 110 | 150 |
| Penalties—Yards | 3-25 | 7-45 |
| Punts—Average | 1-30 | 2-39 |
| Fumbles—Lost | 1-1 | 2-1 |

## GAME ELEVEN—10/9/76 SHARON OLD EXPRESS 10, WHITETAIL BUCKS 9

BUCKS—Ends: Jones, Pheasant. Tackles: Roefaro, G. Walker. Guards: McNeish, Anto. Center: Siegel. Backs: Miller, Rockmore, Good, Kizina. Subs: Potter, Shoop, Keith, Slabon, Gordon, Rutter, Ullein, Spizzirri, Mancuso, Gregg, Kessler, Grissinger, Houghtaling, Marlett, R. Skillings, J. Wales, Garito, Kline, Kurtz, Kritzer, Jeffries, Gibbons, Blowers, Futrell.

## SCORE BY QUARTERS

| | | | | |
|---|---|---|---|---|
| Old Express | 0 | 0 | 0 | 10 - 10 |
| Bucks | 0 | 6 | 3 | 0 - 9 |

CP—Rockmore 20 run (kick failed, no attempt)
CP—FG Shoop 32
E—Ellebie 91 pass from Scrim (Moser kick)
E—FG Moser 28

| TEAM STATISTICS | S | CP |
|---|---|---|
| First Downs Rushing | 11 | 8 |
| First Downs Passing | 0 | 6 |
| First Downs Penalties | 0 | 1 |
| Net Rushing Yardage | 191 | 176 |
| Passes Att.—Comp. | 10-3 | 29-11 |
| Passing Yardage | 93 | 111 |
| Passes Intercepted By | 3 | 0 |
| Penalties—Yards | 1-24 | 4-41 |
| Punts—Average | 5-31 | 4-34.5 |
| Fumbles—Lost | 5-2 | 3-1 |

## INDIVIDUAL STATISTICS

**RUSHING—Old Express:** Ellebie 18-89, Green 11-51, Scrim 12-39, Dugan 3-12. **Bucks:** Rockmore 26-163, Good 9-30, Miller 2- minus 7, Shoop 1- minus 10.
**PASSING—Old Express:** Scrim 10-3-0, 93. **Bucks:** Miller 29-11-3, 111.
**RECEIVING—Old Express:** Ellebie 1-91, Green 2-2. **Bucks:** Jones 6-74, Pheasant 2-34, Kizina 1-3.

# 1977

## 1977 BUCKS GAME-BY-GAME

| | | | |
|---|---|---|---|
| **7/23 Jersey Oaks (H, Non-League)** | L | 6-32 | at State College |
| 7/30 Washington Generals (A) (cancelled) | W | (Forfeit) | |
| 8/6 Youngstown Hardhats (A) | L | 2-47 | |
| **8/13 Allegheny-Kiski All-Stars (H)** | W | 25-12 | at DuBois |
| 8/20 Pittsburgh Ironmen (A) | L | 13-33 | |
| **8/27 Brooklyn Golden Knights (H)** | L | 3-27 | at State College |
| **9/3 Washington Generals (H) (cancelled)** | W | (Forfeit) | |
| **9/3 Pittsburgh Black Knights (H)** | W | 29-0 | at Curwensville |
| **9/10 Youngstown Hardhats (H)** | L | 7-41 | at Clearfield |
| 9/17 Allegheny-Kiski All Stars (A) | W | 11-6 | |
| **9/24 Pittsburgh Ironmen (H)** | L | 0-11 | at Philipsburg |

### GAME ONE—7/23/77 JERSEY OAKS 32, WHITETAIL BUCKS 6

**SCORE BY QUARTERS**

| | | | | |
|---|---|---|---|---|
| Oaks | 17 | 6 | 0 | 9 - 32 |
| Bucks | 0 | 0 | 0 | 6 - 6 |

J—FG Ormosi 27
J—Winters 85 punt return (Ormosi kick)
J—Henry 76 pass from G. Morgan (Ormosi kick)
J—Henry 29 pass from G. Morgan (kick blocked)
J—Safety snap went out of end zone
J—Parker 50 run (Ormosi kick)
CP—M. Morgan 40 pass from K. Rutter (kick failed)

**GAME TWO—7/30/77 WHITETAIL BUCKS WON BY FORFEIT OVER WASHINGTON GENERALS**

**GAME THREE—8/6/77 YOUNGSTOWN HARDHATS 47, WHITETAIL BUCKS 2**

## SCORE BY QUARTERS

| | | | | |
|---|---|---|---|---|
| Bucks | 0 | 0 | 2 | 0 - 2 |
| Hardhats | 13 | 21 | 0 | 13 - 47 |

| TEAM STATISTICS | BUCKS | HARDHATS |
|---|---|---|
| First Downs Rushing | 4 | 4 |
| First Downs Passing | 3 | 11 |
| First Downs Penalties | 6 | 0 |
| Net Rushing Yards | 22 | 78 |
| Passes Att—Comp | 25-12 | 22-16 |
| Passing Yardage | 75 | 240 |
| Punts—Average | 3-26 | 2-41 |
| Penalties—Yards | 3-15 | 10-90 |
| Fumbles—Lost | 6-4 | 1-1 |

## INDIVIDUAL STATISTICS

**RUSHING—Bucks:** Shivery 5-16, Shoop 5-13, Good 10-13, Clark 3-4, Miller 1- minus 6, Detwiler 4- minus 18. **Youngstown:** Stringer 9-29, Fant 10-26, Kelson 1-14, Dunklin 5-11, Ellebie 3-8, Smith 3-4, Preston 4- minus 14.

**PASSING—Bucks:** Miller 20-9-1, 67 yards, Detwiler 5-3-0, 8. **Youngstown:** Wireman 18-13-1-180, Preston 4-3-0, 66.

**RECEIVING—Bucks:** Morgan 2-24, Brown 1-13, Gibbons 1-11, Shivery 1-10, Shoop 1-6, J. Crestani 1-5, Skillings 1-4, K. Rutter 4-2. **Youngstown:** Kelson 7-84, Morris 4-67, Stringer 2-35, Smith 1-33, Taylor 2-27.

**GAME FOUR—8/13/77 WHITETAIL BUCKS 25, ALLEGHENY-KISKI STARS 12**

## SCORE BY QUARTERS

| | | | | |
|---|---|---|---|---|
| Bucks | 13 | 6 | 0 | 6 - 25 |
| Stars | 0 | 0 | 6 | 6 - 12 |

| TEAM STATISTCS | CP | A-K |
|---|---|---|
| First Downs Rushing | 9 | 8 |
| First Downs Passing | 2 | 4 |
| First Downs Penalties | 2 | 2 |
| Net Rushing Yards | 184 | 128 |
| Passes, Att.—Comp. | 12-6 | 27-8 |
| Yards Passing | 88 | 129 |
| Punts—Avg. | 5-38 | 2-38 |
| Penalties—Yards | 5-51 | 7-65 |
| Fumbles—Lost | 1-1 | 1-1 |

## GAME FIVE—8/20/77 PITTSBURGH IRONMEN 33, WHITETAIL BUCKS 13

### SCORE BY QUARTERS

| | | | | |
|---|---|---|---|---|
| Bucks | 6 | 7 | 0 | 0 - 13 |
| Ironmen | 7 | 13 | 13 | 0 - 33 |

CP—Rockmore 63 run (kick failed)
P—Howard 18 run (Ross kick)
P—Orendi 2 run (Ross kick)
P—Farmer 10 run (kick failed)
CP—Morgan 20 pass from Miller (Shoop kick)
P—Thompson 4 run (kick failed)
P—Brosky 2 run (Ross kick)

| TEAM STATISTICS | CP | PITT |
|---|---|---|
| First Downs Rushing | 4 | 11 |
| First Downs Passing | 3 | 3 |
| First Downs Penalties | 1 | 2 |
| Net Yards Rushing | 129 | 201 |
| Passes, Att—Comp | 25-6 | 21-6 |
| Yards Passing | 65 | 40 |
| Punts—Ave | 7-37 | 6-39 |
| Penalties—Yards | 4-53 | 9-60 |
| Fumbles—Lost | 1-1 | 0-0 |

## INDIVIDUAL STATS

**RUSHING—Bucks:** Rockmore 12-116, Shivery 6-14, Good 8-8, Detwiler 2-8, Miller 1- minus 1, Shoop 1- minus 16. **Pittsburgh:** Thompson 13-92, Howard 4-44, Brosky 11-38, Farmer 7-28, Shook 7-18, Orendi 3-5, Bulger 2- minus 24.

**PASSING—Bucks:** Miller 20-5-2-55, Detwiler 4-1-0-10, K. Rutter 1-0-1-0. **Pittsburgh:** Bulger 9-2-0-17, DeMao 12-4-2-23.

**RECEIVING—Bucks:** Morgan 2-31, Brown 1-14, Crestani 1-10, Rockmore 1-8, K. Rutter 1-2. **Pittsburgh:** Koch 2-23, Graham 2-17, Brosky 1-2, Farmer 1- minus 2.

### GAME SIX—8/27/77 BROOKLYN GOLDEN KNIGHTS 27, WHITETAIL BUCKS 3

#### SCORE BY QUARTERS

| | | | | |
|---|---|---|---|---|
| Golden Knights | 7 | 13 | 0 | 7 - 27 |
| Bucks | 0 | 0 | 3 | 0 - 3 |

B—West 27 run (Waters kick)
B—Smith 1 run (kick blocked)
B—Phillips 9 pass from Green (Waters kick)
CP—FG Shoop 24
B—Wenton 11 run (Waters kick)

### GAME SEVEN—9/3/77 WHITETAIL BUCKS WON BY FORFEIT OVER WASHINGTON GENERALS

### GAME EIGHT—9/3/77 WHITETAIL BUCKS 29, PITTSBURGH BLACK KNIGHTS 0

#### SCORE BY QUARTERS

| | | | | |
|---|---|---|---|---|
| Black Knights | 0 | 0 | 0 | 0 - 0 |
| Bucks | 9 | 7 | 13 | 0 - 29 |

CP—Safety snap went out of end zone
CP—M. Morgan 50 pass from Slabon (Shoop kick)
CP—Rockmore 4 run (Shoop kick)
CP—Brown 5 pass from Detwiler (kick failed)
CP—Good 1 run (Crestani pass from Slabon)

| TEAM STATISTICS | P | CP |
|---|---|---|
| First Downs Rushing | 3 | 13 |
| First Downs Passing | 4 | 3 |
| First Downs Penalties | 0 | 4 |
| Net Yards Rushing | 39 | 164 |
| Passes Att.—Comp.—Int. | 20-4-4 | 9-6-0 |
| Yards Passing | 111 | 121 |
| Punts—Ave | 3-19.7 | 1-39.0 |
| Penalties—Yards | 9-67 | 5-25 |
| Fumbles—Lost | 4-1 | 4-2 |

## INDIVIDUAL STATISTICS

**RUSHING—Pittsburgh:** Lee 8-39, Krajewski 2-2, Strong 4-2, Dutrieuille 1-1, McMillen 1- minus 5. **Bucks:** Clark 11-63, Good 13-55, Rockmore 12-39, Detwiler 5-18, Kritzer 2-14, Shoop 1-5.

**PASSING—Pittsburgh:** Lee 20-4-4, 111. **Bucks:** Detwiler 4-4-0, 51, Slabon 1-1-0, 50, Miller 4-1-0, 10.

**RECEIVING—Pittsburgh:** Dutrieuille 1-61, Jones 2-40, Moye 1-10. **Bucks:** Morgan 2-66, Brown 4-55.

## GAME NINE—9/10/77 YOUNGSTOWN HARDHATS 41, WHITETAIL BUCKS 7

### SCORE BY QUARTERS

| | | | | |
|---|---|---|---|---|
| Youngstown | 21 | 13 | 7 | 0 - 41 |
| Bucks | 0 | 0 | 7 | 0 - 7 |

Y—Morris 13 pass from Wireman (Andrews kick)

Y—Smith 1 run (Andrews kick)

Y—Kelson 26 pass from Wireman (Andrews kick)

Y—Fant 9 run (kick blocked)

Y—Kelson 29 pass from Wireman (Andrews kick)

CP—Morgan 102 punt return (Slabon run)

Y—Kelson 4 pass from Preston (Andrews kick)

| TEAM STATISTICS | Y | CP |
|---|---|---|
| First Downs Rushing | 12 | 6 |
| First Downs Passing | 6 | 0 |
| First Downs Penalties | 0 | 1 |
| Net Yards Rushing | 219 | 82 |
| Passes Att.—Comp.—Int. | 15-11-1 | 14-2-2 |
| Yards Passing | 224 | 12 |
| Punts—Ave | 1-40.0 | 3-34.7 |
| Penalties—Yards | 4-31 | 1-5 |
| Fumbles—Lost | 2-2 | 5-4 |

**INDIVIDUAL STATISTICS**

**RUSHING—Youngstown:** Fant 8-95, Ellebie 8-64, Taylor 4-32, Smith 8-16, Wireman 4-12, Dunklin 1-11, Preston 2-minus 11. **Bucks:** Good 14-60, Clark 6-12, Shoop 4-9, Slabon 1-6, Detwiler 2-5, Gibbons 2-minus 10.

**PASSING—Youngstown:** Wireman 9-8-1, 161, Preston 6-3-0, 61. **Bucks:** Detwiler 5-2-1, 12, Miller 4-0-0, 0, Shoop 5-0-1, 0.

**RECEIVING—Youngstown:** Kelson 7-160, Morris 2-39, Banks 1-14, Smith 1-11. **Bucks:** Morgan 1-8, Brown 1-4.

## GAME TEN—9/17/77 WHITETAIL BUCKS 11, ALLEGHENY-KISKI 6

**SCORE BY QUARTERS**

| | | | | |
|---|---|---|---|---|
| Bucks | 0 | 6 | 0 | 5 - 11 |
| Stars | 6 | 0 | 0 | 0 - 6 |

AK—McCloud 25 pass from Graybeagle (run failed)
CP—Clark 2 run (kick blocked)
CP—FG Shoop 24
CP—Bailey safety, tackled Graybeagle in end zone

## GAME ELEVEN—9/24/77 PITTSBURGH IRONMEN 11, WHITETAIL BUCKS 0

**SCORE BY QUARTERS**

| | | | | |
|---|---|---|---|---|
| Ironmen | 0 | 0 | 3 | 8 - 11 |
| Bucks | 0 | 0 | 0 | 0 - 0 |

Pitt—Dolfi, FG, 36
Pitt—Brosky, 2 run (Kick failed)
Pitt—Barroffio safely, tackled Jim Stoneberg in end zone

| TEAM STATISTICS | PITT | BUCKS |
|---|---|---|
| First Downs Bushing | 6 | 3 |
| First Downs Passing | 4 | 2 |
| First Downs Penalties | 1 | 1 |
| Net Rushing Yards | 74 | 47 |
| Passes Att—Comp | 20-7 | 9-3 |
| Passing Yards | 78 | 47 |
| Punts—Ave | 7-41 | 9-31 |
| Penalties—Yards | 3-25 | 5-35 |
| Fumbles—Lost | 2-0 | 1 |

## INDIVIDUAL STATISTICS

**RUSHING—Pittsburgh:** Orendi 5-62, Thompson 19-60, Brosky 4-14, Howard 3-minus 2, DeMaio 2- minus 28, Dolfi 1- minus 32. **Bucks:** Rockmore 13-32, Clark 6-21, Shivery 4-14, Shoop 3-8, Good 6-4, Stoneberg 1- minus 3, Detwiler 10- minus 29.

**PASSING—Pittsburgh:** DeMaio 20-7-1, 78 yards. **Bucks:** Detwiler 7-3-0, 47, Jim Stoneberg 1-0-0, Slabon 1-0-1.

**RECEIVING—Pittsburgh:** Koch 2-32, Thompson 2-22, Graham 2-13, Cleis 1-11. **Bucks:** Morgan 1-31, Brown 1-10, Rockmore 1-6.

# 1978

## 1978 GAME BY GAME

| | | | |
|---|---|---|---|
| **7/15 Erie Express (H)** | L | 14-19 | at State College |
| **7/22 Chambersburg Cardinals (H)** | L | 6-71 | at DuBois |
| **7/29 Brooklyn Golden Knights (H) (cancelled)** | | | |
| **8/5 Cleveland Academes (H)** | L | 0-36 | at DuBois |
| 8/12 Washington Generals (A) | W | (Forfeit) | |
| 8/19 Youngstown Hardhats (A) | L | 6-46 | |
| 8/26 Erie Express (A) | L | 0-53 | |
| **9/2 Pittsburgh Black Knights (H) (cancelled)** | | | |
| 9/9 Cleveland Academes (A) (cancelled) | L | (Forfeit) | |
| 9/9 Pittsburgh Black Knights (A) | L | 0-28 | |
| **\*\*Team folded 9/10/78** | | | |
| **9/16 Washington Generals (H) cancelled** | | | |
| **9/16 Franklin County Minutemen (H) cancelled** | | | |
| **9/23 Youngstown Hardhats (H) cancelled** | | | |

### GAME ONE—7/15/78 ERIE EXPRESS 19, WHITETAIL BUCKS 14

**BUCKS—Ends:** Morgan, Gibbons. **Tackles:** McClincy, George Walker. **Guards:** Rusnak, J. Wales. **Center:** Siegel. **Backs:** Lightner, Primerano, Kritzer, Clark. **Subs:** Crestani, Shoop, D. Rutter, Mancuso, Graham, Stoneberg, J. Williams, G. Williams, Davison, Kurtz, Challingsworth, Slabon, Detwiler, Wilcox, Appleton, Greg Walker, Crotzer, Noel, Rehmeyer, Lane, Arthur, Mickey.

## SCORE BY QUARTERS

Erie Express    6      7      0      6 - 19
Bucks           0     14      0      0 - 14

E—Green 1-yard run (Kick failed)
E—Overton 11-yard pass from Scott (Comer kick)
CP—Morgan 47-yard pass from Lightner (Shoop kick)
CP—Morgan 68-yard interception return (Shoop kick)
E—Ford 57-yard punt return (Kick failed)

| TEAM STATISTICS | ERIE | CP |
|---|---|---|
| First Downs Rushing | 11 | 7 |
| First Downs Passing | 1 | 4 |
| First Downs Penalties | 0 | 2 |
| Net Yards Rushing | 244 | 79 |
| Passes—Att—Comp | 12-5 | 25-8 |
| Yards Passing | 57 | 145 |
| Punts—Average | 2-16.5 | 2-34.5 |
| Penalties—Yards | 9-80 | 0-0 |
| Fumbles—Lost | 2-1 | 4-2 |

## INDIVIDUAL STATISTICS

**RUSHING—Erie:** Green 25-157, Gamble 11-48, Scott 10-27, Lyons 2-9, Nolan 1-3. **Bucks:** Rehmeyer 4-22, Clark 4-21, Primerano 4-16, Shoop 9-14, Lightner 8-6, Kritzer 4-0.

**PASSING—Erie:** Scott 11-5-1, 57 yards, Green 1-0-0. **Bucks:** Lightner 13-5-0, 100, Shoop 12-3-0, 45.

**RECEIVING—Erie:** Johnson 1-19, Thomas 1-15, Overton 1-11, Reighard 1-7, Bibbs 1-5. **Bucks:** Morgan 2-68, Crotzer 2-31, Detwiler 1-21, Crestani 2-17, Rehmeyer 1-10.

### GAME TWO—7/22/78 CHAMBERSBURG CARDINALS 71, WHITETAIL BUCKS 6

**BUCKS—Ends:** Morgan, Crestani. **Tackles:** McClincy, Greg Walker. **Guards:** Rusnak, Appleton. **Center:** Siegel. **Backs:** Lightner, Kritzer, Primerano, Rehmeyer. **Subs:** Mancuso, Stoneberg, Graham, McCoy, J. Williams, G. Williams, Davison, Wilcox, Kurtz, Slabon, Detwiler, Lane, Arthur, Noel, Mickey, Shoop, Clark, Gregg, Snow, Crotzer, Shaw.

## SCORE BY QUARTERS

| | | | | |
|---|---|---|---|---|
| Chambersburg | 7 | 21 | 16 | 27 - 71 |
| Bucks | 6 | 0 | 0 | 0 - 6 |

C—Posey 12 run (Schminke kick)
CP—Morgan 74 pass from Lightner (kick failed)
C—Posey 4 run (Schminke kick)
C—Posey 1 run (Schminke kick)
C—Williams 33 pass from Hare (Schminke kick)
C—Brown 11 run (Schminke kick)
C—Boykin 62 pass from Rydbom (Schminke kick)
C—Safety (Bucks' punt snap went out of end zone)
C—Brown 2 run (Schminke kick)
C—Forman 26 pass from Rydbom (Schminke kick)
C—Williams 35 pass from Rydbom (Schminke kick)
C—Fesler 21 interception return (kick failed)

| TEAM STATISTICS | CARDS | BUCKS |
|---|---|---|
| First Downs Rushing | 9 | 1 |
| First Downs Passing | 4 | 0 |
| First Downs Penalties | 1 | 0 |
| Net Yards Rushing | 252 | 27 |
| Passes Att—Comp—Int | 18-10-2 | 25-8-2 |
| Yards Passing | 253 | 93 |
| Punts—Average | 2-23.5 | 8-36.6 |
| Penalties—Yards | 7-45 | 8-69 |
| Fumbles—Lost | 5-3 | 3-2 |

## INDIVIDUAL STATISTICS

RUSHING—Chambersburg: Posey 19-176, Brown 7-63, Grove 1-10, Duncan 1-8, Rydbom 3- minus 5. Bucks: Rehmeyer 6-22, Kritzer 8-21, Shoop 7-14, Primerano 2-0, Mickey 2- minus 5, Lightner 3- minus 10.
PASSING—Chambersburg: Rydbom 10-6-1, 161 yards, Hare 8-4-1, 92. Bucks: Lightner 19-8-2, 99, Shoop 5-0-1, 0, Kritzer 1-0-0, 0.
RECEIVING—Chambersburg: Boykin 2-77, Williams 2-68, Brennan 2-23, Grove 1-37, Forman 1-26, Harris 1-20, Posey 1-2. Bucks: Crestani 3-11, Morgan 2-81, Crotzer 2-4, Detwiler 1-3.

## GAME THREE–8/5/78 CLEVELAND ACADEMES 36, WHITETAIL BUCKS 0

### SCORE BY QUARTERS

| | | | | |
|---|---|---|---|---|
| Academes | 12 | 12 | 6 | 6 - 36 |
| Bucks | 0 | 0 | 0 | 0 - 0 |

C—Brewer 2-yard run (kick failed)
C—Brewer 1-yard run (kick failed)
C—Davis 20-yard run (kick failed)
C—Davis 1-yard run (kick failed)
C—Brewer 5-yard run (kick failed)
C—Chamberlin 21-yard pass from Patrick (kick failed)

| TEAM STATISTICS | ACADEMES | BUCKS |
|---|---|---|
| First Downs Rushing | 14 | 3 |
| First Downs Passing | 8 | 1 |
| First Downs Penalty | 1 | 1 |
| Net Yards Rushing | 166 | 12 |
| Passing—Att.—Comp. | 25-11 | 14-1 |
| Passing Yardage | 195 | 19 |
| Punts | 0 | 5-37 |
| Penalties | 12-75 | 2-25 |
| Fumbles—Lost | 2-0 | 2-2 |

### INDIVIDUAL STATS

RUSHING—Cleveland: Brewer 19-122, Carter 12-53, Davis 14-53, Bailey 5-3, Dean 1-minus 3, Hughes 1-2. Bucks: Rehmeyer 6-17, Shoop 4-16, Kritzer 2-7, Clark 4-4, Snow 6-2, Lightner 2-1, Primerano 1-1, Mickey 1- minus 4.

PASSING—Cleveland: Patrick 11-25-0-195. Bucks: Lightner 0-10-1-0, Snow 1-4-0-19.

RECEIVING—Cleveland: Chamberlin 6-105, Bailey 2-13, McCoy 2-52, Brewer 1-16. Bucks: Rehmeyer 1-19.

## GAME FOUR–8/12/78 WHITETAIL BUCKS WON BY FORFEIT OVER WASHINGTON GENERALS

**GAME FIVE—8/19/78 YOUNGSTOWN HARDHATS 46, WHITETAIL BUCKS 6**

**GAME SIX—8/26/78 ERIE EXPRESS 53, WHITETAIL BUCKS 0**

**GAME SEVEN—9/9/78 CLEVELAND ACADEMES WON BY FORFEIT OVER WHITETAIL BUCKS**

**GAME EIGHT—9/9/78 PITTSBURGH BLACK KNIGHTS 28, WHITETAIL BUCKS 0**

# INDEX